Researching Crime and Justice

This book provides an introduction to research and some of the methods in the field of crime and justice and related areas, including police, prisons and criminal justice policy making.

Less a dry 'how to' book, it is concerned rather to provide a wide-ranging discussion that illustrates the kind of research that has been done in particular areas, the findings of previous studies, the pitfalls of 'real life' research (and some potential solutions) and the range of possible research methods and approaches – both qualitative and quantitative. It shows how appropriate methods are chosen for particular studies and explores the theoretical underpinnings of the studies, including how and why researchers use theory; the political and ethical issues; and the role of emotions such as fear and danger in researching the field of crime and criminal justice.

Key features include:

- First hand interviews with leading 'hands on' academics
- Examples, excerpts and sources of original research
- Analysis of the theories, methods and outcomes of previous research

Throughout the book there is an emphasis on the often troublesome (and often ignored) relationship between the topic of study, desired outcomes and suitable methods, with a wide range of illustrative case studies. Here the approach is practical – pointing out the different approaches various studies have used and how their outcome is often determined by their choice of methods. The book also reflects on the philosophies of research and includes discussions about the way the choice of methods will be reflected in the findings and vice versa (which seems obvious but is often forgotten).

Researching Crime and Justice: Tales from the field will be an essential source of inspiration and ideas for criminology students and other researchers on crime and justice.

Louise Westmarland is Senior Lecturer in Criminology at the Open University. She has written widely on police and policing, specifically on various aspects of police culture such as in her book *Gender and Policing: Sex, Power and Police Culture* (Willan Publishing 2001) – and on violence and police culture, ethics and integrity. Most recently she has co-authored *Creating Citizen-Consumers: Changing Publics and Changing Public Services* (Sage 2007).

Researching Crime and Justice

Tales from the field

Louise Westmarland

LONDON AND NEW YORK

First published 2011 by Routledge
2 Park Square, Milton Park, Abingdon, Oxon, OX14 4RN

Simultaneously published in the USA and Canada
by Routledge
270 Madison Avenue, New York, NY 10016

Routledge is an imprint of the Taylor & Francis Group, an Informa business

© 2011 LOUISE WESTMARLAND

Typeset in Sabon by TW Typesetting, Plymouth, Devon
Printed and bound in Great Britain by TJ International Ltd, Padstow, Cornwall

All rights reserved. No part of this book may be reprinted or reproduced or utilised in any form or by any electronic, mechanical, or other means, now known or hereafter invented, including photocopying and recording, or in any information storage or retrieval system, without permission in writing from the publishers.

British Library Cataloguing in Publication Data
A catalogue record for this book is available from the British Library

Library of Congress Cataloging in Publication Data
A catalog record for this book has been requested

ISBN 13: 978-1-84392-317-6 (hbk)
ISBN 13: 978-1-84392-316-9 (pbk)
ISBN 13: 978-0-20382-401-6 (ebk)

Contents

	Preface	ix
1	**Problematising criminological research**	1
	Introduction	1
	What are 'criminological methods'?	1
	'Real' research	4
	Is researching crime and justice criminology?	6
	What are criminological research methods?	7
	If this is criminology, what is research?	8
	How and why to research?	9
	Who or what to research?	10
	What is criminological about certain types of research?	13
	What happens in 'real life' research?	14
	Organisation of the book	20
2	**Quantitative versus qualitative methods**	22
	Introduction	22
	Choosing and using research methods	23
	Is this criminology?	24
	Types of research methods	26
	How to choose methods that fit	32
	Researching the 'truth' about rape	35
	Reliability	37
	Validity	39
	The science of research methods	42
	Conclusion	47

3	**Quantitative methods**	**49**
	Introduction	49
	What are quantitative criminological methods?	50
	Primary and secondary data	53
	Interrogating official statistics	59
	Interview with John Muncie	60
	Critiquing government statistics	64
	Summary of secondary quantitative data methods	72
	Primary data research	74
	Summary of primary data research	80
	Conclusion	81
4	**Qualitative methods**	**82**
	Introduction	82
	Versions of qualitative research	84
	Interviews	89
	Interview with Ben Bowling	93
	Interview with Laura Piacentini	96
	Focus groups	100
	Mixed methods	102
	Interview with Sandra Walklate	103
	Interview with Lynn Hancock	110
	Conclusion	116
5	**Soft and semi-structured research**	**117**
	Introduction	117
	Ethnography	118
	Insider/outsider research	123
	Interview with Rob Hornsby	128
	Interview with Simon Winlow	133
	Conclusion	138
6	**Ethics, emotions, politics and danger**	**140**
	Introduction	140
	Research ethics	141
	Ethical restrictions on criminological research	147
	Crime and justice specific ethics?	148
	The politics of researching crime and justice	157

	Emotions	162
	Danger in the research process	166
	Conclusion	168
7	**Analysing evidence of crime and justice**	**169**
	Introduction	169
	What the interviewees said	169
	Analysing evidence	173
	Theoretical concerns	174
	A short guide to criminological theories	176
	The themes that have arisen from the interviews	178
	The writing up process	182
	Conclusion	184
	References	186
	Index	192

Preface

This book has arisen from numerous discussions about the gap between the 'realities' of research and the practicalities of finishing (or even starting) a project. It has come from a growing realisation that while many of us can 'talk a good proposal' the actual doing of the research can be a different matter. As a result, many of the examples in the book are based on discussions I have had with colleagues and students past and present, and experiences over the past ten years or so, especially with Dick Hobbs, John Clarke and Janet Newman. Particular thanks are due to them because the discussions and examples in the text are largely based upon 'real life' experiences of mine or others. In fact, this is where the book is located as something slightly different from dry 'how to' text books because it pivots on a number of interviews with 'real life' researchers – people who actually go out and get their hands dirty, collecting original data or developing new ideas about the world of crime and justice.

Throughout the book I have developed these discussions from the interviews with academic researchers who have experience in a range of crime and criminal justice fields in order to elicit their advice. In the course of a series of short interviews with key players in current criminology I have tried to relate the main points they raise about research in the 'real world-view'. The accounts are not examples of how to do the perfect project and the interviewees do not claim to be experts on every field of criminology. What is worked through in these conversations, reproduced throughout the book, aims to provide a fly-on-the-wall experience for others who might be curious about why or how researchers and colleagues choose the methods they do. As part of these accounts I have tried to give a flavour of a 'warts and all' description of research projects the respondents have carried out in order to try to learn from the mistakes and pitfalls of others in the attempt to avoid them for ourselves.

Due to the central importance of these interviews in the book I would first like to thank the interviewees in order of appearance: John Muncie, Ben Bowling, Laura Piacentini, Sandra Walklate, Lynn Hancock, Rob Hornsby and Simon Winlow. It goes without saying that without them this project would have been a much less entertaining and interesting exercise, and the book would not have been written. I would like to thank them not only for giving up their time but also for being so accommodating and enthusiastic about the whole project and the idea behind it. Second, I would like to thank my colleagues and friends at the Open University, especially Deborah Drake, Reece Walters, John Clarke and all the people in the Department of Social Policy and Criminology who have listened to my woes while writing this book. Once again I would like to thank Brian Willan for being, as ever, a great publisher of extreme patience and also Julia Willan for being so encouraging and sympathetic when deadlines have slipped.

Finally I would like to thank my partner Paul for his patience and cups of tea and coffee, without which this book would never have been completed, and my family, parents and daughters Nicole and Amy.

1 Problematising criminological research

Introduction

This book is intended to be an informative and sometimes comforting yet often disconcerting introduction to research in the field of crime and justice. It has not been written as a 'how to' handbook but rather as an inspiration, source of ideas, and hopefully an interesting journey around the area of what is broadly termed criminology. The main type of information it contains is to do with the nuts and bolts of various methods employed by researchers. These workings are illustrated using a series of first-hand accounts, in the form of interviews with leading 'hands on' academics, as well as examples, excerpts and sources of original research. The idea of the various chapters is to explore the way research happens in 'real life' and to analyse the various theories, methods and outcomes of previous research. Reflections of the key academics whose wise words are reproduced as interviews throughout the text are intended to be enlivening and inspirational, as well as comforting as they explain how things went wrong during their projects, and how they put things back on course.

What are 'criminological methods'?

Although this book has the title *Researching Crime and Justice*, both 'crime' and 'justice' are contested terms and neither can be easily defined. In asking 'what is crime?', we are not only referring to those activities that are prohibited by criminal law, but really talking about the power to criminalise, to define what sort of behaviour is to be sanctioned, regarded as inappropriate, unwelcome, troubling. Similarly, 'justice' has been claimed as a difficult, nebulous, sometimes philosophical term. What is meant by 'obtaining justice' or seeing 'justice to be done'? To take the word crime, for example, to simply mean the breaking of laws is too simplistic. If this simple lawbreaking view of crime is adopted then the following conditions must be met. As Muncie *et al.* (2010: 4–5) explain:

- The act must be legally prohibited at the time it is committed.
- The perpetrator must have criminal intent (*mens rea*).

- The perpetrator must have acted voluntarily (*actus reus*).
- There must be some legally prescribed punishment for committal of the act.

Three important consequences flow from such formulations of crime as law violation:

1. Definitions of crime depend on the prior formulation of criminal law sanctions. No behaviour can be considered criminal unless a formal sanction exists to prohibit it.
2. There can be no official recognition of an individual offence until an offender has been proven guilty in a court of law. No behaviour or individual can be considered criminal until formally decided as such by the criminal justice system.
3. By focusing on certain behaviours, criminal law tends to concentrate on identifying individual offenders, rather than offences committed by state or corporate organisations.

Furthermore, the concept of crime and justice varies over time, with laws being introduced or removed from statute books, and across place – certain activities are against the law in some countries but not in others. The simple and uncritical acceptance that crime is simply the legal definition of lawbreaking is too narrow for the development of research in the arena of crime and criminal justice. As the following list of potential areas for crime and justice research shows, to concentrate exclusively on lawbreaking as a focus is to miss a great deal of the field.

In the following list a series of possible areas for research areas that can be classed as being within the boundaries of crime and justice are outlined. This is not an exhaustive list, but they are the type of areas and questions upon which this book will focus.

- The purpose of the criminal justice agencies, such as the police, courts and prisons, and the measurement and analysis of their activities and effectiveness.
- Public views about the criminal justice agencies, victims and perpetrators.
- Human rights and the way people in the system are processed and the outcome of those processes.
- Crime fighting and prevention.

To begin with, some questions that might seem to have obvious answers may cause difficulties when researchers actually come to address them. These include:

- What is criminology?
- What is 'research'?

- How and why to research?
- What and who to research?
- What is 'criminological' about certain types of research?
- Is criminological research different from other types of research?
- Does criminological research demand different methods?

Just as with the concept of 'crime', justice is also an ambiguous term, as Drake *et al.* (2010) explain:

> The concept of justice defies any straightforward definition. It often appears as abstract and opaque and it clearly means different things to different people. Yet it is frequently evoked as some sort of social ideal to which nation states aspire, or make claim to, in seeking legitimation of their own authority. It conjures up a multitude of competing images of fairness, equality, human rights, just deserts, deserved punishment, moral worth, personal liberty, social obligation and public protection. It is a concept that has been the subject of continual philosophical debate. Is it something universal, derived from fundamental natural or divine principles, or is it indelibly tied to specific social and political conditions?

As the following example suggests, 'justice' as a philosophical term is often appropriated by those campaigning to change the law or to see people who have committed crimes against them punished.

The 'Justice for Julie' campaign

Julie Hogg, a pizza delivery girl and mother of a three-year-old boy, went missing from her home in Billingham, Stockton-on-Tees, in November 1989, sparking an extensive police hunt. The body of the 22-year-old was eventually found the following February by her mother, Ann Ming, hidden behind a bath panel, when the keys to her daughter's flat were returned to her. Billy Dunlop, with whom Julie had previously had a relationship, was charged with her murder but acquitted after a trial. Nine years later he confessed to the crime and was jailed for perjury.

But he was not jailed for her murder, because according to the law of double jeopardy as it stood, dating back 800 years to the middle ages, Dunlop could not be tried twice for the killing. It ruled that a person acquitted by a jury could not be tried again on the same charge, not even if new evidence came to light.

Mrs Ming, from Norton, Stockton-on-Tees, who worked as a nurse at Middlesbrough General Hospital, fought for more than 15 years to change the law on double jeopardy and launched the Justice for Julie campaign. Finally, in April 2005, the rule was altered under the 2003 Criminal Justice Act. Dunlop was jailed for life after pleading guilty at the Old Bailey in

September 2006, and became the first killer to be convicted under the new legislation (BBC News 2007).

As this example suggests (adapted from Drake *et al.* 2010: 3–10), 'justice' can mean something very personal and individual, such as a parent fighting for the rights of their child, and yet have wider legal connotations. These issues make researching crime and justice 'real' in the sense that they can influence policy, practice and legislature, but also that there are 'real' victims whose lives are devastated by the events criminologists make their subject area.

'Real' research

In a world where yoghurts are advertised as containing 'real' strawberries, or ice cream is covered in 'real' chocolate, this book is about 'real' research, or perhaps more correctly about the 'realities' of research. It is based on a series of interviews with leading academics who are involved in research projects and have had long experience of the problems and pitfalls. In the interviews they talk about how they chose particular methods, how successful they were and if they might have done anything different or would do so in the future. The 'realities' in the discussions throughout the book are based on some studies I have conducted alone or with colleagues, as well as examples from other researchers' work. While the book attempts to cover different and competing methods and to explain why some might be more appropriate than others, it cannot provide a complete overview of all methods used by criminologists. Rather, the key and most popular are explored with helpful insights as to the benefits and disadvantages to each approach.

It is clear, of course, that 'real' is an ambiguous term. How can philosophers, academics or ordinary researchers agree what is 'really real', because in a way, everything we know or do is socially constructed, or as a result of things we already know about society? So although this book cannot claim to be able to reinvent or redefine what is 'real', it takes a 'real' approach to what happens when everyday, ordinary researchers decide to investigate a particular problem or question that interests them. The key to this approach is, as Roy King argues, that researchers have to 'be there' and 'do your time' to understand prisons and prison life (King 2000: 297–8). While this book does not assert that observation is the only or a superior method, it gives some suggestions as to the meaning of 'real'. Were you there? Did you see for yourself, smell and hear things, feel fear, embarrassment, emotions?

Feeling the frustrations of real research also extends to statistics, the data from prisons, homicides and so on, as each number represents a real person, victim or crime, or worker within the criminal justice system. One of the reasons this is important and included in this book is that 'real' research asks questions that can be answered using statistics, may be based on face-to-face interviews, such as in the British Crime Survey, which is discussed in Chapters 2 and 3, and will be used in the informing of other research, such as observations.

In sum, this volume attempts to provide a thought-provoking guide to 'being there' – smelling fear, sweat, spit, spew and semen – research. This may sound extreme but the fairly new PhD student or early career researcher at whom these discussions are aimed may need some help to think through some of the more unpleasant aspects they might encounter. It takes the reader through some of the problems that 'real' life research throws up, sometimes literally, exploring some of the difficulties other, more established, researchers have faced. As explained earlier, the book is a guide to the sort of issues researchers in fields of crime and justice might encounter, and what to do in those difficult situations, rather than a 'how to' handbook. Where the detail of 'how to' goes beyond the scope of this text, other works are suggested and can be found in the references at the end of the book.

This is not to say that the interviews with established researchers in this book are intended as a behind-the-scenes 'back story' *exposé* of what happens in 'reality', however that is defined. Rather, the discussions cover the most straightforward processes of research, and the basic advantages and disadvantages of using various methods. For instance, what sort of underlying theory or philosophy of inquiry suits your research questions? Will the proposed methods allow you to discover any sort of answer to the questions you propose (or have had set for you)? The nuts and bolts of the 'realities' of these methods and how and why to choose which method are the most crucial questions researchers face and they are explored in a number of ways throughout the chapters, which aim to discuss the appropriate tools and research design.

This is not to say that this book positions itself as regarding this form of 'real' or 'realistic' research as superior to research that claims to be conceptual, philosophical, theoretical or political. Quite the reverse, as no good, solid piece of research can ignore these aspects in its design and implementation. Nor is it true to say that the book suggests that research that does not involve 'real' processes, such as interviews, observations and investigations that might be called 'empirical' (from the idea that science requires experiments, observations and senses) or 'applied', in the 'leaving your desk or library to investigate' sense, is inferior. There are indeed discussions in this book about statistics, evaluations and quantitative studies that do not involve dirty hands, but this is not the main focus of the book. The focus is to talk about what it is like to conduct research: to knock on doors, to ask people to take part in interviews, or a focus group, to ask people questions that they may find unpalatable. To arrive at a prison reception to be searched, or a police station, or court on a Monday morning, and try to persuade 'gatekeepers' to allow you access to the people they deal with; once that is agreed, to approach the individuals themselves, to convince them that your study is worthwhile and that they will be 'safe' (in several senses) if they agree to talk to you about their experiences.

Of course, it is hoped that many decisions will have been made before this moment of confrontation with a 'real' person arrives. This may have involved discussions with academic supervisors, funding bodies, the Home Office, colleagues, university ethics committees and potential funders. Some of the people who kindly agreed to share their research experiences and stories for this book can attest to these problems – time spent 'hanging around' waiting for permission to interview people, for example (see Piacentini (2004) and Bowling (2010) in later chapters for examples of these frustrating times).

As a result of a series of interviews with experienced academic researchers, this book has many examples of studies that illuminate the problems and pitfalls of 'real' research. The examples have been chosen to give a flavour of what established academic researchers do, how they rationalise their choice of methods, and some illustrations that provide contrasting ways of going about investigating a particular problem or question. Very often the question or problem the researcher is investigating, particularly in the case of the interviews in later chapters of this book, is one that has defined or troubled the lives of the investigator. In some cases it is this 'troubling' aspect that has prompted the researcher to carry out (and to continue carrying out) research in a particular area. In some cases it is the result of a series of questions that others have posed, in others it has to do with the political situation at the time or place, in others it is a long-standing or tangential aspect of other research they are conducting.

The book examines a wide variety of research experiences, but does not suggest or promote any one particular way or method of conducting research. Quantitative (counting), qualitative (understanding) and mixed methods are all included. Interviews, focus groups, observations, surveys and statistical methods are considered using a wide range of crime and justice issues. The more obvious crime and justice topics are covered, such as police, courts and prisons, as are 'victimisation' surveys, and 'official' statistics, as well as some more diverse areas at the edges of what might be considered 'criminology'.

Is researching crime and justice criminology?

Researching crime and justice inevitably raises questions around the methods used, and the existing base of literature and framework in which it can be placed. One of the common ways to place a broad umbrella over these topics is to use 'criminology' as an organising discipline. The conditions for accepting articles from one of the world's major criminology journals show that this is quite a wide remit to cover:

> *The British Journal of Criminology: An International Review of Crime and Society* is one of the world's top criminology journals. It publishes

work of the highest quality from around the world and across all areas of criminology.

BJC is a valuable resource for academics and researchers in crime, whether they be from criminology, sociology, anthropology, psychology, law, economics, politics or social work, and for professionals concerned with crime, law, criminal justice, politics, and penology. In addition to publishing peer-reviewed articles, *BJC* contains a substantial book review section.

The *Journal* welcomes submissions from a variety of perspectives focusing on crime and society; and especially articles written from sociological, historical, philosophical, geographical, psychological, jurisprudential, cultural, political, or policy standpoints. The interests of the extensive Editorial and International Advisory Boards are catholic, neither narrowly ideological nor limited to rigid conceptions of what criminology either should be, or is currently, about.

The two main criteria according to which articles submitted for publication will be assessed are: the degree to which the article contributes new knowledge to an understanding of crime and society, the overall quality of the argument and its presentation.

(www.oxfordjournals.org/our_journals/crimin/about.html)

As this statement suggests, one of the main sources of current criminological debate does not limit the study to a narrow definition of crime or justice. It is open as to the methods used and a brief tour around the website reveals the range of both subject matter and ways of researching it that are classed as 'criminological' enough to be of interest to the *British Journal of Criminology*.

What are criminological research methods?

Throughout this book a variety of methods will be explored, and although this will not comprise an exclusive or exhaustive list of possibilities, some pertinent examples will explain why and how certain methods are chosen. The main reason for choosing any particular method is, as this book hopes to show, that the methods fit the research questions. In other words, the sort of methods that are proposed will have the ability, at least in theory, to discover and collect data that will be able to answer the questions the study aims to illuminate. As some of the 'real life' examples in the book illustrate, however, sometimes this does not work to plan, and sometimes happy and insightful outcomes are the result. A word of both caution and encouragement to any new researchers reading this book: even the most experienced and well respected professors have made mistakes, have often had to revise their studies' outcomes and results, and have had to accept that as criminology often involves 'real' people in the real world, things will go wrong.

In this book a key division is made between quantitative studies, which tend to be concerned with large data sets, counting and measuring, and qualitative methods, which aim to discover the how and why of the world, people's actions and behaviour, and so on. A key feature of this criminological research, however, is that it is embedded in the 'real' world, in the sense that it often tries to solve 'real' problems. To talk of an embedded criminology, as Walters suggests, is 'somewhat tautological' (2007: 19). He argues: 'Criminology's origins reveal that it has been an intellectual enterprise largely dominated by a scientific causation of state defined crime for the purposes of developing a more efficient crime control apparatus.'

Although Walters is being critical of the way some criminology has historically been tied to solving the state's problems of social control, he says that there are encouraging new forms of knowledge and critical resistance in evidence. There are, therefore, multiple challenges and tensions in criminological research, as Sandra Walklate explains in her outline of the key features of the discipline (1998: 13).

1 As a discipline it is held together by a substantive concern: crime.
2 This means it is multidisciplinary in character rather than being dominated by one discipline. As a consequence, in order to make sense of what criminologists might be saying it is important to understand the conceptual apparatus with which they might be working.
3 Thus criminologists frequently disagree with one another.
4 Despite such disagreements, it could be argued that there is some consensus around some features of what constitutes the crime problem though much less agreement on how to 'solve' the crime problem.
5 Nevertheless criminologists have been historically (and still are contemporaneously) concerned to offer some sort of intervention in the policy making process.
6 These features or criminology sometimes resonate with popular (common-sense) thinking about crime and sometimes challenge such thinking. Such tensions are a perpetual challenge for the discipline.

As Walklate suggests, there is much disagreement within the discipline, and indeed some argue that what purports to be criminology is simply the sociology of crime, or deviance or policing or prisons. Similarly, what is research is also hotly debated, as the reasons some methods are chosen over others is a matter of personal and often political choice. The following section explores some of these issues.

If this is criminology, what is research?

We all do research almost every day. From picking the best bananas at the supermarket to choosing a life partner, we consciously or unconsciously take in and process data. We then proceed to make decisions based on our assessment of the results of our analysis. What is different about the various types of research we carry out each day depends to some extent on the purpose of our investigations. Something like choosing bananas will have a fairly immediate cost–benefit analysis result. In other words, if the bananas you choose are not tasty, you'll know straight away when you get them home and eat them. Academic research is likely to be a longer process, involving the collection and consideration of various pieces of data from different places and people, longer-term analysis and the presentation of findings to others.

This sort of research will often require some sort of comparison, although this is not always the case. Defining academic research is difficult because of the multiple forms it takes, and as new methods emerge, it is always changing. We might ask, for example, whether academic research has to be 'scientific' in the way that developing a cure for cancer might be described, or an attempt to pinpoint the 'causes of crime'. Indeed, the impossible task of providing policy-makers or governmental bodies with answers to this question is often heralded as one of the purposes of criminological research. Walters and other critics are scathing about this sort of approach because, they argue, 'crime science' represents 'a new form of right-wing positivist criminology' (Walters 2007: 19).

Any academic research field such as criminology, researching sensitive areas of crime and justice associated with policy, will always be essentially a political activity. This is not simply the political in the sense of right and left, or government, political parties and so on; the realities of research mean that someone somewhere will have an axe to grind or a position to defend. This position might be connected with the research process itself – as later chapters show, quantitative versus qualitative methods can be a hotly debated topic – but also to do with the outcomes, use, or even initial topic itself of the research. Chapter 6 illustrates that the political and ethical concerns of crime and justice research will not be resolved easily, as Hughes has argued:

> All too often research publications fail to tell us about the hidden difficulties, constraints and limitations behind the apparently smooth and detached appearance of the research process ... All social science has a political dimension, in the non-party-political sense. All aspects of research necessarily involve the researcher in both the analysis and practice of power and, in turn, have the potential to generate conflicts of interest between a whole host of interested parties. (Hughes 2000: 234–5)

How and why to research?

Very big and daunting questions, even for experienced researchers. In fact, although it might not be immediately obvious, they are politically loaded questions, even concerning simple decisions such as the approach (meaning the methods and ideas underpinning the research) or the choice of topic (think, for example, of choosing to look at victims or perpetrators of crime and the implications of how this might be viewed). Academic researchers continually argue about the political and ethical issues surrounding research methods in all social sciences disciplines. This is potentially confusing when attempting to ascertain the 'best' method to use for any particular study.

Indeed this idea of a 'best' method for each study is confusing and controversial for a number of reasons, which will be taken up later in the book. Put simply, it is a matter of political and ethical choice overlaid by the requirements of practicalities, such as available resources. While certain methods would definitely not work in answering some research questions, others can be a matter of choice. In later chapters researchers will give examples and illustrations of why they chose certain methods and what happened as a result of those decisions. They explain the choices that were open to them (given what they wanted to know) and those that seemed inaccessible.

A note of caution here about 'scientific' methods, however, as it was raised in this section. Some researchers claim that the search for 'scientific' legitimacy – in other words, 'provable', often numerical results – is a false and misguided chase. They argue that human beings (both the researched and the researchers) do not fit into scientifically researchable categories, such as microbes or molecules. These researchers claim that it is more profitable to look for the meaning in people's behaviour, which is harder to count and 'prove' than simply looking at figures of how many people do certain things in given circumstances. More of this interesting debate in later chapters.

Who or what to research?

Another potentially daunting question, to which the answer is often, 'take your choice', or 'it depends'. Some projects are set in stone from the beginning, others offer a choice and the chance to develop ideas of how to do the research as part of the study. It usually depends upon whether the project is 'yours' or belongs to someone else – from being given a predetermined question, methods and database or 'population' to research, to an almost free rein, to study 'some topic in criminology'. Typically these two extremes represent at one end the research assistant who is employed to carry out a particular study on a fixed-term contract and at the other a student dissertation where the only parameter might be that it has to be in the subject area – criminology.

Even where projects involve agreed parameters, perhaps as the result of winning money from funders such as the government's administrators of grants, the Economic and Social Research Council (ESRC) or the Ministry of Justice or the Home Office, there are often difficult decisions to make.

In other words, the question to be answered might be set, the methods and groups to be researched fixed, yet there are often subtle ways of individualising the research and manipulating the way it is carried out. A simple worked example of such a project is given below. Try to follow the steps and make decisions for the researcher. It is a very simple beginning to the sort of initial thoughts researchers have when they are faced with a problem or question to answer.

Project title: Police and Community Support Officers (PCSOs) and their value to local communities.

Aims of the project: To examine how effectively PCSOs have been working to help local communities.

(Question 1 for the researcher: What sort of questions would be required to fulfil these aims?)

Research questions:

a. To what extent are PCSOs proving to be cost-effective?
b. What sort of tasks do the PCSOs carry out?
c. Are local communities broadly in favour of PCSOs?

(Question 2 for the researcher: Will this study try to look widely right across the country, looking at as many areas as possible, or focus on just one or two?)

Proposed methods: This project will use a combination of methods to elicit answers to the questions that are posed. These will include a questionnaire sent to all police forces to find out how many PCSOs they have. The questionnaire will be aimed at finding out the main strengths and weaknesses of employing PCSOs. This will be followed by a more in-depth study of two selected police forces. The individual forces will be chosen on the basis of the information in the questionnaires. The project will aim to study one force where PCSOs have been embraced and are deployed successfully and another where the reception seems to have been less favourable. The in-depth part of the study of the two identified forces will be ethnographic. This will involve following and observing PCSOs during their daily work on the streets.

(Question 3 for the researcher: Can these methods answer the questions and fulfil the aims of the project?)

As this brief exercise suggests, there are numerous decisions to be made that will probably be answered by 'real world' constraints such as time and available resources (financial and personnel). There will also be the requirements of the funders of the project (if any) and the methods might be determined by self-interest. If the research is being paid for by a local force they will want the focus to be on them, plus possibly one other comparative force. If the money is being put up by a national organisation or a body with wider interests, such as the Home Office, then the project may need to be more widely drawn. This is aside from the ethical and political concerns, which are explored later in the chapter.

By way of contrast, the following extract is from a study of police officers that discusses the cultural beliefs about the wider police 'family' including PCSOs (Loftus 2008: 766–7).

> Front-line officers have a clear sense of the uniqueness of their role. This self-understanding engenders feelings of solidarity and perpetuates the opinion that they are set apart from others within the organisation (Young 1991). The expansion of civilian employment was another source of contention among the rank and file. Although my research focused primarily on sworn constables, I did note some themes with respect to how civilianisation is currently shaping police culture. In particular, officers bemoaned the appointment of 'civies' working in dispatch control and custody suites, and likewise articulated opposition towards the recruitment of PCSOs. The principal objection was that these groups lacked any 'real' understanding of the special rudiments of the police role. The following extract records a group of officers discussing the use of PCSOs within the Force:
>
> *Graham*: They can only really be the 'eyes and ears' for us so we can get on with doing real policing . . .
>
> *Jake*: But they get £15k a year. I would rather they employ one real police officer than two PCSOs. But apparently they are going to employ another sixty of them just in Lowerbrook Division . . .
>
> *Kate*: But the kids, they all know that they've got no powers and make fun of them. So now they are too frightened to go out on their own and will rely on us to come and get them!
>
> *Jake*: I have been off-duty and I have seen PCSOs walking down roads that are access only. There is a garage, a couple of houses and a graveyard! How on earth do they see that as policing?
>
> *Andy*: But they are not proper police. The uniforms look like something from the Thunderbirds! 'Yes, Officer Plastic' . . .

Graham: Plastic Police ...

Jake: But they'll make the police redundant.
(Group discussion – Southville, September 2005)

This brings in another important aspect to what is criminology and how it can be researched. Aside from the political and ethical considerations mentioned above, this book uses many examples such as this from the real world of research. Each of these studies, whether obvious or not, will have these issues and also theoretical aspects to be considered. In addition to the main methods the book examines, such as quantitative versus qualitative, the use of surveys, interviews, and observation methods, Chapter 2 provides a short discussion of the underlying theoretical position of the examples included. This is intended to be a 'light touch' guide to the sort of theories new researchers might be considering as part of their own study, rather than a full blown theoretical guide. At the same time it emphasises that no study, however instrumental, exists in a vacuum. Even evaluations of other studies, such as those often carried out by the Home Office, have an underlying purpose, approach or set of assumptions. These collections of existing ideas or culminations of shared knowledge are important for the understanding of the study and its findings. Researching crime and justice within a criminological framework cannot ignore these understandings; as the book will show, making decisions about methods is based upon the acceptance or rejection of certain theories.

The first decision that often has to be made, as Chapters 2 and 3 illustrate, is whether the study will be mainly 'quantitative' – that is, count how many PCSOs there are and how many forces think they are a positive influence – or qualitative. The qualitative aspects of the example above are the observations of the officers carrying out their work on the streets, to assess how the community and their colleagues seem to appreciate their work (or not). As examples later in this book will show, at a very simple level it is possible to use both these methods, to use a combination of quantitative (counting) and qualitative (understanding). The point of this illustration is to show that quantitative methods give a 'broad brush' picture, giving wide coverage of the problem to be researched. Qualitative methods, due to being time-consuming and expensive, can look in depth, but not across the horizon of the general picture.

What is criminological about certain types of research?

As explained earlier in this chapter, the defining of criminology and criminological research is more difficult than might be first imagined. This vexing and some might argue irresolvable area of dispute hinges on the debate about who is doing the defining and if criminology exists as a separate entity from, say, sociology of crime, deviance, policing, prisons and so on. Furthermore, due to its crossing boundaries with academic disciplines such as social policy, psychology, geography, politics, health and philosophy, to name but a few, some have argued that 'criminology' does not exist. It is argued to be a made-up discipline, drawing scholars and research funds from other more established areas of research and claiming a place that is more appealing to potential students, funders and people purchasing volumes such as this.

Just as 'sex sells', it seems that criminology catches the customers by being the academic equivalent of the television cop show or newspaper headline about crime. Crime and criminality, lawbreaking, the police, prisons and courts may have a superficial appeal; it is alleged, when students or researchers choose to study crime, that 'everyone wants to be Cracker'. The reality, of course, is much more mundane than the glamorous image of the television series from which that fictional character is drawn. Just as many people join the police because they want to 'help people', criminology students may begin by thinking that they want to find out 'why people commit crime' but end up realising that criminology is a much more multifaceted area of research than this question suggests.

What happens in 'real life' research?

Conducting original research can be the most exciting part of academic life. Researchers dream about their ideal project – finally discovering a way to convince people how much crime 'really' exists, or to prove that they know an answer to the question, 'why *do* people commit crime?' Once an idea sets seed, alliances between likely collaborators are forged, proposals are written, and a 'gap in the market' is identified to obtain funding from wherever seems most appropriate, depending upon the amount of money sought, or the social values or 'worthiness' (or otherwise) of the proposed outcomes.

This is, of course, an idealised version of what happens in many research spaces, including universities, throughout the country and indeed the world. Very often more practical concerns come into play, and this book is also aimed at researchers who might have other motives than simply 'wanting to know'. The practicalities of why a study is to be conducted and who is to pay for it are important starting points. Both of these mundane yet crucial questions need to be considered before looking at how the research is to be conducted, because they are as important as any other question we will ask throughout this book. Furthermore, as the chapters proceed, it will be obvious that although this book is not a 'how to do research manual', it certainly covers a number of 'how nots' to do it.

> **How does the research process work?**
> Idea
> Identify problem
> Formulate research questions
> Bid for money – Ask for/negotiate access
> Development of theories – Collection of data – Development of theories
> Collection and analysis of data
> Findings/results – Write up – Publish

As the next chapter will show, this process of research is similar, if not the same, as research that is conducted in other academic disciplines in universities such as sociology, psychology, history as well as geography. Cross- and trans-disciplinary research is often focused upon the doing of crime, its causes and control, and justice, including courts and prisons, community safety, crime prevention and more recently globalisation. The discussions throughout this book provide some suggestions as to how to decide which methods will best lead to the possibility of answering the questions. Again this seems a very simple corollary – it would be obvious that if we want to find out why people burgle pharmacies, for example, we could simply ask people caught doing so. Finding out the obvious answer, however, of 'it's where the drugs are' would be a waste of time. Similarly, using in-depth methods to find out the number and pattern of pharmacies that had been targeted would be useless, and expensive, and would not answer the question.

Sometimes criminological research questions are more complicated than simply finding out how many and why. In some cases they involve knowing the answer to questions about secondary issues, and whether these have an effect on, for instance, offending and the life course or social deprivation. To simply ask why people do or do not commit crime raises issues of independent variables, such as if a certain life event happened to a certain type of offender. For instance, does being sexually abused as a child increase the likelihood that someone will go on to abuse others? Again, there are at least three problems with this type of approach. First, whether it would be possible to find a sample and how likely it would be to access such sensitive information. Second, whether it would be ethical to ask the questions as it might revictimise the offender. And third, whether 'cause and effect' (does (a) plus (b) necessarily equal (c)?) is a valid way to draw conclusions.

Very often these studies build upon, or develop, an existing idea or finding in order to extend current knowledge in an existing field, or find a niche that has not been explored to date. In many cases these initial research ideas tend to fall into two categories. The first is where a great deal has

Table 1.1 Examples of how and why different types of research are funded

Why?	Who pays?
'Just want to know' (sometimes called 'blue skies' research)	Sometimes large research councils such as ESRC/AHRB, sometimes university internal
Theoretical studies of existing phenomena	As above
Studies of general 'social' problems	Funding councils/Home Office/charities
Studies of more specific social/criminal issues	Interested individual agencies/charities
Degrees: PhD/MA/BA	Funding councils/universities/individuals

been already done about the subject and so the problem of finding a new angle is difficult (think of all the research on the police); the second category, where very little is known about the phenomenon, has its own problems as literature on the subject is scarce. Examples might include recently 'discovered' or categorised crimes such as male rape, stalking or cybercrime. Both polarities present problems, in terms of 'new' knowledge we might want to discover, because research often builds upon a corpus of work in a particular field, being the 'pioneer' causes problems. Some such studies are examined in later chapters of this book where we discover how researchers have overcome the difficulties.

Overcoming these difficulties and problems is partly the reason this book has been written; it has arisen from numerous discussions about the gap between the 'realities' of research and the practicalities of finishing (or even starting) a project. It has come from a growing realisation that while many academics can 'talk a good proposal' or study, the actual doing of the research can be a different matter. This is not to say that methodologists do not have much to theorise about considering the ways and means of research, but the discussions in this text are based upon 'real life' experience. They are aimed at developing discussions between academics and practitioners who have experience in a range of representative areas of research within crime and criminal justice fields in order to elicit their advice. In the course of a series of interviews, key players in current criminology relate some of their experiences about research from their 'real world-view'. The accounts are not perfectly organised and the interviewees do not claim to have worked out the best 'methods', but these conversations aim to provide a fly-on-the-wall experience for others who might be curious about why or how researchers and colleagues choose the methods they do. These accounts provide a 'reality' based description of the research projects respondents have carried out; it may be possible to learn from the mistakes made and pitfalls encountered by others in order to avoid them ourselves.

Aside from these issues which are not specific to criminology, which is not to say they are unimportant, this book also tackles an interesting and largely irresolvable dispute in the social sciences about quantitative (hard, counting) and qualitative (soft, no numbers) research. Which is 'better' in any given circumstance, and whether it is possible or advisable to mix these methods in any given study is a debate this book covers but does not claim to solve. Also, despite the outline above of the types and sources of funding for research, there is considerable dispute about what 'criminology' covers in terms of research theory and method, or even whether 'criminology' exists as a discipline separate from those mentioned earlier as its academic feeder subjects. It might be questioned, for instance, whether the efficiency of the police in an increasingly privatised marketplace is within the remit of criminology, or is it within political science or economics. In effect, this leads back to deeper questions of what is 'crime' and 'justice', and how studying these issues fits into a coherent whole.

In order to explore this important question, the next section looks at three introductory areas: what can and cannot be known through conducting research; problems surrounding gaining access to groups who are both inside and outside the law; and issues around access to institutions such as prisons and the police.

1. What can and cannot be known through conducting research

Some fundamental questions need to be asked at the beginning of any research study. Clearly, the most obvious of these is that, as with many other forms of social life, we can never know how much crime there is or the validity of the reports of its effects. This is partly because criminal behaviour is by its nature usually hidden from view, or at least this is the aim of the perpetrator to avoid detection.

Another associated problem is that crime is difficult to define, and therefore impossible to measure, classify or quantify in a way upon which everyone can agree. This position or approach, sometimes referred to as 'constructivist' in criminological fields, is considered later in the book and is based on the notion that what one person (such as a police officer) might regard as 'criminal' (such as polluting the environment) may not be seen as such by another. Even to take Home Office or 'official' statistics, such as those produced by police forces to count the number of recorded offences, as unproblematic is to misunderstand the nature of criminological research. This is because a significant amount of 'hidden crime' – white collar crime, 'domestic' violence and minor, uninsured losses through theft, for example – will never come to the attention of the authorities who record such statistics. This so-called 'dark figure' of crime statistics, while now regarded as something of a cliché, nevertheless remains a constant reminder of the value of maintaining a critical approach to all crime data, quantitative or qualitative.

One of the reasons this is so crucial is that so-called crime 'scientists' or evaluative researchers make claims about being able to find out the most effective methods to control crime. They address the problem from a 'what works?' perspective, believing that value for money, recorded crime reduction and the systematic quantitative investigation of the causes of crime can benefit society. Many examples of this type of approach to research can be viewed on the Home Office website and some of the studies in later chapters explore this issue of validity.

2. Problems surrounding gaining access to groups who are 'inside' and 'outside' the law

Those 'inside' the law, the policy-makers, police, prison and probation workers, all have ready access to data for their own studies. They are sometimes less willing to make this data available to 'non' police or prisons personnel, and even less willing to allow researchers to collect their own data within the organisations, although over the past ten years or so this has become easier, for various reasons explained by the researchers interviewed later in this book. An even more challenging situation, however, is to find and interview perpetrators, suspects and rule and law violators who might not have come to the attention of any criminal, legal or regulatory authority. These include those involved in activities such as people trafficking, tobacco counterfeiting, the environmental crime debate, for example. The obvious problem for researchers that follows from questions of how much crime there is and (supposedly) therefore is it an 'issue' worthy of research, is where to find the 'criminals'. There is no accessible databank of names and addresses such as *Yellow Pages* (although access to the Police National Computer would be a handy equivalent), and the difficulties of finding individual offenders committing crimes, due to the hidden behaviour mentioned above, are obvious; and an advert in the local or national press asking 'Have you committed a crime lately? Talk to us!' might not be a great investment.

The ingenuity shown in finding such inaccessible groups, particularly those involved in crimes of censure such as child sex abuse or crimes committed by those in positions of authority, such as police corruption, is to be commended. Later in the book some researchers explain how they managed to gain access to groups of offenders who have many reasons for not coming forward, other than to be found out. This raises the final problem in this section, the issue of how to access groups who are either 'beyond' the law, who will never be charged with an offence, or those who have committed a crime but have not been found out. This latter group probably includes most of us – occasionally exceeding the speed limit, underage drinking, making a personal phone call at work, accepting too much change from a shop are minor everyday activities that we do not acknowledge as a crime, so this is a difficult area to research. Even the parameters that might be set at the beginning of the study might be difficult to decide upon. (Some companies allow 'short personal calls' to be made, but 'no mobiles', so is phoning your partner to let him or her know you're going to be late home, on what may be the only means of contact, a crime?)

Some of the most inaccessible people for researchers are elite groups such as city traders, or employees of large companies which typically employ their own investigators to trap workers who are committing fraud or other misdemeanours. The employee can be dismissed or required to resign, with no publicity and subsequent detrimental effect to the company. This also means that they escape the attention of the law or the justice process and, usually, researchers. Similarly, violence in the home between partners used to be a 'hidden' crime, with vigorous political campaigns being needed to raise awareness, not least in the eyes of victims and survivors, but also for the police to acknowledge that this is a crime. Accessing the perpetrators of these crimes would and can be difficult, not just because of it being purposefully hidden but also because of its conception and definition as 'criminal'.

3. Access to institutions such as prisons and police

Researching crime and criminal justice is not just about perpetrators, the prisons and the police. There are numerous 'public' displays of justice enacted every day in almost every sizeable town in Europe. These are the courts, where offences from the 'minor', such as driving misdemeanours, right up to the most serious, such as homicide, are tried. Courts are generally open to the public and any researcher can access the front areas of the court and its processes. Once the researcher wants to go beyond these 'front' public areas, however, negotiation with the criminal justice gatekeepers usually has to begin. If this research aims to reach the very heart of the process – the jury room, for instance – these negotiations would be protracted and at the highest levels of the Home Office. In the following chapters various researchers describe the trials and tribulations of their journeys to negotiate the hurdles, including accounts of abortive or unsuccessful approaches; sometimes compromises are reached that make the process acceptable to both researcher and researched.

The difficulties of accessing other criminal justice institutions can be similarly fraught with difficulties. Few organisations would voluntarily air their dirty linen in public and yet this is potentially what prospecting researchers ask when they approach the gatekeepers of the policing or prison system. Organisations may claim to be protecting the rights of those they serve, and some may be doing so legitimately; it is often difficult to determine whether this is also being used to protect themselves. It could be argued, therefore, that 'insider' research might be preferred in these circumstances, where employees of the organisations become 'semi-detached' workers. In distancing themselves they enable informed yet objective research to be conducted. Some of the case studies in this book explore the problems and advantages of this type of approach.

Organisation of the book

The next chapter explores a debate in the social sciences that often causes researchers to divide themselves into two camps. Whether or not counting the frequency of a problem, event or behaviour using numerical methods is 'better' than investigating why this happens is not the aim of this book. The discussion examines the various arguments for and against quantitative and qualitative methods, their underlying philosophies and practices, but also 'realistically' what they are said to be able to achieve. In asking the fundamental questions about what research is for, whom it can benefit or harm and how it can be justified, the chapter takes a practical approach, without arguing that either method, or a combination of both, can be advantageous. This is illustrated by using real and speculative studies that employ contrasting methods, in order to explore the advantages and disadvantages of each approach.

Chapter 3 explores quantitative methods and evaluative research more closely using studies such as the British Crime Survey. There are explorations of a quantitative international study on police corruption, and a contrast of the advantages of primary (self-researched) and secondary data. John Muncie is interviewed about his international studies of youth imprisonment and his extensive work on the subject is used to discuss the topics he raises.

Chapter 4 follows on with an introduction to qualitative methods with discussions of illustrative projects. Ben Bowling is interviewed about his research on policing the Caribbean, and Laura Piacentini talks about accessing Russian prisons. The chapter then moves into mixed methods discussions and uses the work of Sandra Walklate and her study of fear of crime and victimisation in two contrasting neighbourhoods. The chapter also draws upon the work and experience of Lynn Hancock and explores her research on how jury members view the criminal justice system and the process of serving on a jury.

Chapter 5 extends this discussion into various aspects of qualitative methods, such as ethnography and some of the more inventive means of studying 'deviant' groups of people such as cigarette bootleggers and bouncers involved in organised crime.

In Chapter 6 ethics, emotions and danger are discussed, illustrated by various case studies where problems could have halted research projects, or did, and in some situations posed a severe risk to the researchers' physical and psychological safety. While these issues cannot always be anticipated, the experience of others is useful when considering the risks of any project, especially where groups of researchers are working together, and some might be less experienced and/or more vulnerable for various reasons. The discussion of ethics includes the problem of gaining ethical approval from institutional committees, the use and abuse of informants and the appropriation of findings of a study once it is published.

Chapter 7 concludes with a summary of what the interviewees were saying about methods and theory fitting with aims of research, and draws together cogent findings of the book as a whole. The chapter also considers how to analyse and write up a research project and the role of theory as part of that process, finishing with some concluding thoughts about the book and its main debates and arguments.

2 Quantitative versus qualitative methods

Introduction

In each of the forthcoming chapters it will be emphasised that there are no 'right', superior or proper methods to use in researching crime and justice. One of the aims of this book is to illustrate that in 'real life' research there are compromises, innovations and ingenious routes that have to be taken to achieve certain ends. This chapter in particular aims to highlight that the choice of methods is important – the question that needs to be asked is, 'Can this method (or methods) have the potential to deliver answers to the sort of questions the project will pose?' You may notice the word 'potential' in this sentence – this is because in the real world not everything goes to plan; sometimes things go wrong, and in some cases happy accidents occur as a result of not being able to control where and when the research takes place. There are at least two examples of this in the interviews that are reproduced in this book and the experienced researchers who describe these instances are suitably philosophical about the outcomes of their studies and the way they overcame various obstacles.

To explore these issues this chapter begins with a general discussion of the ideas or philosophy behind research methods, with an emphasis on how to think about choosing and using particular methods. This includes how and why certain approaches can only discover what they set out to do, as an aid to choosing wisely. The limitations of research methods are shown by using examples from various studies that illustrate real life research. These discussions involve talking about what can and cannot be achieved using quantitative and qualitative methods, and the sort of studies that are better suited to each. This is followed by a section on formulating research questions, and the necessity to reformulate them as the project proceeds in the light of do-ability, within budget and time restraints. This latter discussion includes cross-references to points in forthcoming chapters where these issues are raised in the interviews with researchers that form the 'research in real life' part of this book.

Choosing and using research methods

To some extent the qualitative versus quantitative debate is an example of a false dichotomy. Quantitative studies measure 'how many' type questions and rely on numbers and calculations to support their arguments. Qualitative studies use data sources that do not normally mean the use of numbers. Although some studies will be purely one or the other – counting or not – in many cases, for pragmatic reasons, projects will use some of each, a little of one and a majority of the other, or be openly 'mixed' in their approach. In designing real life projects researchers usually want to consider the following issues:

- Will these methods answer the question posed?
- Do they have the potential to cover all the angles necessary?
- Are resources available to use these methods?
- Will the cost of the study be justified in terms of the potential findings?

Among other considerations, answering these issues satisfactorily will rely upon the ability to pose the sort of questions required by the researcher, or whoever is funding or requests the study to be carried out. This is not to say that the research question has to be necessarily decided before the methods are chosen. A researcher might decide that they are keen to conduct a qualitative study looking at the culture of prisons. The researcher knows that they want to spend time understanding or appreciating prison life, to conduct an in-depth study for instance, but may not have a specific question in mind. Sometimes research questions need time to be developed and this may require some preliminary or pilot research. Preferably the research questions and methods should be developed in parallel, one informing the other.

Having said this, as explained earlier, this chapter does not claim to be a definitive guide or explanation of all possible research methods. It should be acknowledged here, as in all projects, that it is subject to researcher bias in that some are selected and others discarded. The main aim of the discussion here is to give an overview as to the various advantages and disadvantages of certain methods and their potential combinations. To do this the chapter draws upon a range of criminological research that has been conducted over the past 20 years or so in the UK and abroad, to give a sense of how the discipline is organised and the sort of topics with which it is concerned. It also aims to dispel the myth that there is one perfect method, from 'pure' counting to 'naturalistic' observational methods that collect data not very different from the sort of information we all collect about general social life.

Is this criminology?

The question which might be contested here is: what makes some research about crime and justice 'criminological'? As the discussion in Chapter 1 illustrated, what is criminology is debatable, and so the methods that define and explore the discipline must also be under dispute. It is true to say that just as some academics deny the existence of a specific discipline called criminology, they must argue that methods used by so-called or self-defined criminologists must be simply those used and developed by other academics in subjects such as sociology and given a different title. I have no dispute with this position. It is clear that as a relatively newly defined area of study, criminology must avail itself of established methods, theories and approaches of previously more established scholars.

A list of contents from the *Handbook on Crime* (Brookman *et al.* 2010: v–viii), for example, contains the following types of headings:

> **'Conventional' property crime:** domestic burglary; vehicle crime; shoplifting; understanding and tackling stolen goods markets.
>
> **Fraud and fakes:** income tax evasion and benefit fraud; theft and fraud by employees; fakes; scams; credit fraud; identity theft and fraud.
>
> **Violent crime:** homicide; domestic violence; street robbery; stealing commercial cash: from safecracking to armed robbery; youth gang crime; violence in the night-time economy; hate crime; stalking and harassment; arson; blackmail, kidnapping and threats to kill; elder abuse; school bullying: risk factors, theories and interventions; institutional abuse and children's homes; animal abuse.
>
> **Sex-related crime:** sexual offences against adults; sexual offences against children; sex work.
>
> **Drug-related crime:** drug- and alcohol-related crime; drug supply and possession; drug trafficking.
>
> **Organised crime and business crime:** corporate financial crimes; middle range business crime: rogues and respectable businesses, family firms and entrepreneurs; human trafficking; money laundering; extortion.
>
> **State, political and war crimes:** state crime; genocide and 'ethnic cleansing'; torture; crimes of the global state; political protest and crime; terrorism.
>
> **Harms, health and safety:** eco-crime and air pollution; corporate violence and harm; driving offences.

This list begs a further question as to the definition and identity of any research carried out on the topics so far determined in this volume, those looking at the police, courts, prisons, law violations, the punishment of offenders, and the treatment of victims of crime. It is true to say that there are (as far as can be ascertained) no methods that are exclusively criminological. Research studies may investigate criminological topics, but use methods from sociology, psychology, history, geography, anthropology or any other appropriate area of social science. As Garland notes:

> Criminologists in Britain, before the development of a university-based profession, were characteristically practitioners. In so far as they had an expertise or a knowledge base it was a detailed knowledge of the institutional terrain and its requirements, together with a general training in medicine or psychiatry, and later, psychology. It was this practical surface of emergence which largely accounts for the individualized, policy based and theoretically limited criminology which was characteristic of Britain before 1935.
> (Garland 1988: 14–15)

Later, in the 1960s and 1970s, one of the most common approaches was to conduct research under a 'sociology of deviance' label, which included studies of gangs, drugs, prisons and prisoners, and police misconduct. It covered a broader remit than acts that could be classed as 'criminal' behaviour, as anything that deviated from society's established norms could be included. These early studies tended to be qualitative because they involved exploring the social world of the so-called 'deviant'. Commencing with a group of researchers in the 1930s in the USA, what became known as the Chicago School popularised the tradition for naturalistic studies of human behaviour which later became prevalent in the UK. This will be discussed in more depth later in this volume in the chapters concerned with qualitative research. These early researchers of deviance differed from what had gone before in studies of crime and justice in that they were concerned with the real lives and lived experiences of the participants rather than simply how many crimes had been committed. They viewed prison life from the perspective of the inmates (Cohen and Taylor 1972); they saw what it was like to be an illegal drug user (Young 1971), how juvenile gangs work and live (Parker 1974), and the way police administer 'justice' on the streets (Skolnick 1975).

These countered the 'official' statistics that had formed the basis of criminological studies previously. Historians have also shown that a fairly continuous system of crime data recording has been in place over a long period (see Sharpe 1988 for a fuller discussion), becoming formalised in England and Wales in the nineteenth century. 'Official' government statistics are available for at least the past hundred years and certainly data were recorded long before that. To call these studies criminological at the time would not have been something the participants understood, yet the same sort of data are used today by those calling themselves criminologists. This is, of course, a tautological argument: that is to say, it is obvious that if scholars and researchers describe themselves and their studies as criminological, then they most likely will be identified by others as such. The object of this book is not to try to sort out the problem of which research method is the best approach, but to explore these issues for the reader to be aware of the concerns.

Chapters 3 and 4 illustrate in depth the aims and objectives of what can be largely classed as quantitative methods (how many, how much, when and where) and those classed as qualitative methods, which generally aim to concentrate on the underlying questions. This makes the distinction appear clearer than it will ever be in practice: for example, qualitative researchers might begin with quantitative data and then start to unpick the meanings and subtleties of the answers the original data suggested. The general philosophy behind these two approaches is often viewed as opposing and irreconcilable, but as the following typology shows (and as the two case studies that follow illustrate) there is crossing and re-crossing of paths in each case.

Types of research methods

Quantitative	Qualitative
Evaluation	
	Ethnography
Crime science	
	Interviews (open-ended questions)
Surveys	
	Focus groups
Interviews (closed questions)	
	Life history
Official statistics	

- **Quantitative methods** involve numbers, counting how many, when, and how much crime, for instance.
- **Qualitative methods** generally involve no numbers data but may use computer software in analysis.
- **Mixed methods** may involve elements of both methods: using counting or a quantifiable method for the analysis of qualitative data.

The sort of questions these methods can address depends upon the topic to be investigated. The following is a list of the type of subjects that researchers have investigated in the studies illustrated throughout this volume.

> **Police**
> Are the police corrupt?
> How do the police decide how to go about solving a murder?
> Are the police racist/sexist/incompetent?
>
> **Prisons**
> Are prisons safe and drug free?
> Do prison officers treat all prisoners fairly and equally?
> Could prisons be more compassionate places?
>
> **Suspects and offenders**
> Contraband smugglers
> Drug dealers
> Cyber fraudsters/white collar criminals
> Paedophiles
>
> **Victims of crime**
> Fear of crime
> Sexual assault
> Domestic violence
> Homicide

There follow three examples of research studies that illustrate the differing nature of the questions that can be posed, answered and investigated using quantitative, mixed and qualitative methods. In each case the study uses each of these three methods. In other words, this is intended to illustrate the relative non-exclusivity of research methods. Quantitative studies often have qualitative aspects and qualitative studies use numbers.

Example 1: Quantitative methods

As the term quantitative usually means counting or using numbers to support the conclusions and findings of a study, in criminology this often means large data sets, such as the number of crimes committed in a particular country over a time period such as a year. These data are discussed at length in Chapter 3. To give a flavour of a smaller and more manageable project, the following example is taken from an article by Tyler (2005). In this article Tyler is testing the theory that the public judge the police relative to their treatment (whether just and fair, for example) of citizens; he is basing his ideas on existing literature about 'process based policing' and social justice. Tyler states: 'This procedural justice-based perspective suggests that the key to public trust and support lies not only, or even primarily, in the ability of the police to suppress crime but in the manner in which the police interact with citizens' (Tyler 2005: 326).

In order that we can judge his evidence more effectively later in the article Tyler explains his sample and the sort of questions he asked his respondents (2005: 327–8).

METHOD
In this study, a multiethnic sample of New Yorkers was interviewed over the telephone concerning their views about the NYPD and about policing activities in their own neighborhoods. The interviews were conducted during the summer of 2002.

SAMPLE
The sample included 1,653 New Yorkers: 550 Whites, 455 African Americans, 410 Hispanics, and 210 other-ethnicity non-Whites (28 respondents declined to give their ethnicity). Those whose ethnicity was other or who declined to give their ethnicity were included in the overall analysis but were not considered as a subgroup. The sample used in this analysis is not weighted, so the results do not reflect population parameters for all of the residents of the city of New York.

QUESTIONNAIRE
An 8-item scale was created that combined responses to three aspects of cooperation. The questions measured were willingness to work with the police, willingness to work with the community, and institutional support for the police department (overall alpha = .73).

Cooperation with the police. People responded to three questions, which asked: 'How likely would you be to call the police to report a crime that was occurring in your neighborhood?' 'How likely would you be to help the police to find someone suspected of committing a crime by providing them with information?' 'How likely would you be to report dangerous or suspicious activities in your neighborhood to the police?'

Cooperation with the community. People responded to three questions, which asked the following: 'How likely would you be to volunteer your time on nights or weekends to help the police in your community?' 'How likely would you be to volunteer your time on nights or weekends to patrol the streets as part of a neighborhood watch program?' 'How likely would you be to volunteer your time on nights or weekends to attend a community meeting to discuss crime in your community?'

Institutional support for the police department. Respondents were asked to agree or disagree with the following questions: 'The size of the

Quantitative versus qualitative methods 29

NYPD should be increased by adding more patrol officers?' 'The officers of the NYPD deserve higher pay?'

As the later chapters of this book will show, many studies tend to limit themselves to either the broadly quantitative or the qualitative, seeking to understand the 'facts' behind the numbers, to explore new ideas or theories or to gain 'deep' knowledge of a small part of the social world (ethnographies), to find out about a bounded area of some aspect of social life (case study), or perhaps to hear about the experiences of a certain group of people (life history research). Some, however, use quantitative data to 'define' or describe the problem before going on to explore the reasons behind the apparent phenomenon they have discovered. As the following example shows, mixing methods in this way can produce a broader picture of the problem to be researched.

Example 2: Mixed methods

A worked example of a proposed project

Research area: The 'problem' of women in the police. Why are they lagging behind in terms of promotion, appointment to specialist posts such as the CID, the cars, guns and horses?

1 Begin by looking at the number of women in promoted posts and specialist departments (both nationally and in individual local forces).
2 Discover from the statistics that very few women make it to the top.
3 Find out that women are clustered in some specialist departments such as Child and Family Protection Units.
4 But then find other statistics that illustrate that compared with their overall presence (i.e. only 20 per cent overall) and length of service they are promoted more quickly than men with the same experience.

Research question (narrowed down from 'research area' above): Are there any structural or cultural reasons for the lack of promotion and specialisation of women officers?

Methods (in an ideal world):

- Analyse the number of women nationally, then by force area in specific posts across individual forces (see for example police

service strength England and Wales 2010, available at www.statistics.gov.uk or www.homeoffice.gov.uk/rds.
- Interview senior officers (including those responsible for human resources and training) to ask them about their policies.
- Organise a series of focus groups to ask front-line male and female officers what they think.
- Use the focus groups as a method of identifying other officers who might wish to contribute their views.
- Interview some promoted women to ask how they managed to be successful.
- Spend some time on patrol with male and female officers to conduct informal ethnographic conversations and interviews about the situation.
- Try to achieve wider coverage by visiting other geographical areas and types of police forces (e.g. rural/city, north/south, poor/affluent).

Alternative methods (quick and dirty – in the 'real' world):

- Find out whether any previous research has been conducted.
- Interview the people who did the previous research and/or identify anything they missed.
- Send out questionnaires to the women officers asking about the issues that might arise in the focus groups (above) but using responses that can be coded in order to count their opinions numerically.
- Carry out a computer-based package analysis of the data.
- Feed back results to officers involved in training/promoting staff to find out if the findings coincide with their view of the situation.

In a mixed methods study such as this, some of the quantitative counting questions can be asked, followed by some further in-depth issues using qualitative methods.

Example 3: Qualitative methods

Women on the door: female bouncers in the new night-time economy

The following extract is from a study of women bouncers or 'door security staff' that aimed to find out about their lives in this occupation that is normally associated with large, muscular men. The study used qualitative methods, interviews and focus groups, and although it asked questions about numbers – such as how many years they had been a bouncer, how much they earn and so on, the main analysis, findings or conclusions, part of which are reproduced below (from Hobbs and Westmarland 2006: 19–20), did not rely to any significant part on the quantitative element of the questions asked.

> In order to explore questions around gender transgression, ambiguity and occupational roles, we asked the women we interviewed about their occupational backgrounds, family lives and reasons for entering the world of door security. We found that they had a wide variety of previous or ongoing jobs in contrast to Hobbs *et al.* (2003) who discovered that male door staff came from a narrow range of industrial working class occupations. The women we interviewed had experience working in door security ranging from 10 months to 16 years, and from working in just one night-time venue, to one woman who had worked across 25 different doors in Manchester, including 'a huge variety of venues and stuff from your softest gay door to the roughest R and B doors' (woman bouncer C12).
>
> In addition to their wide age range (18 to 'past 50') and diverse ethnicities (20 per cent were of mixed or black origin or from countries other than white British), there were also variations in the amount of time women spent working on the doors, from just one shift of approximately five hours, to over 50 hours per week. For a few women, therefore, this was their main or only job. Their previous work experience ranged from being an ex-Metropolitan police officer, a woman working as a 'kissagram', a model turned club dancer, an office worker, civil service customer service manager, a city council regeneration policy officer and a call centre worker. There were two care workers, a night centre manger for the terminally ill suffering from AIDS/HIV, a prison officer, a recruitment consultant (dealing mostly in 'fork lift truck drivers'), a matron at a girls' private school, a newspaper delivery van driver, a bus driver, someone who 'does whatever needs doing' at a club during the day, and a manager with the Inland Revenue. One woman was a shop floor worker for a DIY chain, there was a football stadium stewards' supervisor, a trainee restaurant chef turned hotel assistant manager, an ex-RAF police officer, an aeronautical engineering student hoping to qualify as a commercial pilot, a life guard at a leisure centre, two glass washers, a gym instructor, and a shop assistant in martial arts shop (n = 27).

> While some of these occupations might seem to be very different from door security and the potentially violent role it entails, others have clear links and similarities. The former Met and military police RAF officers and the football stadium steward might be seen as relatively obvious routes into door security. Our interviewee who worked in the martial arts shop said that she had become interested in security work through talking to male customers in the job who encouraged her to apply. These diversities aside, the biggest occupational group from which the women were drawn was bar work, or as one of them called it, going from 'from barmaid to bouncer' (n = 13). These women, working behind bars in busy venues, would often be involved in control functions within the pub or club and are therefore 'used to seeing the violence'. Several of these women said they had been encouraged by other door security staff to train for their security badges, and remarked that it was better paid than bar work. Furthermore, they liked the 'control' aspect of doorwork in that rather than having to smile and be helpful and subservient as 'sellers' they could be thanked for letting the customers in, and so they had exchanged their 'service with a smile' role that Hochschild (1983) describes as being physically and emotionally draining, to one where they were thanked and respected and held some power.

How to choose methods that fit

In 'real life' research any combination of the above three methods or approaches will be part of the way the researchers try to find out the 'truth'. It is obvious that different methods will discover different reasons for the lack of women in policing, confidence in the police or why some women become bouncers, although in some cases there may be a certain amount of cross-over in the findings. It is plain, therefore, that research methods can rarely be placed in a box labelled 'qualitative' or 'quantitative'. In classic descriptions of research methods there is a continuum of methods, with extremes at each end.

Collecting numbers and displaying them in tables with little explanation or analysis, such as 'official' figures the police record on crime and clear-up rates (see *Crime in England and Wales 2009/10* for example, available from http://rds.homeoffice.gov.uk) are at one end of the quantitative or 'hard' end. Statistics from findings such as these, which are a combination of data from the British Crime Survey (BCS), are explained later in this chapter. At the 'soft' or qualitative extreme are the 'full immersion' ethnographies where researchers might 'live the life' of the police as far as possible and become accepted as part of the scenery; and also perhaps life history, where a researcher asks the respondent to recount a part of their life and experience in a free-flowing description.

This book aims to illustrate that criminological research covers the range of these methods and to provide a flavour of these approaches. They can broadly be grouped into 'paradigms', which help to decide whether the study is 'nomothetic' – that is, theory driven, testing existing hypotheses – or alternatively 'ideographic' – that is, developing theory as part of the creative process of the research. In effect, this means you either start out with an existing theory to test, or carry out a study to develop a theory.

These seemingly complicated terms simply refer to the way that theory is dealt with in the study. Some research projects begin with a theory, perhaps a general one about the world pertaining to crime and justice, or a more specific one that is closely related to the proposed project itself. An example might be the theory that is known in criminology as 'labelling theory'. This theory is most commonly associated with Howard Becker (1963) who argued:

> ... the central fact about deviance: it is created by society. I do not mean this in the way it is ordinarily understood, in which the causes of deviance are located in the social situation of the deviant or in 'social factors' which prompt his action. I mean, rather, that *social groups create deviance by making the rules whose infraction constitutes deviance*, and by applying those rules to particular people and labeling them as outsiders. From this point of view, deviance is *not* a quality of the act the person commits, but rather a consequence of the application by others of rules and sanctions to an 'offender'.
>
> (1963: 8–9, emphasis in original)

In the search for the causes of crime and trying to understand why people commit criminal acts, it was quite a radical idea that the acts and the actors themselves are called 'criminal' simply because society so labels them. In terms of a research project, then, a researcher might commence with this theory and aim to construct some research questions to explore the validity of Becker's ideas. For instance:

- To what extent might Becker's ideas hold water today?
- Does race and/or gender make a difference to the labelling process?
- Who has the power to create labels, and apply the rules?
- How does social class affect the application of rules and sanctions?

In contrast to research projects that begin with a clear theory to be tested, some may be intended to explore a theory that is primarily connected to the study itself. For example, that young people tend to 'grow out of' crime, with a peak age for offending for girls being between about 15 and 18, and for young men between 16 and 24. This theory could be linked to a number of 'bigger' theories, such as gender theories, biological theories, social learning theories, or theories about social class such as Marxism. The sort of project that uses theory in this way might aim:

- To explore the role of families in the timing of commencement and termination of criminal careers.
- To examine the way families without fathers may find their juvenile boys in trouble with the police.
- To investigate the way young people from more privileged backgrounds experience the criminal justice system.

These potential projects are using their own theories about the world to create research questions. They are making assumptions about the way families and young people live their lives, drawing on theories about families and their support systems; men and masculinity and their role in the family; the role of class in the way young people might be treated by the police and courts. At the same time they have their foundations in the bigger theories mentioned above, such as differential association (how crime is alleged to be passed down through the generations), gender theory (the role of fathers), and Marxism (that people at the bottom of the social class system will be more readily criminalised by the justice agencies).

Finally, a third approach to theory is to begin the study with a broad approach or set of theories that the research will be based around. This is often the case where 'appreciative' naturalistic or observational studies are conducted. It is sometimes difficult to predict which theories will be useful. Sometimes data collection needs to be commenced before general patterns of the emerging ideas can be ascertained. Once the general feel for the sort of issues that will be important for the study emerge, they can be marshalled into categories and given headings. This will lead to the development of theories about the data, the social situation and the problem or questions the study first aimed to address. This sort of approach is often likened to a 'funnel' because large amounts of data are collected and gradually the question or theory is narrowed down to a point. It is the opposite of the approaches above where a narrow idea or theory is then widened out with data sources and collection.

All three approaches, and various combinations of them, are illustrated in the examples in this book, but this is not to suggest that they are fixed or rigid approaches. The next part of this chapter looks at two studies that have differing paradigmatic approaches yet seek to discover facts about broadly similar topics. In order to draw out the comparisons the stated aims and objectives of each study are reproduced here and the methods are explored in some detail. There is then an opportunity to think through the match between research questions and method in each case, followed by a discussion of what can and cannot be learned from the findings of each piece of research.

It is not always possible to begin a project with a set theory. As might be obvious from the examples that follow, it is generally the nature of the research questions that determine which methods are to be used. In some cases this will be predetermined because someone else, such as the funders of the research, has set or designed the question or questions. In others there might be one 'set' question, perhaps a problem that needs investigation, with some flexibility about the sub-questions, or the questions to ask that will attempt to answer the main question. Whatever the case, the role of theory cannot be ignored, as the assumptions and value judgements that will become obvious as this discussion progresses are firmly rooted within theory.

Researching the 'truth' about rape

In this section two studies are compared to illustrate the way researchers have tackled the difficult and sensitive issue of rape. One study is quantitative and the other is qualitative.

Jennifer Temkin's article 'Reporting rape in London: a qualitative study' (1999) aimed to seek the experiences of rape victims in a particular area of the London Metropolitan Police (MPS), following published changes in police procedures in the treatment of women who had been raped. From a list of rape victims deemed suitable to be asked to take part in the study (see Temkin 1997, 1999 for a more detailed explanation), 13 women agreed to be interviewed. In addition, four women come forward as a result of a local newspaper advert. As Temkin acknowledges:

> Thus 17 women in total were interviewed. This does not claim or aim to be a quantitatively representative sample, but it is sufficient to reveal a number of important issues about the police processes ... Twenty-one police officers were also interviewed. Eight had been involved in cases in the victim sample.
>
> All interviews, which were conducted by a female researcher and lasted for approximately two hours, were tape-recorded and transcribed. Victims were asked specific questions about their reactions to police processes at each stage from reporting until the trial ... Police officers were asked, inter alia, about their attitudes towards rape cases in general and the extent to which they felt the police were able to provide a proper service for rape victims.
> (Temkin 1999: 21)

Temkin argues that her findings show that despite the new regime, 'most victims, however, were wholly or partly dissatisfied with the follow-up provided by the police ... Complaints concerned lack of information and lack of contact both of which aroused particularly bitter feelings' (1999: 29). Her findings also acknowledge the severe stress women officers are placed under due to the nature of the crime and its reporting and the volume of cases. These findings are presented in her article using the words of the women victims she interviewed. As she explained (1999: 34–5):

> Women in the study were asked to sum up their feelings about the service provided for them by the police. Some of the criticisms and conclusions were scathing and several mentioned that, in the event of a similar occurrence, they would not report again. L02, whose rapists were eventually imprisoned for twelve years, nevertheless summed up her experiences with the police as follows:
>
>> I didn't have a positive response from the police who didn't believe me. I felt really, really awful. I regretted terribly ringing them up and I thought: 'Why the hell did I pick up that phone and make that call?' I was so fed up with it all. I just wanted to see the back of the police and never see them again ... I talked about my experience with the police (with a counsellor at University College Hospital) and how I was made to feel like I was the criminal ... I felt the whole thing was negative.
>
> L12, whose case also resulted in a conviction, said that if a similar thing happened again:
>
>> I'd be very wary of going down to the police about it because I'd think they'd let me down. I feel they have let me down badly. They just wanted to get a result. They wanted him to be found guilty. You know: 'He's guilty. That's it. Don't bother with her any more.'
>
> L15 concluded:
>
>> The police could have been a bit nicer, more caring. I don't think a lot of them to tell the truth. I don't think they're very competent many of them.
>
> L14, whose rapist was convicted, said:
>
>> I believe they're trying but they're doing it in an amateurish way ... They don't want to do it this way but they've got to because of all of these women's groups and everything else. You know, I just don't think their hearts are in it. All these nice little suites with nice furniture and flowers and cups of tea and people in plain clothes don't convince me. It's attitudes that convince me.
>
> L05, whose case was transferred to the British Transport Police, regretted ever reporting the matter to the police. She said:
>
>> The British Transport Police just made a mockery of the whole thing. They made me feel worse actually.

L07 said:
> I thought they would be on my side but I think it's a lousy system.

Despite some women saying very positive things about individual officers, Temkin's research is clearly damning of the new system, which is supposed to be supportive and believing of women who report rape. One response, perhaps from the Metropolitan Police that are the subject of this criticism, might have been the way she selected the interview data or the respondents, or how she asked the questions. Another criticism might have been regarding her sample size and composition. She interviewed 13 women of a possible total group of 143, with a booster sample of four, drawn from the wider population. Even with these additional interviewees, her sample was just about 10 per cent of the women who reported rape in that district at the time of the study. This could mean that the 90 per cent not represented, whose voices are not heard in the study, might have been quite satisfied with the new service.

This is one of the main problems facing any research: does the study 'tell the true story' or situation? This is sometimes referred to as 'validity' – does it seem to reveal the truth, does it have evidence that seems to support the position or argument the author is putting forward, is it plausible and believable? For instance, from Temkin's evidence in the section of the article above, is it plausible that the women who encounter the Met's rape investigation system are largely unhappy with how it worked for them? In other words, how does the research hold up to scrutiny in a number of ways that include the three Rs: reliability, representativeness and replicability?

Reliability

Are the data and the findings reliable? The answer to this question may be based on the following two Rs:

Representativeness: Is the group from which the data was collected a representative subset of the whole? In other words, is the 'sample' of the relevant population?

Replicability: Could the study be carried out again, using the methods described by the original researchers, to obtain a similar result?

This means that for the findings of a study, particularly one that relies upon quantities and counting for evidence, although not exclusively, the 'reliability' or plausibility or claims to 'truth' having to pass the test of representativeness and replicability is easier. The sample (presuming the whole possible population has not been surveyed) has to have been chosen in a way that means it is an approximation, a reflection, and so can be said to 'represent' the total population. Otherwise, critics of the study will say that whatever the findings are, they do not apply to everyone who could be in that group. 'Replicable' means that following a model of the natural sciences, for research findings to be reliable another researcher could carry out a study using the same methods (possibly with another representative sample of the same population) and find broadly similar results.

One of the answers to this conundrum is to have a statistically representative group or 'sample' drawn from a wider population. Take, for example, the methodological note of another study looking at women's experiences of rape and sexual assault, conducted by Myhill and Allen for the British Crime Survey (BCS) in 2002.

> A nationally representative sample of 6,944 women aged 16 to 59 answered the 2000 self-completion module. The response rate was 98 per cent of those eligible to participate. The responses of these women were used to estimate the extent of sexual victimisation. In order to examine the nature of incidents, the 1998 and 2000 modules were combined, to give a total of 1,183 female victims. The authors carried out extensive checks on the data before combining the modules, to ensure that minor question changes had not led to different types of incident being recorded.
>
> (Myhill and Allen 2002: 6)

This shows the comparison between the two methods. The BCS survey that Myhill and Allen describe had an initial sample size of nearly 7,000 women. As the following explanation of the key points from the findings show, in the year of the survey approximately 61,000 women said that they had been a victim of rape. Of these, just 20 per cent of the rapes came to the attention of the police, of which 32 per cent were 'very satisfied' and 22 per cent were 'very dissatisfied'.

Key points
- 0.4 per cent of women aged 16 to 59 in England and Wales said they had been raped in the year preceding the 2000 BCS – an estimated 61,000 victims.
- 0.9 per cent of women said they had been subject to some form of sexual victimisation (including rape) in this period.
- Around 1 in 20 women (4.9 per cent) said they had been raped since age 16, an estimated 754,000 victims. About 1 in 10 women (9.7 per cent) said they had experienced some form of sexual victimisation (including rape) since age 16.
- Age is the biggest risk factor for experiencing sexual victimisation; women aged 16 to 24 were more likely to say they had been sexually victimised in the last year than older women.
- Women are most likely to be sexually attacked by men they know in some way, most often partners (32 per cent) or acquaintances

(22 per cent). Current partners (at the time of the attack) were responsible for 45 per cent of rapes reported to the survey. Strangers were responsible for only 8 per cent of rapes reported to the survey.
- 18 per cent of incidents of sexual victimisation reported to the survey came to the attention of the police; the police came to know about 20 per cent of rapes. 32 per cent of women who reported rape were 'very satisfied' with the way the police handled the matter, 22 per cent were very dissatisfied.
- Less than two-thirds (60 per cent) of female rape victims were prepared to self-classify their experience as 'rape' and less than three-quarters (70 per cent) of women who self-classified themselves as having been the victim of 'attempted rape' also self-classified this incident as a crime.

(Myhill and Allen 2002: 1)

One of the ways quantitative research aims to justify or support its claims is to rely upon large numbers of people saying the same thing. As other examples will illustrate in Chapter 3, numbers can be very powerful and persuasive. It depends upon your point of view as to which study is more convincing – personal accounts or large numbers of people agreeing that a particular statement is true or false. There are no definitive rules about sample size and validity. For example, one woman's intimate recounting of her horrific experiences as a victim of rape (see Saward 1995, for instance), and subsequent processes of the police and criminal justice system, can be as powerful as the large numbers of women who claim that they were dissatisfied with the police in the survey above.

So what can be said is the truth about rape? How survivors experience the justice system, including the initial police contact when they report the incident, obviously varies. These two different studies tell different stories, but is either (or both) telling 'the truth', or what might be termed 'a truth', about the situation they have researched?

Validity

In research terms truth is often discussed as the study's 'validity'. In other words, do the conclusions seem to answer the question the research aimed to answer? Do they contribute to theory, or possibly policy or practice in the field? One of the ways this is judged is by the credibility of the evidence upon which the conclusions are based. In a sense this is the meat of the research, because the truth that the study has unearthed might not be obvious. This shows that the evidence and how it is presented is often the place where 'truth' or validity is determined. At a simple level an unconvincing research study is one where the reader finds the conclusions unbelievable, unsupported or can think of another explanation, which the researcher has not addressed. Consider the question of 'who commits crime?'

Validity relies upon:

Plausibility: We have many years' data and several studies that show that young men between the ages of 16 and 24 are the main lawbreakers.

Credibility: Given the nature of the problem, the data that were collected, and the way the researchers carried it out, is this likely?

The following statistics, taken from a Ministry of Justice publication (2010) about juvenile reoffending rates, suggest that this might be the case.

Reoffending by gender

Between the 2000 and 2008 cohorts, the proportion of female offenders in the cohort increased from 20.9 per cent to 25.2 per cent. Females have a much lower frequency rate than males. In the 2008 cohort it was 68.6 offences per 100 offenders compared to 129.2 offences per 100 offenders for males. However, males have seen the largest reduction in frequency rate of 24.0 per cent from 170.0 in the 2000 cohort, compared to a reduction for females of 15.2 per cent from 80.9 in the 2000 cohort (Figure E).

Comparisons with the most recent cohort, 2007, show that the frequency rate for males has fallen, from 131.0 to 129.2 offences per 100 offenders. There has been a decrease in the frequency rate for females over the same period, from 71.4 to 68.6 offences per 100 offenders.

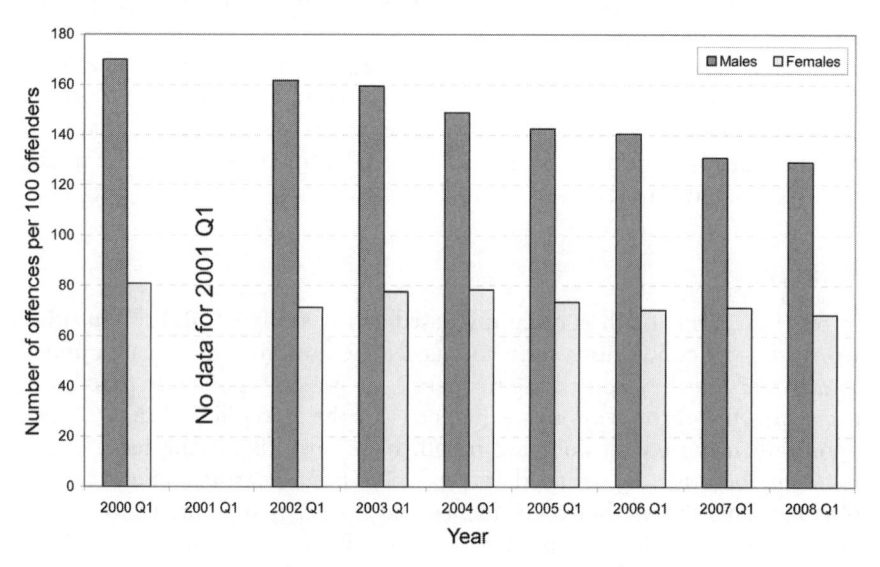

Figure E Number of proven offences per 100 offenders by gender, 2000, 2002–2008 cohorts

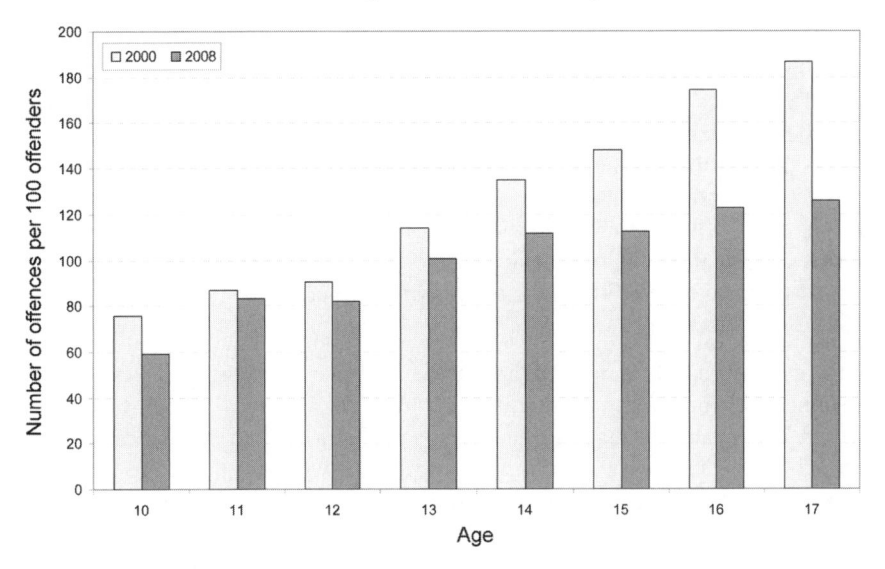

Figure F Number of proven offences per 100 offenders by age, 2000 and 2008 cohorts

Reoffending by age
Age is taken to be the age of the offender at the index date, i.e. the date on which the offender entered the cohort (sanctioned or released from custody).

All ages saw a reduction in the frequency rate between the 2000 and 2008 cohorts. Reoffending has fallen the most amongst 16 and 17 year olds – the frequency rates for these age groups fell by 29.7 per cent and 32.6 per cent respectively. However, these two age groups still had the highest frequency rates, at 122.7 for 16 year olds and 125.8 for 17 year olds in 2008 (Figure F).

What role, if any, does 'common sense' or personal experience play in the role of believing the findings of the studies that suggest this is the truth? There are a number of problems that could mean this is not the whole truth about the incidence of crime. For example, which groups might not be recorded as lawbreakers? Why might young men be so obviously involved in crime? In addition, a number of questions can be asked about any study before it can be classed as 'valid', or if not 'the truth' at least having conclusions that speak of 'a truth'. This is part of the consideration of whether the findings are plausible, credible, or essentially believable. Basing social science research on the scientific model raises a number of problems. For example:

- Despite some assertions, 'truth' varies depending upon interpretations.
- 'Facts' (or at least their presentation) are influenced by values.

- Knowledge that may have been gathered and built upon may appear objective but could have begun with a false premise.
- If variables, such as gender, are used in this quasi scientific method, are they valid?
- Is it possible to be objective when measuring people, their beliefs, actions and motives?
- Is it possible to escape the politics of such research?
- Is it ethical to use 'scientific' methods (for instance, to separate twins at birth to see whether one turns out more criminal than the other)?

On the other hand, it depends upon the purpose for which the research is designed. If the study is intended to provide an initial 'how many' or 'where' or 'when', perhaps some initial 'facts' before the research can begin, it might be described as 'descriptive' research. It would still need to be valid; plausibility would rely upon a number of factors, perhaps the coverage of the research. Did it ask everyone available or design a reasonable sample? Did the researchers consider all the options and available information? Is the data presented as being suitably analysed to lead to the conclusions, even if they simply describe a particular situation?

The science of research methods

Why not simply replicate 'science', then? Surely researchers would have no further problems with validity if they simply used methods employed by physicists and chemists.

In fact, being 'scientific' in the social sciences does not necessarily mean trying to replicate the methods used by 'natural' scientists. This is one way of delineating the difference. Sometimes there is a distinction used that talks about 'hard' and 'soft' science – the factual, replicable, non-human participant type of research with inanimate objects as opposed to the type of research that involves decision-making human beings and more ambiguous questions and answers.

In reality, though, there are few definite borders because 'hard' scientists are still human and have to interpret results, and 'soft' social scientists have methods that replicate 'hard' or objective studies. These methods include those used by the government collecting 'official' statistics, discussed in the next chapter, and the British Crime Survey.

These studies rely upon large 'sample' populations – that is, a large number of people are interviewed to form a 'representative' group. If the population was 50 million, the BCS would aim to interview 50,000, and they need to be from various backgrounds: towns and cities and the countryside, with an age, gender and ethnicity mix that approximates to the overall population. In a smaller study, perhaps of an organisation of a few thousand, it might be acceptable to choose every tenth person on a list of staff. This sample would then need 'standardising', however; for example, counting the number of women overall in the organisation and then making sure that the male to female ratio in the final sample matched the overall population. If the sample chosen at random does not match the characteristics of the overall population, it is usual to select a 'booster' sample to add to the original group.

The 'harder' end of qualitative research tends to involve a set of pre-designed questions, delivered either by questionnaire or (in the case of the BCS) by interviewers trained and instructed to ask questions and record answers in a standard format. Commercial market research companies use similar methods when collecting a large amount of cheap data. There might also be a 'softer', qualitative section where the respondent might be asked to answer a more open-ended question. The following is an extract from a Home Office online document detailing how the BCS collects its information (http://rds.homeoffice.gov.uk/rds/bcs-methodological.html).

Methodological information about the British Crime Survey

The British Crime Survey (BCS) is a well-established study and one of the largest social research surveys conducted in England and Wales. It is a victimisation survey in which adults living in private households are asked about their experiences of crime in face-to-face interviews . . .

The BCS currently interviews over 51,000 people aged 16 or over every year. This includes around 47,000 interviews in the main survey, with an additional boost to the number of interviews with 16- to 24-year-olds. The survey was also extended in January 2009 to include 4,000 interviews with children aged 10–15 each year.

Previous sweeps of the BCS were carried out in 1982, 1984, 1988, 1992, 1994, 1996, 1998, 2000 and 2001. The first survey was carried out in England, Wales and Scotland (hence the study was referred to as the *British* Crime Survey), as was the third survey. Scotland now has its own survey (Scottish Crime & Justice Survey), as does Northern Ireland (Northern Ireland Crime & Victimisation Survey).

Although there have been changes to the design of the survey over time, the wording of the questions that are asked to elicit victimisation experiences has remained constant throughout the life of the BCS.

At present, the sample is designed to provide adequate numbers (around 1,000 interviews) in each Police Force Area. The overall response rate is currently 75 per cent – one of the highest for the large continuous government surveys.

Technical reports

We produce a technical report providing information on survey design, weighting and survey response every survey year.

Basically the questions the British Crime Survey asks are about victimisation. They try to determine who has been a victim of crime in the past year, and because of the large and representative sample, covering the whole country and 'weighted' to make sure that those within the sample represent the general population, they can claim to be rigorous, representative and therefore have a high claim to validity or 'truth'. Of course, the accusations levelled at the 'softer' end of research are that they cannot match this sort of level of resource. Furthermore, as the debate regarding the 'truth' about rape illustrates, this is also a political, theoretical and philosophical issue. Who can claim to know the truth is a contentious issue; researchers from what is called the 'positivist' tradition have been challenged by feminist critics, for example. They argue that the findings of 'hard science' – created by studies that use methods copying the natural sciences such as physics and chemistry – make overblown claims as to their rigour, and the 'power' of their claims to truth. As Powell explains:

> The positivist proclaims a detached disinterest in any consequences emanating from 'his' research. Sensitivity to any emotional impact the research process or outcome may have on the 'researched' is not an issue and any such impact on the researcher goes unacknowledged. His job is merely to 'tell it like it is' and if the 'truth' hurts someone – well so be it.
>
> (1996: 4)

The critique or rejection of 'positivist' science based on value-free 'facts' is challenged by feminist researchers, among others. Punch argues that the 'value neutral' or value-free positivist position has been challenged over the past 20 years (2005: 48):

> [The] rejection of the positivist view comes from several quarters. Feminist scholars, for example, have repeatedly challenged the 'persistent positivist myth' (Haig 1997) that science is values free, and critical theorists and feminists alike regard the distinction between facts and values as simply a device which disguises the role of conservative values in much social research. Instead of value-free research, critical theorists especially argue that research should be used in the service of the emancipation of oppressed groups: in other words, that it should be openly ideological. (Hammersley 1993)

This sort of 'political' argument, the positivist 'scientist' versus their critics, is evident throughout this volume, but will not be resolved. Aside from these higher philosophical concerns the methods that are chosen for any particular study depend upon practical considerations – time, money, availability of people to interview, existing data and so on – but more importantly it depends on the intended purpose of the research. Some of these purposes might be as follows.

- Descriptive and informative – simply aims to sketch the existing picture or situation.
- To work out whether an existing theory or set of ideas is credible.
- Policy led – to find out what the current situation is and perhaps suggest solutions.
- To carry out research that also instigates changes.

Some of these types of research lend themselves to quantitative methods, as discussed above, others more towards qualitative methods, which are explored in the following section. As you will have begun to realise, however, much of the research in criminology, with the exception of the Home Office tables and official statistics, combines qualitative and quantitative methods (see Chapter 4 for a fuller discussion of this).

As this suggests, there are a number of things the British Crime Survey cannot achieve, and the authors do not claim to achieve. First is the nuances and experience of being the victim of crime. The definition of what is crime is not the least of these. The simple question, 'Have you been a victim of crime?' will mean different things to different people. The BCS aims to find out the 'real' level of crime by asking people, in their own homes, to relate their experiences of the past year – a reasonable time to remember. Of course, this does not mean it captures all events, but it does reveal about twice the number of crimes that are recorded by the police each year.

A more qualitative study of crime victimisation might rely on personal contact and trust. Reflecting on her pioneering study in the 1980s, which is explored in her interview in Chapter 4, Sandra Walklate says that 'positivist' criminology or victimology has a certain focus and an understanding of the 'victims' in a certain way:

> It reflects a traditional view of science and the scientific knowledge-gathering process which is concerned to separate that which is knowable – the observable, the measurable, and the objective – from that which is not knowable – belief. Hence the methodological focus on the construction of victim typologies and the search for patterns of victimisation through the use of the criminal victimisation survey. This process, positivist victimology presumes, equips us with objective, measurable information. This does not mean that such information is without its applied uses, in the spheres of either politics or policy. The development of the criminal victimisation survey was clearly influential

in placing the question of criminal victimisation on the political and policy agendas.

(Walklate 2000: 186)

As her interview illustrates, she has some insights to share that are crucial to the way 'real' life research is carried out, including the problems and pitfalls of encountering 'the public' as respondents to a survey. She explains one of the problems of these encounters for researchers in the following extract.

> The interviewers we used were not stereotypical university students. They were all mature with northern connections; some were from Salford itself. And although they were going into houses with traditional survey instruments we ensured that the students remained sensitive to the process they were engaging in. We trained the interviewers to pay particular attention to the importance of informality and of asking questions as if they were part of a conversation. We asked them to be fairly informal in their dress and not to carry clipboards or briefcases but to carry the questionnaires around in plastic bags. This was done as a way of trying to increase their safety on the streets as well as helping the respondents to feel more relaxed and confident about the process.
>
> (Walklate 2000: 194–5)

Here the emphasis is upon using a quantitative 'research instrument' to measure and gather 'hard' data, namely a questionnaire used by the interviewers to ask a predetermined set of questions; but its effect is 'softened' by training the researchers to elicit responses that would be as close an approximation as possible to the 'truth' by making the respondents comfortable, confident and hopefully open and responsive. The distance between the researcher and the researched and their relationship, even for the brief time period of an interview or 'conversation', as Walklate describes the delivery of the questionnaire in her survey, is something that qualitative researchers consider important. As the detailed discussion in Chapters 4 and 5 will show, where qualitative methods are considered in more depth, this aspect is something that separates qualitative and quantitative research. Quantitative measures often rely on objective, sometimes non-human contact (questionnaires delivered by post, for example), whereas qualitative studies almost always have a personal, if not emotional, attachment between the researcher and researched. They will often rely upon a personal approach, achieving access to the person or group of people to be researched. This may require the negotiation of access via a 'gatekeeper', someone with the power or authority to allow the person to be interviewed. Finally, as Walklate suggests, gathering the data will rely upon a personal rapport or feeling of confidence or comfort between the people involved.

Within criminological research there are many situations where the problem of negotiating access to particular groups and then negotiating confidence and rapport between the researchers and respondents might be problematic. This book is full of topics where there are complications associated with accessing the respondents, not simply because they are difficult to find but also because they lie behind a barrier that needs to be negotiated. Sometimes this barrier is physical – the person in charge of a prison (and usually the Home Office), for example, has to give permission for a researcher to talk to prisoners or prison officers. In other cases it is psychological – for example, in the area of police corruption, not many police officers would admit to being corrupt or want to tell of colleagues' corrupt practices, and this would, of course, cause difficulties for the organisation. Certain groups of victims would also be difficult to access because of sensitive issues. Interviewing the family and friends of murder victims, for example, while not impossible, would require great sensitivity to build up a rapport because of the emotional pain involved in being reminded of the events associated with the loss. Even the initial contact would have to be managed extremely sensitively as the trauma resulting from such an approach might cause the victims to be revictimised. This chapter has offered a flavour of these difficult topics in its exploration of rape and sexual assault, and the crime victimisation studies and there are many more throughout the book.

Conclusion

This chapter has aimed to introduce the idea that real life research, with its practical demands, might require a range of methods to address the question it is trying to answer. It has suggested that although there are no 'superior' methods or any one particular approach that is better than others, the important point is to consider how appropriate the particular method is for the particular study: its aims, theoretical approach, available resources and so on. The central points from this chapter will be revisited throughout the forthcoming chapters.

One of the main strengths of quantitative research is that by using numbers and counting its claim to validity or truth is immediate and obvious – these studies can claim to be easily replicable and therefore provide 'scientific' results.

Qualitative methods provide more depth, understanding and can use 'scientific' methods, with representative sampling, replicability and so on, but are more open to criticisms of researcher bias.

Mixed methods, or those not fitting neatly into one or other category, can have advantages, unless they mean that resources are spread too thinly for meaningful data, analysis and results.

This chapter has also introduced the philosophies that underlie the choice of any particular method. Research cannot exist in a vacuum away from political and ethical concerns, and the theoretical approach that is chosen, or within which the project exists, draws upon or develops, will influence the outcome. These latter points will be explored and developed in later chapters, where the 'real life' examples described will help to further these debates.

3 Quantitative methods

Introduction

In this chapter the quantitative – counting or evaluative – aspects of criminological research are considered and explored in terms of their 'real life' applications. To make this large topic manageable, the discussion is divided into a series of smaller sections, which include the way 'official statistics' are collected by the government to describe the number of crimes reported to the police that are recorded and processed. The problems with these processes, and the way people have criticised the way they are used, are compared with some other types of secondary data such as the British Crime Survey (BCS), which attempts to illustrate the 'real life' crime experiences of people who may or may not report incidents or offences against them to the police.

These secondary data sources – in other words, the statistics that are largely gathered by official governmental organisations – are compared with methods and uses of primary data – that is, data collected by the researcher for use by the researcher, which provide questions and inform projects that are largely within the control of the researcher. The latter can be just as valuable as the large data sets available from 'official' sources and can provide a useful critique of the bigger picture.

Taking these types of research together (primary and secondary) this chapter begins with the more 'public' side of criminological research. It reflects the way statistics are used, studies that 'count' and the growing importance of evaluation in criminological research. One reason why these studies or data are considered public is that they are often considered 'official' statistics – that is, numbers of crimes or incidents collected by public bodies such as the police, prisons and courts, and made available (usually free of charge) to any researcher who wishes to access the data. In addition, they are often the studies from which conclusions are drawn that lead to government policies and, ultimately, new laws. In this sense this chapter is about the way statistics are used in quantitative studies, using some examples of existing and potential research projects.

This chapter begins with some observations on the general nature of crime statistics, government figures on levels of different types of crime, police clear-up rates, and so on. It is these figures that are often referred to as the 'official' statistics of crime. There follows a discussion of the problems with this type of published research and the basic methods that are used to collect the statistics the government (and many others) use to base decisions about new legislation and policies. The collection of statistics that can contradict these 'official' criminal justice data are then discussed. The main source of these 'critical' statistics has traditionally been the British Crime Survey, the BCS. These are also collected by the government, in the sense that they are collected by a government-funded agency, and so it is slightly misleading to differentiate between the two. They way they provide a comparison with, or sometimes contradict, 'official' statistics is that they give a picture of what people say has happened to them rather than facts from organisations such as the police. This is explained in more detail below. Then the chapter moves into 'non official' statistics, and the principles guiding the collection and reliability of these figures which may become 'facts'. Finally the work of the first interviewee in this volume is discussed, to illustrate the problems, pitfalls and potential solutions to problems of research using statistics.

What are quantitative criminological methods?

Before launching into the types of statistics that criminologists use and how they are collected, it is useful to think about the type of research covered by the term 'quantitative'. As might be suggested, it implies quantities to be measured, counted, added up and analysed. Aside from data that criminologists might collect themselves there are many different types of statistics already in existence that are readily available, and many quantitative methods by which to analyse and collect further data. Using these statistics is sometimes referred to as 'secondary analysis'. According to Coleman and Moynihan (1996) there are three main types of data – 'official' statistics – that is, the data on police prisons, reported crimes and so on; self-report studies, where people are asked about their 'criminal' activities; and finally victimisation surveys. They argue that each of these types of data is haunted by what they describe as the 'dark figure'. They describe this problem in relation to understanding crime data and that:

> In this preliminary sketch of the major developments in perspective on crime data over nearly two centuries, it should be clear that the dark figure has been a haunting presence. It might be thought that, with the advent of self-report and victim surveys in recent years we have been getting closer and closer to a 'total picture' of crime and criminals, with the dark figure exposed for what it is. This is not our view. Crime and dark figures are not simply 'out there' waiting to be counted by the application of a simple rule to unambiguous events in a laboratory setting by neutral observers. Instead, any concerns and objectives use a

set of definitions, rules and procedures (on which there may not be agreement) in a complex environment to arrive at that product.

(Coleman and Moynihan 1996: 20)

As explained earlier in the introductory chapter, quantitative methods have been moving from the centre to the periphery and back to become increasingly important in the UK criminology world. As Cresswell documents, prior to the 1970s in Britain, with a few exceptions counting and statistics were the main social science 'method', while from the early 1980s onwards qualitative methods, books and studies began to develop (2010: 15–16). Although there had been studies such as Banton's ethnography of policing in 1964, and in the 1930s some sociologists in the Chicago School had looked at 'criminological' or sociology of deviance areas of interest, mainstream criminology was located in counting things. Since the early 1990s, with the rise of what is described as 'administrative' criminology, led by the Home Office's demand for evaluation, evidence-led research and so on, it has undergone a resurgence. This was partly led by New Labour's demand for knowing the 'causes of crime' and 'what works', in response to earlier right-wing assertions that 'prison works'. Over the past ten years or so in the UK, because of a series of political decisions about the 'problem' of crime and how to seem to be solving it, the demand for 'hard' statistical data has increased. A brief search of the UK Ministry of Justice website illustrates the way governments attempt to work out what the problem is, the so-called 'causes of crime', and how to find out if anything can help. The following is their mission statement (see www.justice.gov.uk/about.htm).

Ministry of Justice Mission Statement

The Ministry of Justice is one of the largest government departments, with around 95,000 people (including probation services) and a budget of £9.2 billion.

Every year around nine million people use our services in 900 locations across the United Kingdom, including 650 courts and tribunals and 139 prisons in England and Wales.

Our work spans criminal, civil and family justice, democracy, rights and the constitution.

The Ministry of Justice works to protect the public and reduce reoffending, and to provide a more effective, transparent and responsive criminal justice system for victims and the public. We also provide fair and simple routes to civil and family justice.

> The Ministry of Justice has responsibility for different parts of the justice system – the courts, prisons, probation services and attendance centres. We work in partnership with the other government departments and agencies to reform the criminal justice system, to serve the public and support the victims of crime.
>
> We are also responsible for making new laws, strengthening democracy, modernising the constitution and safeguarding human rights.

While they seem to give equal weight to qualitative, in-depth studies, a brief examination of the studies published since 2001 shows that the majority of past commissioned and published studies contain some element of counting. This is not a specific criticism, just an observation that few studies, even the most in-depth qualitative ones, can escape counting, at least initially, the scale of the problem to be addressed. Nor is it the case that all Home Office/Ministry of Justice studies are conducted by researchers employed directly by the government. Often there are tenders or calls for expressions of interest from independent researchers, and/or established academics in their field, who are invited to carry out research on behalf of the Home Office/Ministry of Justice. The subsequent report will be prefaced with the disclaimer that the views expressed do not necessarily accord with the funders – ultimately the government.

In some ways this is a positive advantage for the average researcher because he or she may not have the expertise or the funds to conduct large-scale statistical analysis of a problem they wish to investigate. In effect, studies may already exist that answer at least some of the basic questions you may wish to ask. The advantages of using already existing quantitative data such as this are that is cheap (and often free), the methods used to collect it will be explicit (usually) and numerous types of criminological and associated data are regularly updated. Such sources include the obvious ones:

- Crime figures
- Police
- Prison
- Courts

There are also some more general social statistics such as:

- Deprivation index
- Employment statistics
- Health
- Births and deaths

Two broad types of quantitative study are examined in this chapter: statistical data and evaluative data. There are some studies, such as the Home Office collections of data on numbers of crimes, police officer strength and so on, that simply count statistics: how many of any particular thing, without having to make any points or judgements about the data. This is sometimes called 'raw data' in that it has not been processed (apart from the collection, analysis and publication). Evaluation is another step, which compares data, or sometimes involves an intervention. This might include a type of experiment, such as changing something about the situation (this is called a 'variable') and then measuring to see if it has had any effect. Two studies later in this chapter illustrate this approach.

The next section of this chapter aims to examine how existing statistics can be used in research, and their drawbacks. The examples included are mainly from large government data sets. Later the chapter moves on to talk about collecting original data, and individual studies are analysed. Where appropriate, the authors are interviewed about their choice of method.

Primary and secondary data

In this section it is secondary data that will be tackled first. This refers to the sort of statistics and figures that count how many crimes are recorded by the police: the 'official' statistics and other large studies that are usually publicly funded and widely available. The topic of primary data will be examined later, as it refers to studies in which the researcher is the first person to lay hands on the information as a result of asking questions, sending out surveys or observations.

There are massive data sets available on a huge range of crime issues in most developed countries. Similar to the way any research may proceed, in the UK the Home Office/Ministry of Justice, and in the USA government-funded organisations such as the Institute of Justice, may call on expert advice and leaders in particular fields of criminology, and also use their own in-house research staff, to carry out studies and collect statistics. These data sets are generally freely available to anyone embarking on a project within any field of criminology, and associated fields of study. The following is an example of one way to begin looking at a problem where existing data sets can be employed as a starting point.

Case study 1: homicide statistics

When beginning a study of homicide, one thing researchers might want to investigate is how many occur per year. Who, how, and what is the result of police investigations? Are there more murders than in previous years? What makes a difference? Does the 'dark figure' exist in terms of homicide statistics? In other words, can people 'get away with murder', can it be covered up? If so, to what extent? Does the problem that 'haunts' other crime statistics apply here? In the sense that because commonly crime is covert, and people do not report some crimes and 'over-report' others (such as items stolen in a burglary to boost their insurance claim), is homicide different? Are homicide statistics more reliable than other crime figures? After all, bodies are difficult to conceal and someone would usually notice if a friend or relative disappeared, and they would report it to the police.

Perhaps more so than for other crimes, homicide and violent crime as statistics are seen as a 'measure' of the health of a country or society. This is because they are used by political parties: governments turn to them to show how well they are doing, or how much more they are about to do, or to justify new policies 'tackling' crime and its associated evils. Violent crime statistics can sometimes make the populace feel 'insecure' and in need of strong, confident policy measures to counteract the threat. Reassurance is a tool of what is sometimes described as 'governing through crime', as the special fears that crime engenders can be used to persuade people that certain measures are necessary (such as anti-terrorist laws that may infringe upon personal liberty). Whichever way they are used, violent crime statistics, especially those for homicide, can convey a political message, whether the incidence is increasing or decreasing. This is very much in evidence in violent crime and the official government statistical machine is geared to separating this sort of activity from other types of crime.

Prior to the data being widely available electronically on the web the Home Office would publish annual statistics in the form of a large volume called *Criminal Statistics England and Wales*. The following extract is from the 1995 edition, when the volume ran to 256 pages.

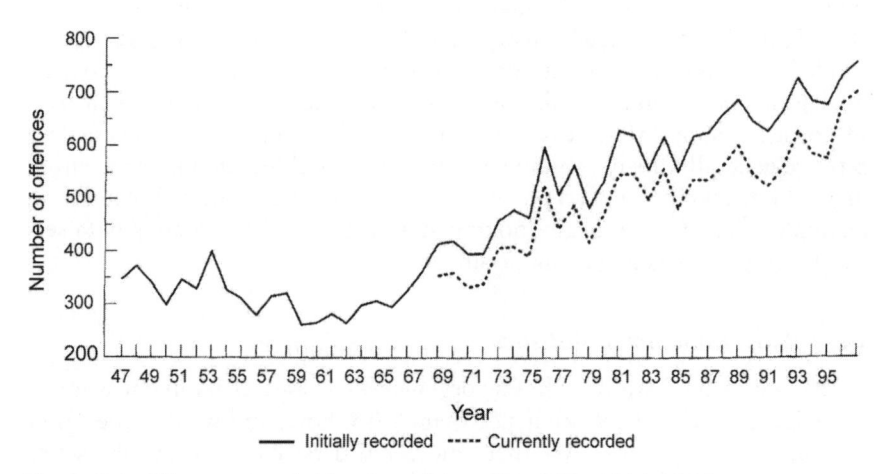

Figure 3.1 Offences recorded by the police as homicide 1946–1995
Source: *Criminal Statistics England and Wales*.

Offences initially recorded as homicide and their outcomes

4.1. Homicide includes the offences of murder, manslaughter and infanticide. At the time of writing, court proceedings were still pending in around one-third of the incidents initially recorded as homicide. The outcome may result in some offences being reclassified when final data is available, for example where it is concluded that death was accidental. The 1994 figures are therefore a better guide to recent trends.

4.2. It would be wrong to place too much importance on any one year's figure because homicides are rare, and considerable year-on-year variation is to be expected both in terms of the numbers and types of homicides recorded. The 754 deaths initially recorded as homicides in 1995 is the highest annual total this century. Over the past 20 years the average increase in homicides was 1.5 per cent, which compares with 6.2 per cent for serious offences of violence against the person. Figure 4.1 gives the number of homicides currently recorded for 1995 as 699, 60 more than the 1994 total.

4.3. Of the 754 offences first recorded during 1995, by August 1996 55 were no longer recorded as homicides. Court proceedings had resulted in findings of guilt in respect of 299 victims and proceedings were pending for a further 246. No suspects had been identified in relation to 88 victims (including 18 cases where all suspects were acquitted). The suspects responsible for the deaths of 50 victims had committed suicide or died.

4.4. Taking the more complete 1994 figures as a guide, around 12 per cent of deaths initially recorded as homicides may be reclassified. For the rest, about three-quarters will result in conviction, there will be no suspect for around 15 per cent and for about 1 in 10, court proceedings will not be initiated or will be concluded without conviction or acquittal, e.g. the suspect died or committed suicide or proceedings discontinued.

The way these statics are recorded is fairly confusing because the classification of homicide relies upon someone being found guilty in a court. So if someone who is suspected of an illegal killing is brought to court but is acquitted, and after the trial the police announce that they are 'not currently seeking anyone else in connection with this case', this usually means that they feel they have irrefutable evidence that the person they caught was indeed guilty of the offence. The jury thought otherwise, however, and so the homicide does not exist in the statistics. This is taken up later in the case study below, but the issue to remember is that statistics rely on 'human' factors, and are only the result of processes that are controlled by events in the 'real' world.

One reason why these figures are important is political, as the discussion above indicates. The news from the Home Office in 1995 that the steady increase in homicides in England and Wales had hit the 'highest annual total this century' could be a statistic used by political parties to suggest that the government was being careless with the nation's personal security, or at the very least that 'something needs to be done about violent crime'. Homicide, although rare, is newsworthy – think about the BBC's *Crimewatch* programme, where each edition almost always has at least one unsolved murder – and plays upon people's feelings of insecurity. Another reason is that the figures can provide a barometer to a nation's comparative ranking in terms of security. How does the UK compare with other countries in Europe, and with the USA?

It might be assumed that a study of the rate of homicide in any particular country would be a fairly straightforward exercise. Unlike other sorts of crime, the evidence is there – the body – and it would be assumed that with very few exceptions the body will be discovered quickly and the death investigated. It will be ascertained whether the death occurred by natural causes or by suicide or by some sort of homicide. In common parlance there are two categories of homicide in the UK and most other countries: killing with intent (usually 'murder'), and killing with some degree of lesser intent, sometimes called 'manslaughter'. Another category exists, which is less common: 'being reckless' as to whether death would result from certain actions, such as arson.

Aside from these difficulties of categorisation, homicide means that someone has died at the hands of another, and it is not a pure 'accident' (such as in a car crash, for example). This would seem to make it easy to count the incidence in any particular country, and perhaps go on to make comparisons with different countries or jurisdictions. The following discussion shows, however, that this is not the case, due to the problems with classification that Brookman and Maguire raise (2004: 329).

> *The discovery of bodies.* We do not know how many killers manage to dispose of the bodies of their victims without trace. It is estimated by the National Missing Persons Helpline that about 250,000 people go missing every year in the United Kingdom, a fair proportion of whom are never accounted for ... More specifically, a large force such as Greater Manchester Police can expect in the region of 11,000 missing person reports each year (Newiss 1999). While many of these will have deliberately sought obscurity, some will probably have become victims of homicide.

Establishing the cause of death. In the case of a discovered body, it is not always possible to determine whether the death was unlawful. One of the purposes of a medico-legal autopsy is to establish whether the mode of death was natural, accidental, suicide or homicide, but distinguishing between these categories is not always straightforward (Geberth 1996). This issue has been well documented in relation to infant deaths, where it is recognised that distinguishing an infant homicide from 'Sudden Infant Death Syndrome' (SIDS) or 'cot death' can be very difficult.

Reclassification of cases. Databases on homicides are normally flexible and subject to frequent adjustment as new information emerges about particular cases. For example, apparent unlawful homicides may later be reclassified as accidents or suicides, or the charges in court may be lowered to, for example, assault, child cruelty, or aiding and abetting suicide. Recording procedures in such circumstances can vary widely between jurisdictions.

In short, the seemingly simple question of how many homicides take place in a particular year cannot be easily answered, and while most jurisdictions produce official statistics pertaining to homicide, these clearly do not include all killings of another human being. In comparing jurisdictions, or in looking at trends over time, careful attention has to be paid to definitions and recording practices.

(Brookman and Maguire 2004: 329)

It is therefore clear that this simple question is much more complex than might be first imagined. The counting of homicides, the way the figures are collected, measured and compiled – for instance, only being 'counted' as a homicide once someone is convicted in a court of the offence affects even these 'raw' data, the number of people killed or suspected to be killed by another person – has ideological and emotional underpinnings. Sometimes the verdict of the court is also unsatisfactory. For the victims' families a 'not guilty' verdict at court literally means that their loved one is removed from the official statistics, and no longer 'exists' as a homicide. For a guilty suspect found innocent in court, this can have the same effect as the Scottish version of this verdict, 'not proven'. In other words, the lawyers or an overly sympathetic jury may have caused him or her to be acquitted, but the police may proclaim at the end of the trial that they are not looking for anyone else in connection with the crime, indicating that they were convinced that the suspect was guilty.

The ideological basis of these statistics can be seen in the way they are described in the 'official' version of crime, as illustrated above in the extract from the criminal statistics for England and Wales. The Home Office says that although the homicide figures are the highest since for over a hundred years, there is no need for alarm. Some homicides will later be removed from the register, and the latest version of the same document talks about homicide figures continuing to reduce from their peak of 1996, emphasising a reduction of 50 per cent by 2010. These figures are available from the year 1898 at http://rds.homeoffice.gov.uk/rds/recordedcrime.

These ideological and practical issues can cause problems for people conducting research because some statistics can only be accessed using 'official' sources: they may be held in a central database, collected by official sources and published only by government departments. For example, it would be very expensive and time-consuming to approach each of the 43 police forces in England and Wales to ask them about their categorisation of each suspicious death they have dealt with during that year. To start with they would probably say that they send all data to the Home Office, and it is collated there. They might just say the data were unavailable, or even refuse to reply at all. For a researcher to do this sort of analysis would create problems of validity – some data might not be available and it would be necessary to negotiate with each force for permission to question particular detectives who had taken the decisions to classify deaths as worthy of investigation based on their own evidence and the verdict of the coroner. Staff may also have moved on to other posts, details will have been forgotten, paperwork mislaid, and so on. Even though each police force publishes official data on 'solved' homicides these are only the superficial facts. It might be possible to find the statistics but would probably take such a long time that the next year's statistics would be appearing before the previous year's had been finished. Another problem with homicide statistics is that they can change after they have been published as 'facts'. According to the law in the UK, until someone is declared guilty of murder, in a court of law, it is not officially a crime. Hence, the note in the appendix of a Home Office document describes the recording practices of the statistics:

> In chapter 4, [Homicide] offences are shown according to the year in which the offence was initially recorded by the police as homicide; this is not necessarily the year in which the incident which led to the death took place, nor the year in which any court decision was made. The statistics all refer to the position at 5th August 1996; subsequent court hearings or other information received will change the figures given.
> (Home Office 1996: 226)

The 'list' of homicides is revised in the light of such convictions and this can take place many years later. In England and Wales, due to the practice of waiting for the coroner to classify a death as homicide, if New Year's Eve falls on a Friday, Saturday or Sunday, and coroners' offices are closed for several days over the holiday period, bodies are stored and are recorded on the first few days of January in the next calendar year. As new year celebrations can be a time where both drink-fuelled street violence and domestic violence peak, the result can be that trends in 'violent crime', based on the number of murders in a year, can increase by as many as 15–20, leading to an apparent increase.

Interrogating official statistics

One way to interrogate 'official' statistics such as the Home Office data sets is, ironically, to use other official statistics. Trends on other countries such as the USA and Europe can be used to compare the numbers of certain crimes, because patterns often cross continents or the world. There are problem with this, however, because of reporting and jurisdiction differences. Even making apparently simple comparisons between England and Wales with the Scottish system is problematic because of the different legal systems, classifications and recording practices.

It is not just legal issues that can vary from country to country; cultural differences can affect the way crimes are classified and recorded. In some countries juvenile or child offenders cannot be held responsible for crimes and because of their age may be viewed as victims themselves. In the following extract John Muncie compares two countries' attitudes to the accountability of children who commit serious violent crimes.

> In Trondheim, Norway, in 1994 a five-year-old girl was murdered by two six-year-old boys. The exceptionality of this case mirrored that of the murder of James Bulger by two ten-year-old boys a year earlier in England. In the seven subsequent years, public, media and political outcry remained unabated in the UK, continually dwelling on the 'leniency' of their sentence, their 'privileged' access to specialised rehabilitation and their eventual 'premature' release under a cloak of fearful anonymity. In Norway the murder was always dealt with as a tragedy in which the local community shared a collective shame and responsibility. The boys were never named. They returned to school within two weeks of the event.
>
> (Muncie 2004: 299)

In order to collect evidence as to which countries and cultures are the most punitive researchers have tried to compare international statistics on the number of young people in prison. This is one way of supporting the notion that some countries are much 'softer' on youth crime. One reason that researchers are interested in this problem is to support the 'what works' debate, as discussed earlier in this chapter. Another reason is that crime and justice policy is political. It is useful for governments in various countries at various times to appear 'harsh' or 'lenient'. As Muncie explains. 'The use of custody appears politically and culturally, rather than pragmatically, inspired. For some jurisdictions prison seems to "work" at a political and symbolic level even when it is a demonstrable failure' (Muncie 2005: 53).

Muncie is implying here that despite so-called 'globalisation' and various international treaties on the rights of the child, individual nation states and local policies are affected by social and economic conditions. He says that the 'key issue to be addressed is not how globalisation is producing uniformity but how it is activating diversity' (2005: 56). Elsewhere, Muncie and Goldson explain some differences of approach to youth crime:

> In England and Wales the numbers of 15 to 20 year olds in prison almost doubled in a decade from some 5,000 in 1993 to nearing 9,000 in 2002. The apparent fall in crime in many US cities has proved to be an irresistible draw for British politicians. Any number of 'zero tolerance' initiatives have targeted anti-social behaviour and incivilities, effectively criminalising non-criminal behaviour. A tough stance on crime and welfare has become the taken-for-granted mantra to achieve electoral success.
>
> (Muncie and Goldson 2006: 202)

Is this the whole story? To what extent are individual nation states more 'punitive' than others? Is the UK the most punitive, and does it 'work'? These are questions that researchers such as John Muncie have asked. In the following interview John Muncie explains the difficulties he has come across in the attempt to do this for the past ten years.

Interview with John Muncie: comparing youth justice

My latest research has been on comparing youth justice systems internationally. I first got into this field as a result of various lectures that I was doing around the country, in England, where the noticeable thing looking at the number of juveniles (that's those under 18) that were being locked up in England and Wales had increased dramatically since the early 1990s. As a result of these lectures people would quite often ask me, 'Well, how does England compare to other countries – is this something specific to England or is it part of a more international or global trend?' So I set about trying to answer this question, thinking that it might be fairly straightforward, to be honest, to find out how many young people, that is, under 18-year-olds as defined by the United Nations, are being held in incarceration in closed institutions in various countries around the world. I started off optimistically with the world and have since pared it down to North America and Western Europe, and now just to Western Europe; in fact my future research will probably just be on the UK for reasons I will hopefully outline to you.

So the major initial source for this research was secondary statistics. Now where do you go for secondary statistics? The most obvious place is the United Nations, which has done a survey for the last 20 or 30 years of inviting every country around the world to enter data about how many police, prisons they have, how many people in them, etc., so I had a look at this database. For a start it's quite clear that not all countries are replying in the same year, let alone the same date, and that might affect how they are reading levels of imprisonment; some countries, for example, for the year that I was looking at, Australia and Canada, had no entry at all. It also became apparent to me that the numbers couldn't be taken at face value. Some of them were obviously a head count of under 18s, some were a head count of under 21-year-olds, often taken at different dates. Now if it is common through the rest of the world, I don't know, but certainly in England and Wales in institutions the numbers that are held over Christmas are much lower than in the summer – so if you take a census date at December you'll get a much lower rate than if you took it in June.

There's a problem generally with international juvenile justice research because what counts as a minor, what counts as a child, what counts as a juvenile, what counts as a young person, doesn't mean the same thing. So, for example, the age of criminal responsibility varies widely around the world, anywhere from around age 7 in various states in the US, to 18 in Luxembourg. Even in the UK we have a distinction between age 8 in Scotland, which may be raised to 12, and currently under review, 10 in England and Wales and Northern Ireland. If Scotland does raise its age to 12, England and Wales will have the lowest age of responsibility in Europe.

So the basic building blocks for generating these statistics is not even secure in itself because they are measuring different populations at different times. Now how they measure them varies as well – sometimes it's just a head count on a particular day and others seem to be measuring how many go in and out in a particular year. So we have a distinction between a stock figure – a one-day head count – and a flow figure – the number going in and out in a particular year. So it's not even clear if they are measuring the same sort of things.

So I then tried to find other databases. The second one is the Council of Europe criminal statistics called SPACE, but this still seems to have the same sort of problems with different ages of criminal responsibility and also different definitions of what 'juvenile' is.

I then turned to a third database, which contains statistics that were initially collected by the Home Office, now collected by the Centre for Prison Studies at Kings College, which give numbers by the rate per 100,000 – but unfortunately it doesn't give separate figures for juveniles. But it does give it as a percentage of the total prison population, so you can roughly work out how many are for under 18-year-olds – and with some exceptions most of them are for under 18-year-olds, so they are comparable.

Of course, the initial thing you find is that there are vast discrepancies in numbers being held in different countries across Europe. So at any one time you might have 2,500 to 3,000 young people being locked up in England and Wales, compared to say 10 in Norway, Finland and Sweden. So to try to make further sense of that I then accessed population and demographic figures for each of those countries, which will tell you the under-18 population for each country. Then do a rate compared to England and Wales, and that'll get you a bit closer to what is happening in each particular country. It will throw up some differences, so on a basic head count a country like the Netherlands will not score highly, where you're not just measuring a simple head count, you're measuring how many per 100,000 of the under-18 population. Now I don't know anywhere else that does this – the United Nations tried, but they just do it as far as I can tell per 100,000 of the general population, not specific youth population.

So once you've got all these figures together – are they then accurate? Well, you then have to start asking yourself whether the institutions in which children and young people are locked up in different countries actually go under the same name. So if you ask in, say, England and Wales, how many people do you lock up, it will include people in young offender institutions, secure training centres and secure children's homes. If you ask this in Finland, it seems to me that they only give the figures for those locked up in prison service establishments; even though a lot of kids may be confined against their will, they'll be in a range of institutions, like those called 'treatment centres' or 'closed care'. They might not be run by the prison department, they may be run by a welfare agency; as all are there against their will and whether or not they are there for an offence condition, it's very difficult to find out.

It means that all these comparative bases are very unstable. And can you try to extrapolate that on the basis of these statistics – can you

> actually say that England and Wales is one of the most punitive, which is one of the common criticisms? If you triangulate the results from the United Nations, with the data from the Council of Europe and data from Kings College, and they are all pointing in the same direction, you can come to a tentative conclusion that compared to the rest of Europe – but not, say, America or Russia – England and Wales is a punitive country as regards the degree it locks young people up in closed institutions and doesn't mind calling them prison, and that's the important point.
>
> References: Council of Europe; SPACE: www.coe.int/t/e/legal_affairs/legal_co-operation/prisons_and_alternatives/statistics_space_ii/PC-CP(2003)6E-%20Space-II.pdf

As you may have gathered, Muncie's position is that official statistics do not necessarily provide a very accurate picture of the nature and extent of youth custody or offending. As he says elsewhere: 'The first and most paramount "fact" about official statistics is that they are both partial and socially constructed' (Muncie 1996: 22). For three main reasons, they should not be simply taken at face value (see Muncie 1999: 16–17):

- Crime statistics depend initially to a large degree on those crimes *reported* to the police by the public.
- Even when an incident is reported to the police it will not count as crime unless the police *record* it as such.
- Changes in law enforcement and in what the law counts as crime preclude much meaningful discussion over whether youth crime is forever rising (or indeed falling).

As Muncie argues, a single set of data may not be reliable, as too many extraneous factors can influence the so-called 'facts' and figures. Furthermore, as these figures are usually collected by national governments or their agencies, they can be open to subtle political influence, such as definitions: 'what is a child?' The ideological issues for John Muncie's work are the way young people are classified and whether they are in institutions called 'prisons'. For homicide statistics, as illustrated earlier in the chapter, it may be about making people feel 'safe' or protecting police criminal justice agencies such as the police and courts from criticism, or the Home Office/Ministry of Justice and government themselves, especially at politically sensitive times such as elections.

Having explored some of the problems with official or government statistics as a starting point, it is clear that a good healthy dose of scepticism is necessary. This is not to say that these data have no value; indeed, as a means of discovering the underlying 'problem', such as the example of women police and promotion in the previous chapter, it is an excellent, quick, cheap and obvious place to start. Once there, what to look for and how to use the statistics may need a bit more thought.

This is because, as the discussion so far has shown, quantitative methods and statistics can be a useful part of criminological studies, but are limited by the ways in which they are collected. Although the focus has been primarily on the use of official statistics, with a warning about how exactly these statistics are gathered, the use of evaluative frameworks by Home Office, and the power and resources that enable governments and officialdom to collect large data sets.

As with the discussion on qualitative data collection and analysis later in the book, this chapter does not aim to be a 'how to' guide to quantitative research methods. Rather it explores what is and is not possible with such methods and the way that research questions and methods need to be considered as a seamless issue for the researcher. In other words, the way that the project is designed needs to keep methods and research questions viewed in tandem, and if either is changed or modified it will have an effect on the other. In the following section one attempt to look behind official criminal statistics is explored, with the aim of trying to unpick the officially reported and recorded version of the facts of crime.

Critiquing government statistics

Often other people's statistics will provide a starting point for more research, rather than be a simple acceptance of the figures. This is especially true of government statistics, where comparative or international studies of offending and imprisonment, as the example of John Muncie's research illustrated. One problem is that the statistics already exist and have been collected and collated in particular ways. Where statistics have been gathered by any large central institution, such as the Home Office/Ministry of Justice, the reliability of the data is based on the belief that the agencies who supply the Home Office with their figures across the UK are collecting them in the same way. As an example, there have to be agreed definitions of 'criminal damage', and agreed methods of differentiating it from, say, attempting to break into a vehicle, which may be recorded as attempted theft. There need to be accepted rules about the difference between 'drunk and disorderly' and 'drunk and incapable', and they have to be judged in the same way by everyone filling in the forms, from charge sheets to annual returns to the Home Office. Aside from the logistical problems of collecting and presenting such large data sets accurately, the 'human' element is inescapable, as discretion is a significant part of policing and therefore in the recording of crime.

This is the problem, that for each case an individual, discretion-bearing, mood and situation-respondent human being is responsible not only for deciding how to record such incidents (often without any checks or balances) but also for transmitting them accurately to a database. Other fallible human beings then have to assemble the statistics and forward them to the Home Office/Ministry of Justice, where some scrutiny does take place (in the form of a police inspectorate acting as an audit system); but this comes too late and is too physically distant for checks regarding their original recording accuracy. One solution to these problems is to have another way of collecting crime statistics: to use the people who are affected by those activities in their daily lives – the public. Another reason to be sceptical about the accuracy of statistics based on what the government publishes as a result of crime recorded by the police is that an unknowable number of offences will not come to the attention of any official source. In other words, these are the crimes that no one reports to the police, or, as indicated above, the so-called 'dark figure'.

In response to a growing awareness of significant omissions from the crime statistics, particularly of crimes such as violence within the family, sexual crimes and fraud, in the 1970s in the USA and early 1980s in the UK, victim surveys developed in order to investigate this unreported crime. As Jupp summarises:

> In part, victim surveys developed as a result of recognised deficiencies of official crime statistics as valid measures of the extent of crime in society. For example, crimes recorded by the police rely to a great extent on members of the public reporting such crimes. There are several reasons for not reporting crime, for example, the sensitivity of the act, triviality of offence or distrust of the police. Victim surveys collect data on the occurrence of criminal acts irrespective of whether such acts have been reported to the police, and thereby, gain some measure of the 'dark figure' of unreported crime. A further impetus came from a direct concern for the victim within criminology and also within criminal justice policy.
>
> (Jupp 2006: 449)

The British Crime Survey

The British Crime Survey, often referred to by its initials, BCS, is one such study, with large numbers of statistically representative samples, carried out in a broadly similar form since 1982. Although it is called a 'crime' survey, it is sometimes referred to as a 'victimisation' survey, as the questions that are posed concentrate on the way the respondents view themselves in relation to crimes committed against them. As stated in the introduction to the 2008–09 survey, below, this is because for its validity the survey relies upon respondents being asked about crimes 'which they themselves have experienced'. In effect, the survey is being lent plausibility and credibility because it reports on people's 'real' experiences, things that have actually happened to them in the past 12 months. Add to this the sample size and lengths to which the survey team go to achieve representative samples, the BCS becomes a forceful piece of research that can be used by policy-makers, political parties and researchers to provide substantive evidence.

The following introduction to the 2009 BCS explains the current rationale for the research they conduct.

> The British Crime Survey (BCS) is a well-established study and one of the largest social research surveys conducted in England and Wales. The survey was first conducted in 1982 and ran at roughly two-yearly intervals until 2001, when it became a continuous survey.[1] The survey is carried out for the Home Office, and is managed by a team of researchers in the Home Office Statistics Unit. They develop each survey in collaboration with an external research organisation. Since 2001 *BMRB Social Research* has been the sole contractor for the survey.
>
> The 2008–09 survey was similar in many respects to previous years but it also introduced a number of new elements. The total sample size was the same as in the previous year, with approximately 46,000 core adult interviews being conducted across the year, and an additional boost of approximately 2,000 interviews with young adults aged 16–24. The survey was designed to achieve a minimum of around 1,000 core interviews in each Police Force Area in England and Wales. This was also similar to the previous year of the survey.
>
> The 2008–09 survey differed in two respects from the previous year. First, it involved a new sample design, with the introduction of a partially unclustered sample, which replaced the clustered design used on all previous surveys. A second important development was the extension of the survey to include interviews with 10–15-year-olds during the course of the 2008–09 survey year. The BCS is primarily a **victimisation** survey, in which respondents are asked about the experiences of **property crimes** of the household (e.g. burglary) and **personal crimes** (e.g. theft from a person) which they themselves have experienced. Following the move to continuous interviewing in 2001 the reference period for all interviews has related to the last 12 months before the date of interview. Although there have been changes to the design of the survey over time, the wording of the questions that are asked to elicit victimisation experiences, have been held constant throughout the life of the survey. (Bolling *et al.* 2009: 1)

1 Previous British Crime Surveys were carried out in 1982, 1984, 1988, 1992, 1994, 1996, 1998 and 2000.

The following explains the BCS questionnaire design and content (see Bolling *et al.* 2009: 37).

3 Questionnaire content and development
3.1 Structure and coverage of the questionnaire

The BCS questionnaire has a complex structure, consisting of a set of core modules asked of the whole sample, a set of modules asked only of different sub-samples, and self-completion modules asked of all 16–59-year-olds. Within some modules there is often further filtering so that some questions are only asked of even smaller sub-samples. The precise modules asked on the survey vary from year to year as do the exact modules asked of the core and young adult boost samples.

The 2008–09 BCS questionnaire consisted of the following sections:

- Household grid
- Perceptions of crime
- Screener questionnaire
- Victimisation modules for incidents identified at the screeners (up to a maximum of six)
- Mobile phone and second home crime
- Performance of the criminal justice system
- Contact with and attitudes to the police (Module A)
- Contact with and attitudes to the criminal justice system (Module B)
- Crime prevention and security (Module C)
- Ad-hoc crime topics (Module D)
- Night-time economy and alcohol disorder
- Anti-social behaviour
- Plastic card and identity fraud
- Demographics and media consumption
- Self-completion module on drug use and drinking
- Self-completion module on inter-personal violence

Where a 'module' is mentioned, this refers to groups of questions around that particular topic area. For example, the following is about the respondent's attitudes to various aspects of the criminal justice system.

Module B: Contact with and attitudes to the criminal justice system

Again, this module included questions that had mainly been asked in previous years, although there were some new questions about the types of sentences that respondents thought appropriate for different types of offenders under particular circumstances. Topics covered in this module included:

- priorities of the criminal justice system;
- where people get information about the criminal justice system;
- knowledge of sentencing practices;
- attitudes to the type of sentence appropriate for different types of offenders under particular circumstances;
- attitude to sentencing policy, including what respondents thought sentences should be for particular crimes and what they thought they actually were;
- recent contact with different parts of the criminal justice system; and
- attitudes to aspects of the youth justice system.

What is interesting about this type of survey is that large samples of the population can be asked about their experiences of crime and this can be contrasted with other 'official' large data sets, such as the government's *Criminal Statistics England and Wales*, and other available data such as the annually published *Police Strength England and Wales*. There is some suspicion that the 'true' figures are the ones collected as 'official' statistics (see Maguire 1994, for example) and due to some such criticisms, since 2001 the two data sources, *Criminal Statistics England and Wales* and the British Crime Survey, have created a joint publication called *Crime in England and Wales*. In an overview of the findings for the year 2009–10 it is stated that:

> There are two main sources of official statistics on crime: the police recorded series and the British Crime Survey (BCS). The BCS is a nationally representative sample survey (now based on more than 45,000 respondents) of the population resident in households in England and Wales. As a household-based survey the BCS does not cover all offences or all population groups. While police recorded crime has a wider coverage of offences (including crimes such as drug offences that are often termed 'victimless') and covers the entire population, it does not include those crimes not reported to the police. Both sources have their strengths and weaknesses but together provide a more comprehensive picture than either on its own.
>
> (Home Office 2010)

In effect, the publication of *Crime in England and Wales* attempts to reconcile the police figures that are incomplete due to the issues discussed so far in this chapter, and the crimes that are reported by people to the BCS interviewers. Typically the trends discovered by the BCS are that both crime and fear of crime are much higher than the 'actualities' of the official statistics or the police recorded version. In an attempt to reconcile these differences – such as the BCS estimate that only 43 per cent of 'comparable' crime is being reported to the police (2010: 19) – the series are adjusted to make comparisons between police recorded crime and the BCS. The 2010 *User Guide to Home Office Crime Statistics* explains how these adjustments are made.

> In order to compare the crime rates measured by the BCS and police recorded crime, a comparable subset of crimes has been created for a set of offences that are covered by both measures. Various adjustments are made to the recorded crime categories to maximise comparability with the BCS but they are not adjusted to exclude victims of commercial offences and offences committed against those under 16. Over three-quarters of BCS offences reported via interviews in recent years fall into categories that can be compared with crimes recorded by the police (Table 4a).
>
> **Crimes excluded from comparable subset**
>
> *Recorded crimes:*
> The violent offences of: Homicide; Attempted murder; Intentional destruction of an unborn child; the five offences of causing death by driving; Endangering life at sea; Possession of weapons; Harassment; Cruelty to or neglect of children; Abandoning a child under the age of two years; Child abduction; Procuring illegal abortion; Concealment of birth; All sexual offences; Non-domestic burglary; Proceeds of crime; Theft in a dwelling; Theft by an employee; Theft of mail; Abstracting electricity; Theft from shops; Theft from automatic machine or meter; Handling stolen goods; Other theft; All Fraud and forgery; Threat etc. to commit criminal damage; All Drug offences and All 'Other' offences.
>
> *BCS:*
> Other household theft and Other thefts of personal property.
>
> **Reporting rates – findings from the BCS**
> The BCS asks a series of questions regarding whether incidents were reported, or otherwise came to the attention of the police. These findings reveal considerable differences in reporting rates between different types of offences and some variability in reporting rates over time. Analysis of reasons given for not reporting crime to the police are also available.
>
> (*User Guide to Home Office Crime Statistics*, http://rds.homeoffice.gov.uk/rds/pdfs10/crimestats-usergui de.pdf)

Table 4a *Comparable subset of crimes*

BCS category		Recorded crime offence included
Vehicle thefts	37.2	Aggravated vehicle taking
	48	Theft and unauthorised taking of motor vehicle
	45	Theft from a vehicle
	126	Vehicle interference and tampering
Burglary	28A	Burglary in a dwelling
	28B	Attempted burglary in a dwelling
	28C	Distraction burglary in a dwelling
	28D	Attempted distraction burglary in a dwelling
	29	Aggravated burglary in a dwelling
Bicycle theft	44	Theft or unauthorised taking of pedal cycle
Theft from person	39	Theft from the person
Vandalism	56	Arson
	56A	Arson endangering life
	56B	Arson not endangering life
	58A	Criminal damage to a dwelling
	58B	Criminal damage to building other than a dwelling
	58C	Criminal damage to a vehicle
	58D	Other criminal damage
	58E	Racially/religiously aggravated criminal damage to dwelling
	58F	Racially/religiously aggravated criminal damage to a building other than a dwelling
	58G	Racially/religiously aggravated criminal damage to a vehicle
	58H	Racially/religiously aggravated other criminal damage
Assault without injury	104	Assault without injury on a constable
	105A	Assault without injury
	105B	Racially/religiously aggravated assault without injury
Assault with minor injury	8A	Less serious wounding
	8D	Racially/religiously aggravated less serious wounding
	8G	Actual bodily harm (ABH) and other injury
	8J	Racially or religiously aggravated ABH or other injury
	8K	Poisoning or female genital mutilation
Wounding	5	More serious wounding or other act endangering life
	5A	Inflicting grievous bodily harm (GBH) with intent

	5B	Use of substance or object to endanger life
	8F	Inflicting grievous bodily harm (GBH) without intent
	8H	Racially or religiously aggravated inflicting GBH without intent
Robbery	34B	Robbery of personal property

Note: The mapping between police recorded offence codes and BCS categories is approximate and categories will not be directly equivalent in all cases.

As the Home Office guide concedes, the difference between the number of crimes reported to and recorded by the police, and those that people tell BCS interviewers about, can vary greatly. What can be agreed, however, is that trends in crimes are often in accordance; in general trends go up or down in generally broadly similar ways. The Home Office statistical bulletin for 2009–10 notes:

> The most striking new finding within this report is that both the 2009/10 BCS and police recorded crime are consistent in showing falls in overall crime compared with 2008/09. Overall BCS crime decreased by 9 per cent (from 10.5 million crimes to 9.6 million crimes), and police recorded crime by 8 per cent (from 4.7 million to 4.3 million crimes).
>
> These results may be seen as surprising given there were expectations that crime, particularly property related crime, could rise in a period of recession. However, neither source shows an increase in levels of property crime during this period (though the full effects will not show through with the BCS until next year) and indeed there have been some notable falls. For example, both sources are consistent in showing marked falls in vehicle crime (BCS vehicle-related theft down 17 per cent and police recorded vehicle crime down by 16 per cent compared with the previous year). In addition, while the 9 per cent fall in domestic burglary from the BCS was not statistically significant it is broadly in line with the 6 per cent reduction recorded by the police.
>
> (Flatley *et al.* 2010: 2)

As Johannson's history of the BCS illustrates, this is an important counter to the 'official' statistics gathered by the police and other criminal justice agencies. Johannson (2010: 4) talks about the origins of the BCS:

> The first victimisation surveys were carried out in the 60s and 70s, designed to examine the 'dark figure' of crime, i.e. crimes that are not reported to or recorded by the police.
>
> The surveys followed debates about whether changes in police recorded crime reflected actual changes in crime rather than reporting

and recording practices. The early victimisation surveys were mainly experimental, for example, a survey carried out in Britain in the early 70s only covered three London areas (Sparks, Genn and Dodd 1977).

The BCS was first carried out to better understand victimisation across the country as a whole. The first BCS was carried out in England, Wales and also Scotland.

The BCS was essentially a research tool designed to:

- obtain a better count of crime (as it included crimes that were not reported to or recorded by the police);
- identify risk factors in victimisation; and
- examine people's worry about crime and their perceptions of and contact with the police.

Over time it also started to provide more reliable information about trends in crime.

> It [the BCS] offered a new way of counting crimes, including those not in police records, and a means of identifying the sorts of people most at risk. It has also provided unique information for this country about the impact of crime on victims, people's fear of crime, their experience of the police, and related topics. (First BCS report, Hough and Mayhew, 1983)

Summary of secondary quantitative data methods

This section has discussed the use of 'official' statistics in the form of government-published data of crimes reported to the police and their outcome. It has also discussed some of the other governmental statistics that can be used to 'triangulate' or check the validity of these statistics, such as victim surveys.

These surveys are certainly useful as they have a particular version of 'truth' that can lend them power. Governments and party politicians like to quote numbers, as they lend validity to their argument. For researchers such as John Muncie, using statistics that others have gathered has certain advantages, being freely available and, some would argue (although not John Muncie), free of ideology or bias.

If a study aims to measure how much of something there is, and then, following some sort of intervention, to see if anything has changed, then statistics and numbers are a good way to approach the job. Counting the number of offences and the outcomes, such as in the prison study above, is usually cheaper and quicker than going into more depth. Even simple percentages can be useful to illustrate a point. Despite the shortcomings of these statistics, counting responses using a standardised questionnaire can permit comparisons to be made across countries, using data sets collected by different research teams. One of the aims of these sorts of studies is to find out, in common parlance, 'what works?' Sometimes these studies are referred to as 'evaluative' in that they try to assess whether an intervention can make a difference statistically. The following example is about the resettlement of prisoners following their release from custody (Lewis *et al.* 2007: 36).

Aims

The evaluation was intended to determine the effectiveness and the cost-effectiveness of the Pathfinder projects in addressing the resettlement needs of short-sentence prisoners, and in reducing reconviction. Key objectives included:

- identifying the main obstacles to the effective delivery of resettlement services;
- determining prisoners' problems and the levels of services received;
- determining the effectiveness of the different projects in addressing practical resettlement needs, and in reducing reconviction.

Methods

To achieve the aims of the evaluation three main strands of work were undertaken:

- a process of evaluation, commencing with an early organisational 'audit' of project design and delivery, followed by a longer-term study of how each project actually delivered resettlement services;
- an investigation of the resettlement needs of short-term prisoners and the level of service provided at each scheme;
- an assessment of the impact of the projects on resettlement problems and on attitudes related to offending.

Various methods were used in conducting these interrelated strands of work. 'Entry' and 'exit' interviews were undertaken with project managers and staff, with whom close contact was maintained throughout the study. Project participants were tracked using detailed case management records (CMRs). Pre- and post-release interviews with offenders, and completed postal questionnaires, provided the participants' perspective. Interim outcome measures were used to determine the impact of the projects. In the longer term a reconviction study was undertaken which provided further information about the effectiveness of each scheme, and of the various types of 'service' provided, in reducing re-offending by short-term prisoners (Clancy *et al.* 2006).

As Pawson and Tilley point out in an excellent book about 'realistic evaluation' (1997), the 'quasi-experimental approach' that they describe was ignited by a 'quake' that occurred with the publication of Martinson's 'What works? Questions and answers about prison reform'. As they explain:

> Martinson's (1974) paper is a summary of a 1,400 page manuscript which itself was a summary of *all* published reports in English on attempts at the rehabilitation of offenders from 1945 to 1967 ... Curiously, he never uttered the verdict 'nothing works' directly in the whole paper, yet he managed to flatten the aspirations of reformers in fields way beyond his own.
> (Pawson and Tilley 2007: 9)

One aim of this sort of evaluative approach is to provide 'evidence' upon which to base policies. As another of Pawson's texts on the subject suggests, the 'realist perspective' can carry out research that designs, implements and systematically reviews policy interventions (Pawson 2006: 9). In Chapter 5 of the book, he outlines how this has happened in the USA in relation to 'Megan's Law', providing a detailed, practical illustration of how this works from a realist perspective.

Having explored the difficulties and shortcomings of secondary statistics, the following section moves on to explore data collection and the uses of primary data.

Primary data research

This chapter has discussed secondary data and the analysis and comparison of large data sets reliant upon the methods and decisions made by various people about what and how to collect this material. These discussions have all been about sources of secondary data: that is, the statistics that other people have gathered, collected and to some extent analysed. It could be argued that one way of avoiding the problem of being constrained by the data collected by others is to collect your own statistics.

The difficulties with this include that it is expensive, it requires access to 'real' sources of data (such as people or files that may be restricted for various reasons such as data protection), and gaining access to them may not be easy, as later interviews in this volume will illustrate. Further, it may require technical expertise such as the use of computer packages that analyse large data sets. Sometimes the only computational skill required may be to work out percentages with a calculator, but anything including variables will normally require a commercial analysis computer package such as SPSS (Statistical Package for Social Scientists).

More complicated analysis of statistics (using a package like SPSS) can provide interesting findings where 'variables' are used to control for differences in the research sample, for instance those of gender. An explanation of the full workings of such a package is not included here; there are numerous excellent books on the subject (see, for example, Brace *et al.* 2009). But to illustrate what can be done, the following study, about police officers' beliefs regarding ethical behaviour, shows the use of quantitative methods. It was originally part of a wider international study. It aimed to ask police officers in 14 different countries about their attitudes to their own and their colleagues' behaviour (see Klockars *et al.* 2003 for a fuller discussion).

The use of quantitative methods was suitable and appropriate because each country was being surveyed by a different team. The questionnaires were translated into the relevant language and administered by different investigators in each country. The sorts of questions that were asked included, among other things, how many officers thought that accepting a free drink on duty was bribery. The idea was to see whether certain behaviours were acceptable to police officers in one country, but taboo in another. In addition, for the UK part of the study one of the variables was gender: how many of the officers who thought certain behaviour unacceptable were women? Did rank or promotion make a difference to the way they answered?

One advantage of studies involving the collection of primary data is control over the questions, distribution and analysis of the final questionnaires. It allows the researcher to ask about the specific issues they want answers to, rather than simply analysing secondary data, which may not cover the required questions. At the same time, a survey is a reasonably cheap, easy and quick way to obtain large amounts of responses and can act as a forerunner to more in-depth quantitative work. In the following survey, the data were analysed using SPSS, which involves inputting and time-consuming coding, but this also facilitated some quite simple analysis of the responses. For instance, it is easy to compare percentages – the number of officers as a percentage of the UK part of the study who indicated certain behaviours were unacceptable, for example, against other behaviours they regarded as 'less serious'.

In order to ascertain these responses the officers were asked to read a questionnaire consisting of 11 scenarios. In each case they were asked to rate their responses to the behaviour outlined in the scenario.

Case study 2: police integrity

The scenarios in the questionnaire were as follows:

1 A police officer runs a private business in which he sells and installs security devices, such as alarms, special locks, etc. This work is done during off-duty hours.

2 A police officer routinely accepts free meals, cigarettes and other items of small value from shopkeepers on his beat. He does not solicit these gifts and is careful not to abuse the generosity of those who give gifts.
3 A police officer stops a motorist for speeding. The officer agrees to accept a personal gift for half of the amount of the fine in exchange for not issuing a summons.
4 A police officer is widely liked in the community, and on occasions such as Christmas local shopkeepers and restaurant and bar owners show their appreciation for her attention by giving gifts of food and alcohol.
5 A police officer discovers a burglary of a jewellery shop. The display cases are smashed and it is obvious that many items have been taken. While searching the shop, he takes a watch, worth about two days' pay for that officer. He reports that the watch had been stolen during the burglary.
6 A police officer has a private arrangement with a local vehicle body shop to refer the owners of cars damaged in accidents to the shop. In exchange for each referral, he receives a payment of 5 per cent of the repair bill from the shop owner.
7 A police officer, who happens to be a very good car mechanic, is scheduled to work during some planned forthcoming holidays. A supervisor offers to authorise these days off, if he agrees to tune-up the supervisor's personal car. Evaluate the SUPERVISOR'S behaviour.
8 At 2 a.m. a police officer, who is on duty, is driving a patrol car on a deserted road. She sees a vehicle that has been driven off the road and is stuck in a ditch. She approaches the vehicle and observes that the driver is not hurt but is obviously intoxicated. She also finds that the driver is an off-duty police officer. Instead of reporting this accident and offence, she transports the driver to his home.
9 A police officer finds a bar on his beat that is still serving drinks an hour past its legal closing time. Instead of reporting this violation, the police officer agrees to accept a couple of free drinks from the owner.
10 Two police officers on foot patrol surprise someone who is attempting to break into a car. He runs off. They chase the suspect for about two streets before apprehending him by tackling him and wrestling him to the ground. After he is under control, both officers punch him a couple of times in the stomach as punishment for fleeing and resisting.
11 A police officer finds a wallet in a car park. It contains the amount of money equivalent to a full day's pay for that officer. She reports the wallet as lost property, but keeps the money.

For each of these scenarios the respondents were requested to circle an answer to a number of questions, on a scale from 1 to 5, for example where 1 is 'not at all serious', to 5, 'very serious'. At the end of the questionnaire they were asked to complete a demographic section about themselves.

1 How serious do YOU consider this behaviour to be?

   Not at all serious   1 2 3 4 5   Very serious

2 How serious do MOST POLICE OFFICERS IN YOUR FORCE consider this behaviour to be?

   Not at all serious   1 2 3 4 5   Very serious

3 Would this behaviour be regarded as a violation of official policy in your force?

   Definitely not   1 2 3 4 5   Definitely yes

4 If an officer in your force engaged in this behaviour and was discovered doing so, what, if any, discipline do YOU think SHOULD follow?

   1 None   2 Verbal reprimand   3 Written reprimand
   4 Fine   5 Demotion in rank   6 Dismissal/required to resign

5 If an officer in your force engaged in this behaviour and was discovered doing so, what, if any, discipline do YOU think WOULD follow?

   1 None   2 Verbal reprimand   3 Written reprimand
   4 Fine   5 Demotion in rank   6 Dismissal/required to resign

6 Do you think MOST POLICE OFFICERS IN YOUR FORCE would report a fellow police officer who engaged in this behaviour?

   Definitely not   1 2 3 4 5   Definitely yes

Table 3.1 Seriousness of behaviour (percentage)

	Not serious	2	3	4	Very serious
Scenario 5: Officer takes watch after burglary (N=270)	0.0	0.0	0.0	0.0	98.5
Scenario 10: Officers punch arrestee (N=270)	1.0	4.0	10.5	17.5	65.5
Scenario 11: Officer takes money from found wallet N=270	0.0	0.0	0.0	1.0	97.0

Source: Westmarland (2005).

The survey found, just in terms of the officers in the UK part of the study (see Westmarland 2005 for a fuller discussion), that the officers who responded thought that the 'acquisitive' actions were more serious than the 'procedural' misdemeanours: 98 per cent of the respondents thought that taking the money or the watch was much worse than the brutality or covering up for a drunk driver.

At the end of the survey the officers were asked to reveal their rank, years service and gender. As the results were being analysed using SPSS, it was possible to introduce these as variables to see if it made a difference. So it was possible to work out whether senior officers viewed certain behaviour more seriously than other ranks, or if gender made a difference. This was done in the following way.

Please circle, underline, or fill out your response.

12　How many years have you been a police officer?

　　1　Less than 1　　2　1–2　　　3　3–5　　　4　6–10
　　5　11–15　　　　6　16–20　　7　Over 20

12a　Are you male or female?　　1　Male　　2　Female

13　How many years have you been employed at your current location in the force?

　　1　Less than 1　　2　1–2　　　3　3–5　　　4　6–10
　　5　11–15　　　　6　16–20　　7　Over 20

14　What is your rank/role?

　　1　Probationer (yr 1)　　5　Inspector　　　　　　9　ACPO rank
　　2　Probationer (yr 2)　　6　Chief Inspector
　　3　Police Constable　　 7　Superintendent
　　4　Sergeant　　　　　　 8　Chief Superintendent
　　Other _____

15　Which of the following best describes your current work?

　　1　Patrol
　　2　Neighbourhood/community officer
　　3　Detective/Investigative
　　4　Special Operations (vice, juvenile, etc.)
　　5　Communications
　　6　Administrative
　　Other _____

16.　Are you a supervisor or non-supervisor?

　　1　Non-supervisor
　　2　Supervisor (shift supervisor, area supervisor, ACPO rank)

> 17 Which of the following best describes your police force?
>
> 1 Very large force (more than 3,000 sworn officers)
> 2 Large metropolitan force (2,001–3,000 sworn officers)
> 3 Medium-sized metropolitan force (1,501–2000 sworn officers)
> 4 Small metropolitan (1,000–1,500 sworn officers)
> 5 Very small metropolitan force (fewer than 1,000 sworn officers)
> 6 Large rural force (more than 2,000 officers)
> 7 Medium-sized rural force (1,500–2,000 sworn officers)
> 8 Small rural force (fewer than 1,500 sworn officers)

Although the sample size was too small to make the variables of gender or years service significant, some interesting trends make this the sort of study that could be used as a pilot, or a small-scale preliminary testing ground for a larger project. The extract from the findings of the articles section describes the issues in brief.

> In a discussion about police loyalties, Punch (1985: 125) argues that some officers he interviewed felt that to discuss police deviance or to express worries about corruption was to appear 'weak' or 'soft'. Some officers he talked to were unclear about whether certain gifts, such as a bunch of flowers to say 'thank you' to an individual cop, were acceptable (Punch 1985: 126–7). It seems futile therefore to discuss police professional integrity without reference to certain beliefs about solidarity and the 'blue code' that are embedded in their occupational culture. Police officers often have to make the best decision they can based on what they might describe as 'professional experience' or 'gut instinct' (Westmarland 2001b) rather than an explicit code of ethics. Furthermore, once 'means justifies the end' principles often described as the 'Dirty Harry' syndrome in police literature are applied, most 'dubious' actions can often be justified by the potential outcome in police cultural terms (Westmarland 2000a). In this survey, however, although limited by the small sample size drawn from only one force, the findings suggest that officers view acquisitive crime (i.e., taking money or property) as very serious and not acceptable, even where the amounts of money are relatively small, such as in the case of the late serving pub, illicit speeding fine or repair shop backhanders. This is the behaviour they would be quite likely to report. Other behaviour, such as excessive force and bending the law to protect a drunk driving colleague, is regarded as serious, but they would be less likely to report it than some of the larger financially rewarding corrupt behaviour. As argued above, this might be simply due to the internal and external pressures of police culture and the demands for results, or

some other concerns about the level of punishment their colleagues would receive.

As explained above, the findings are limited in terms of their generalisability, but these are all issues that need further investigation as this is the first survey in the United Kingdom to ask these questions. Overall the respondents displayed high levels of understanding of what professional integrity requires of them; they know the 'rules' and have firm beliefs about some types of behaviour being 'very serious'. This survey of officers' attitudes towards integrity and certain types of rule infringements provides evidence that research into the motivations behind the reporting of 'very serious' behaviour is needed. In effect, why acquisitively corrupt behaviours are seen as so serious compared to actions such as assaulting a suspect or allowing a drunk driver to go unpunished are also areas of research that could be developed from this study. Perceptions about police officers' acceptance of unnecessary brutality, bending the rules by accepting small gifts or favours, seem to be reinforced by the findings here, but the motivations, actual occurrence of such behaviour and the reasons officers do not report others' misdemeanours remain unanswered. (Westmarland 2005: 162–3)

Summary of primary data research

Although this survey was administered to a fairly large number of police officers across the world – about 14,000 in total – in the UK only 28 per cent of the 1,000 questionnaires were returned. The findings from the UK part of the study were therefore based upon the responses of only 280 officers. In comparison to the thousands surveyed for the BCS, or the data sets for the official crime statistics, it is a very small study. One benefit of primary research, however, is that even for small numbers it can reveal trends, such as the very high number of officers who thought that taking the watch and the money was very serious. In its defence, it could be argued that if a larger sample was surveyed – say, half of the serving officers in England and Wales – the percentage of officers believing these scenarios to be 'very serious' would be similar.

This last section of the chapter has aimed to illustrate that quantitative studies can be illustrative and relatively easy to administer and can reveal some interesting findings. Unlike the large data sets and the 'official' statistics examined in the earlier part of the chapter, they cannot claim to be so robust, however, in terms of generalisability. One reason for this is that unlike the BCS, for instance, the sample was not representative of the population as a whole. Further, the sample was drawn from one police force only and it might have specific local issues that could affect the results.

Overall, the benefit of primary research is that it provides original data that can be to some extent verified in terms of the processes of collection and context, and this can lead to some satisfying results, and new contributions to knowledge.

Conclusion

As stated earlier, this book aims to provide a discussion starting point for students or professionals; they might be beginning conversations with supervisors or funders about how a project might be conceived, conducted and completed. This chapter has aired the possibilities of the types of research questions criminologists might pose using statistics, in order to ask how many, how much, and so on in their projects. There is, of course, a long tradition of criminologists who have aimed to find out how much crime there is, whether or not particular crimes are increasing, and whether justice and punishment are being meted out 'fairly' (or at least evenly). These are all important questions, and as the examples in this chapter illustrate, within the terms of reference the studies adopt they are often successful. It is important to keep in mind throughout this discussion, however, the point made in Chapter 2 about social constructionism and the 'unknowable' figure of crime. The basic premise of the constructionists is that crime is historically and geographically contingent. As shown above in the data from the table from *Criminal Statistics, England and Wales*, the footnote explains that a homicide does not exist until someone is found guilty of the crime in a court of law. Social constructionists would ask, 'Was this not a crime before it was coded as such?' Criminologists such as John Muncie might demand to know why some countries would punish the child perpetrators of this crime much more severely than in others.

Overall this chapter has aimed to illustrate the advantages, pitfalls and problems of quantitative research in the real world. In most cases, for criminologists this will generally involve some sort of engagement with secondary data in the form of 'official' statistics, even if this leads to their own primary research. This has not intended to imply secondary meaning 'second rate'; indeed, the excellent resource that is the government statistical machine and its associated BCS are invaluable to criminologists, especially now that they are available freely online. What needs to be remembered, however, is the circumstances under which the data were collected and collated: namely, the result of a discretionary decision to arrest, and an arbitrary decision to record, within a police station, and to prosecute, within a court in front of a jury. All of these decision-making processes and stages have to be enacted for the statistics criminologists are interested in to exist. As Muncie argues in this chapter, this means that the integrity of the data has to be questioned, as the basis upon which it is gathered, the context or culture in which it is situated, may render it unstable and hence unreliable.

4 Qualitative methods

Introduction

As explained in Chapter 2, there are no perfect studies, methods or research designs. In the real world of research all sorts of unexpected issues and problems arise. Furthermore, although some researchers or organisations will advocate the benefits of perhaps quantitative research over qualitative methods, this can be a political decision. This is also outlined in Chapter 2 and explored in more depth in Chapter 6. In other words, sometimes the debate around which methods are best for investigating any particular question can become bound up with a particular professional expertise or group of researchers who argue for a certain view of the world. Set these against another group of researchers with different ideas and the debate becomes 'politicised' in the sense that such beliefs about what is right or wrong are held passionately. Add to this mix the various theories that underpin the methods of research and the potentially explosive and controversial nature of choosing which method becomes more understandable.

These issues are important but more important is to be clear as to whether the methods chosen will deliver the goods – in other words, is it possible to reach plausible conclusions using the proposed methods? If the answers to the questions require respondents to reply using one word (or one tick), or rely on large numbers of people answering a series of questions that are unambiguous ('Have you been the victim of crime in the past 12 months?', for example), quantitative methods may be very useful. If the study is trying to get some more considered answers to questions, however, such as whether or not people have confidence in the criminal justice system, more in-depth or qualitative methods will be required.

This chapter and the following one are concerned with the exploration of various aspects of qualitative methods. As illustrated earlier, in comparisons between quantitative and qualitative methods, in the past it has seemed that government or official statistics were the gold standard. To find out how many crimes are committed in any particular time or place, or how many police officers are available to solve those crimes, how many are cleared up, how many suspects are punished and/or how many reoffend would once have been the central element of criminological research. It cannot be said that these quantitative studies still dominate the world of criminological research to the detriment of others, although it sometimes seems to be where the funding for research resides. One reason for this is that statistics have the power of 'science' behind them, and can be difficult for the lay person to argue against. To some extent, it is possible to explain the basics of quantitative research more succinctly, whereas the complexity of qualitative research may lend itself to a longer discussion.

To recap, from the analysis and examples throughout the previous two chapters it might be assumed that quantitative research is concerned with 'proving' things and evaluating interventions, so it may follow that qualitative methods do not try to provide conclusive or hard evidence of social situations or 'facts'. This would seem to rule out anything that involves systematic or quasi scientific methods such as having propositions or hypotheses to prove or theories to develop, test or undermine.

This is, of course, to misrepresent the nature of qualitative research, which in its basic premise seeks to ask the deeper 'why' questions that lie behind the 'how many, where and when' of quantitative methods. The following gives a very brief explanation of what quantitative methods have traditionally tried to explore.

Quantitative methods:
Ask questions such as: How many? When? Who? What? Where?
Sometimes there will be an intervention (variable).
The study will then count any changes in the how many, when, who, what and where.
The results may lead to possible predictions of how many, when, who what and where.

The example in Chapter 3 illustrated how prisoners were offered help in resettlement when leaving prison. A fairly large group of respondents was selected, they were interviewed, then the intervention took place (the variable of receiving help or not). The results were compared, with the aim of finding out whether it made a difference to their reoffending rates. The idea was to explore the 'what works' debate. As the researchers discovered, however, the results of the quantitative data analysis needed refinement. Essentially, the study found that for some people in some circumstances, some interventions 'worked', but the picture was too complicated to be a simple mathematical 'proof'. So what sort of qualitative material would need to be explored in order to make sense of the experiences of the resettlement of inmates? One solution would be to ask some questions that qualitative studies do best:

> **Qualitative methods:**
> Ask questions such as: Why? What if?
> *Sometimes there will be an intervention (variable).*
> Has this made any difference?

Due to the investigative nature of qualitative methods they have traditionally been seen as lacking substance, science and therefore validity, or what social science often calls 'rigour'. This refers to the robustness of the data that result from any research: can it stand up to scrutiny, criticism, and to some extent replicability, although this is not a primary concern for qualitative research. This refers to a more natural sciences type of approach which would make claims to samples being able to be taken in other situations, perhaps in drugs trials for instance.

In qualitative studies, one way round the expense of collecting lots of data on different things in different places is to conduct a case study (see Gomm et al. 2000 for a discussion of case study and generalisation). This implies that the research is carried out in a particular case, with a particular group of people, and does not claim to apply to all people in all places at all times. This said, to be rigorous and convincing it should be internally consistent, if not externally representative. This means that although the results may not be able to claim to apply to all cases everywhere to everyone, in terms of its findings as one example of the situation, it must be plausible. Traditionally case studies take one small part of an organisation or place and do some in-depth research, reporting on that particular situation and then explaining the differences or similarities that could make the research more or less generalisable to the whole organisation, or the bigger picture.

Versions of qualitative research

Interviews

Interviews may be one to one, or take place in groups, or be ongoing 'conversations' that often occur naturally during fieldwork or observations.

Focus groups

Focus groups usually involve more than two people who may be a pre-existing established group (such as a local residents' action group), or may consist of people brought together for the purposes of the research, or within an organisation could involve people who know one another and might form groups, but who could be selected to form a group.

Observational studies (such as ethnographies)

This broad category includes any study where the group or scene to be researched is observed by researchers. This can be either with or without their knowledge.

Case studies

Case studies tend to be self-contained and concern people who have some pre-existing relationship with one another. In this sense it could be argued not to be a 'method', because case studies may involve any of the research processes discussed in this book, although as Gomm *et al.* observe, 'quantification of data is *not* a priority. Indeed qualitative data may be treated as superior' (2000: 4, emphasis in original).

Diaries

These are sometimes also called 'reflexive' or 'reflective' notes by the researcher. They are data that allow the researcher to record information that may be extremely useful later in writing up the findings of a study, to add context. In some cases it might be argued that ethnographies consist of this sort of data almost entirely. Notes describing the scene, what people say, how they behave, the environment, the researcher's feeling and emotions, are all part of the reflexive diary. They act as an *aide mémoire* but also as a record of how it felt to be there.

Life history

This type of research involves interviewing or asking respondents to make a recording of their personal experiences, usually with reference to the topic of enquiry of the study. Interviewees may be asked to talk about their experiences in prison, for example.

Visual

This method is becoming increasingly useful and popular, as recording technology becomes more accessible and easy to use. There are particular ethical issues and problems, as with all of the above methods, which will be discussed later in Chapter 6.

Case studies

The following example could be called a 'case study' because it takes a particular minority group and examines quite deeply the lives and beliefs of this particular group. It is about women door staff or 'bouncers'. Only 50 women in total were interviewed, which at the time of the study (2004) was a small proportion of the 7 per cent of door staff in the UK who are female. The study covered a reasonable number of towns and cities, primarily major centres where clubs and pubs would be likely to employ women. In a fuller account of the project, Hobbs *et al.* (2007) explain more about these locations and the types of women the researchers encountered. The rationale for using interviews was to elicit the sort of information that would explain how and why women work in the door security business. The following extract is from the end of project report, and below the questionnaire used is reproduced.

> We developed an interview schedule (see below) to elicit demographic information regarding age, years working in the industry, working hours (including other 'day' jobs if appropriate), family circumstances and so on. Our questions then led to discussing their motivation for working, the violence they had experienced, and the attitudes of friends, family, customers and colleagues towards them as women in this traditionally male role.
>
> Discussions often turned to ways they had learnt to deal with violence, how they prepare or protect their bodies, the difficulties they perceive inhabiting a 'weaker' female body, conceptions of their lack of physical capital, and whether they involved themselves in body modification, in terms of body-building fitness training in order to develop their capabilities, confidence or strength. Women were often keen to discuss the ambiguities they felt regarding their performance as agents of social control, and in particular their appearance as 'masculine' or 'butch'. Especially for those who were working in gay or lesbian venues, this often led to discussions concerning sexuality. (Hobbs and Westmarland 2006: 16–17)

Questionnaire

We're doing research on women who work as door staff. We'd be really grateful if you could take a few minutes to complete our questionnaire. All answers will be kept strictly confidential.

How long have you been working as a door supervisor? (Please tick one)
Less than a year   1–2 years   3–5 years   more than 5 years

How did you get into it?
Contact at a gym/sports club   Approached by venue/agency
Replied to advert   Other (please specify)

Do you work on your own?
Sometimes   Always   Never

Are you usually: Inside the venue   Outside the venue   It varies

Do your duties include:
Meeting and greeting   Choosing customers
Checking toilet areas   Evicting customers   Body searches

Do you always work at the same venue?   Yes   No

Are you employed by: An agency   A venue

How would you describe the venue(s)?
Pub   Club   Bar   Other

Is the venue:
Gay   Lesbian   Straight   Mixed

Do you train or work out (for instance at a gym), or play sports?
Yes   No   If yes, how many hours per week?

Do you take part in:
Martial arts   Body building   Weight training
Boxing   Other physical training (please specify)

Have you done the police/local authority door supervisors' course?
Yes   No

Have you been physically injured at work?
Yes   No

If yes, how many times in the past 12 months?
1   2   3   4   5   More than 5

How many hours do you normally work per week?
5 or less   6–10   11–20   More than 20

Is this your only job?
Yes   No

If this is not your main job, what else do you do?

How much do you usually earn per night?
Less than £50   £50–£75   £80–£100
£100–£125   More than £125

> How old are you?
> 18–24   25–30   31–35   36–40   41–45
> 46–50   Over 50
>
> Would you describe yourself as:
> Gay   Lesbian   Bisexual   Straight
>
> Anything else you'd like to tell us?
>
> *Thank you for taking the time to answer our questions. We might want to talk to you about your job. If you would be willing to see a researcher very briefly to ask more about what you've said here, please leave us a contact number.*

Sometimes the criticisms that are levelled at qualitative work for being non-representative or non-replicable can be countered by the claim that although a representative sample was not possible, the size and demographic make-up of the group was known (and hopefully turned out to be reasonably representative) and could be applied to other areas, if tested. In some situations, a case study can use an unrepresentative sample, because a small and unusual group of people are chosen, such as vicars' wives (Finch 1984), search and rescue volunteers (Lois 2003), armed robbers (Gill 2000), or as in the case above, women bouncers. Because they are part of a relatively rare, exceptional group it would be difficult to find a representative sample, and so instead their demographic status is reported as part of the methodology of the study. The point being, as with the report above, the researchers do not claim representativeness and have a reason for not striving for it. If the group is extremely rare, and they are spread out over a large area and difficult to count as a total population (for instance the women bouncers who work casually, or trafficked women for whom there are few agreed statistics), then the sample is impossible to verify as representative.

In effect, qualitative researchers are aiming for something different from quantitative researchers. They are aiming to validate and obtain plausibility through in-depth knowledge of a smaller group or situation, rather than a larger, broader number of respondents. Quantitative studies often use a brief set of responses to questions: one word, or very short response such as agreeing or disagreeing, or placing a circle around a figure to indicate a place in a scale. Case studies can also use these methods, but will lay less emphasis upon the quantitative data alone. For instance, the questionnaire above was used as an *aide mémoire* or prompt for the interviews, rather than a survey that the respondents filled in themselves. The women bouncers were encouraged to elaborate and it was the taped interviews that provided the data for the reports and articles that resulted from the project (see for example, Hobbs *et al.* 2007; O'Brien *et al.* 2007).

To summarise, therefore, surveys can be quantitative or qualitative, and in both there may be similar sorts of approaches to questions, such as how many people have confidence in the police and the criminal justice system, for instance. For qualitative researchers the validity and plausibility of the study would not rely upon having large numbers of people filling in questionnaires and answering questions with codeable one-word responses; they would want to find out in depth which types of people have confidence in the police, and whether class, age and ethnicity make a difference. Again, this could be asked in a quantitative study, using a tick box, but the qualitative researcher would be interested in why people of a certain category might have more or less confidence – what, if anything, makes a difference to the way people feel about the police and criminal justice system in general.

Interviews

The interview process

Interviews are often regarded as the quintessential qualitative method. They are sometimes thought of as an easy method of obtaining lots of useful thoughts and ideas that can be written up neatly and quickly after they have been completed. Think of a few questions to ask everyone, make appointments, position the microphone, ask the questions and write up the findings. In some ways this is straightforward, but there are in fact many things to be considered, especially in researching areas connected with crime and justice.

The following questions were devised for the writing of this book, and were used as a guide to the conversations, and a prompt if the interview dried up or strayed too far from the topic.

> **Research methods interview schedule**
>
> I'm interested in a study you did in the past, and, briefly, what methods you used, how easy it was to gain access (where applicable) and major successes and failures of your research. In particular I'm interested in how you solved problems you encountered along the way, as I'm writing a book about 'real life' research; in other words, the story behind the study, or the sort of things that often happen on the way to the final report.

> **Questions**
>
> 1 Did your study investigate an area where there are large amounts of existing data, or very little of relevance upon which to base your initial ideas?
> 2 What was the initial research 'idea', i.e. briefly, what did you want to know?
> 3 Were there any particular problems with access? If so, how did you overcome them?
> 4 Were there any ethical problems, and if so, what did you do to solve them?
> 5 Which methods did you use (quantitative/qualitative/mixture)?
> 6 Did the methods you used turn out to be appropriate?
> 7 What were the main successes of the study?
> 8 What were the main difficulties and how were they overcome?
> 9 Were the findings published, and where?
> 10 Anything else we haven't covered?

This type of set of questions and the earlier questionnaire for women bouncers are examples of an interview schedule. Interviews that follow a fairly rigid pattern with 'closed' questions, such as, 'How many hours a week do you work?', are sometimes called 'structured' interviews. There is a list of questions to be answered, usually in a given order. Semi-structured interviews tend to have more 'open-ended' questions, such as those beginning, 'Do you think . . .', 'Can you tell me about . . .'.

In terms of time, compared to ethnographic research, interviews are usually a very efficient way to carry out qualitative research: as appointments can be arranged in advance, and usually take about an hour to conduct. If they are well prepared, a great deal of useful data can be obtained. Sometimes setting up the interviews can be more time-consuming than the interviews themselves; it can be difficult to gain access to certain interviewees (such as those in a senior position, as in Ben Bowling's experience, and also as Laura Piacentini describes in her account of accessing Russian prison officials – both later in this chapter).

Things that can go wrong in interviews

In addition to the 'normal' human aspects of arranging meetings, such as people not being available on the phone, or unable to make the appointment, there are particular access problems for researchers who wish to conduct interviews. The sort of things that go wrong can include:

Technology

Sometimes tape recorders malfunction, batteries are suddenly dead, or the situation is too noisy to make a good recording.

Interviewees who are hostile or defensive

It seems unlikely at first that someone would agree to be interviewed and then refuse to answer questions, or act in a very negative way. But there are people who may agree to be interviewed to 'make a point' or to display their power to say 'yes', and then go on to be uncooperative. Some interviewees, particularly in organisations, although they may claim to have freely consented, may have been told to take part in an interview, and worse, instructed 'not to give anything away'. It can be difficult to find out why someone appears uncomfortable and defensive in an interview. Sometimes it is not until later that the researcher discovers some reason in the personal or political background to the interview that makes this clear.

People who agree with everything you say

Perhaps even more difficult than dealing with hostility, it can be impossible to conduct an incisive, useful and productive research interview with a respondent who just wants to agree with the questioner or has no opinion on the topic of the conversation. The researcher may have to accept that a particular interview will not be useful in the final data analysis and not be included in the writing up.

Ethical issues

This is discussed in Chapter 6, but it is worth pointing out here that the interview can be a situation where respondents feel that they are in an intimate relationship or environment. Sometimes this can lead to disclosure about some personal and occasionally upsetting or distressing information.

How to prepare

As far as technology is concerned, there are precautions researchers can take, but short of having two of everything, technology may be the thing that defeats at least once in a project.

Be ready to defuse hostility. Try to anticipate who might have an axe to grind, and in advance work out a way of disarming the hostile. For example, it might be useful to check that people have 'really' given their consent to the interview rather than being forced into it. Switching off the tape recorder (or offering to do so) can sometimes help defuse people's anxieties.

Be prepared for the 'yes' people. Try to find out about the interviewees. If they have written or published anything, read it. If they have certain responsibility in an organisation, find out all you can about it. Then, if the conversation dries up with a series of 'yes' and 'no' answers, you can introduce something different that may spark a discussion. This way you can appear to have done your homework, but do admit anything you really don't know about, and try not to be a know-it-all.

Sometimes interviews have a dual purpose, such as the example by Ben Bowling below illustrates. It is a reflection on one of the interviews he conducted for his book *Policing the Caribbean* (2010). Developing his earlier work on transnational policing (see Bowling 2009) he was setting out to investigate how the Caribbean islands are an important area for analysing the trafficking of goods and people, and other illicit transactions. The book concentrates on how various agencies, such as police and customs, respond to what is often seen as 'insecurity', because while 'some islands are relatively safe, violent crime has been rising across the region since the 1980s and in some parts, the murder rate has reached startling proportions' (Bowling 2010: 3). His approach was broadly that of a case study, using interviews and observations, looking not only at the war on drugs throughout the islands but also at the 'associated harms of money laundering, corruption, armed violence, murder and mayhem' (Bowling 2010: 34). In order to do this research he wanted to interview the Commissioner of Police, but through that meeting also to gain access to other people in the organisation. These 'gatekeeper' meetings with key interviewees can thus be very important; the occasion can be a chance to hear it from the top, but also to convince the main player of your intentions and capabilities and to persuade them you are 'safe' to have around their organisation and people.

Preparing for these first meetings, which may be set up as 'interviews' of key personnel, can be disarming. It is not uncommon to be put 'on the spot' with difficult questions at these encounters. At my first meeting to set up access for an ethnography of women in the police (see Westmarland 2001b: 529) the first question fired at me was, 'What will you do if you see a police officer assault a suspect and they call upon you to be a witness?' In these situations it can be difficult to be suitably prepared and to know what to say that will not have a negative effect on the prospective research relationship. This issue of ethical dilemmas in the research process is discussed in Chapter 6.

Ben Bowling discusses these problems and others surrounding access and credibility. As his interview illustrates, just getting to the point where you can meet and convince the appointed liaison person can be problematic.

Interview with Ben Bowling: accessing the Commissioner

The police headquarters' public face is the Central Police Station, a solid and authoritative stone building, behind which is the Commissioner's office, a wooden building in the colonial style. At a sentry post, I was asked whether I was in possession of a firearm or a knife and then given a thorough search with a very sensitive metal detector. It beeped when it detected a coin in my pocket and again when it discovered the metal eyelets on my shoes. Entering through the central archway, away to the left I could see the cell-block, guarded by an officer in a white uniform holding a cane that he was whacking smartly against his left hand. To the right lay the quartermaster's stores and shop with a sign saying 'Kit available' and giving the times that equipment can be picked up.

Walking through a further archway, I passed into a traditional cobbled courtyard with the various departments coming off to left and right built variously of stone and wood and with shutters that were falling apart. It had something of the appearance of a garrison or colonial military barracks. The officers wore a khaki uniform and had a strong military air about them.

On my way to the Commissioner's office, I watched a troupe of new recruits going through drill. These were again officers in khaki uniform – which I understand are the paramilitary section of the police – who were marching up and down with rifles over their shoulders. I noticed that the recruits included a number of women. The person supervising the drill seemed to be a classic sergeant major with crisp uniform, narrow waist and good voice shouting marching orders.

The entrance to the Commissioner's office was also guarded by a sentry on the ground floor; behind him sat a plain clothes administrator who pointed me up two flights of stairs. At the top of the stairs was a waiting room where about eight or nine people were sitting, supervised by two uniformed officers acting as receptionists. I explained that I had a meeting with the Commissioner and was pointed to the far end of the corridor. There was yet another receptionist to whom I gave my card. She then telephoned the Commissioner's secretary who, after a few minutes, came out to see me. She looked at me sternly and told me that she had instructed me to 'call, not come' and that the Commissioner had a full diary today and could not see me. I explained that I had written an email to say that I would like to see the Commissioner today, that I had confirmed this by telephone with her last week, and had again emailed over the weekend to confirm a time, 2 p.m., which it now was. Nonetheless, she said that the Commissioner couldn't see me today, but could perhaps later in the week. I explained that this was frustrating since I would like to speak to members of his staff, and perhaps could I be referred to them. Yes, that would be fine, she replied, but I would have to speak to the Commissioner first. Probably tomorrow afternoon, she suggested. I agreed to call in the morning to confirm a time.

When I phoned the next morning, I was unable to reach the Commissioner, but was instead put through to the office of the Assistant Commissioner, who was willing to see me and suggested that we meet at 2.30 p.m. that day. After going through the same security procedure as the previous day, I found myself outside the Assistant Commissioner's office. Unfortunately, on my arrival, he turned out to be in a meeting with the Commissioner, and I agreed to wait for his return. I sat and waited, taking in my surroundings.

The anteroom at the top of the stairwell where I was sitting had a patterned lino floor, brick red doors and cream walls lit with a fluorescent light. There were four red fire buckets filled with sand. The wooden panels on the staircase were rotten and there was a general sense of decrepitude. It was stifling, far too hot for my grey wool suit, white shirt and patterned tie. A gentle breeze blew tantalisingly for a few seconds before disappearing into the heat.

After about an hour, the Assistant Commissioner returned from his meeting and explained that he couldn't meet me that day, but invited me to come back at 11.30 a.m. tomorrow.

At half past one the following day, fully two hours after the time of my appointment, I found myself still sitting outside the Assistant Commissioner's office. Tropical rain was falling hard outside, the dense tropical foliage dripping, compounding the uncomfortable sensation of the rivulet of sweat running down my back. While waiting, I examined the foul contents of the sand buckets in front of me, watched the paint flake off the decrepit walls, observed the comings and goings of the police administrators (most of them women) and endured the raised eyebrows of the passers-by.

Finally, two hours and five minutes late, the Assistant Commissioner for Administration and Training arrived at his office. Without apology, noting simply that he had been in a meeting with the Commissioner, he showed me into his generously proportioned office. It was in a state of extraordinary disarray: a three-piece suite was entirely covered in disorderly piles of files strewn higgledy-piggledy; cabinets and shelves were covered in files and folders. On the desk there were five or six rather neater piles that had items of paperwork on top of them awaiting signature.

We sat at either side of the desk and I prepared to commence the interview, but before I could start the Assistant Commissioner crossed the room and turned on the television. This was showing the cricket – the West Indies were on the back foot against a touring England team. (Despite Brian Lara's record 400 not out, the home team suffer an unprecedented and humiliating 3–0 series defeat.) That the Assistant Commissioner watched the match over my left shoulder for the duration of the interview made it somewhat difficult to keep the flow of the conversation going and was disconcerting to say the least. He was unwilling to be taped, so I took notes instead as he spoke.

I started by asking what the Assistant Commissioner saw as the major security threats facing the Caribbean region and the island in particular. He replied that he couldn't comment on that because he was Assistant Commissioner (Administration and Training) and therefore crime fell outside his ambit. I then asked him if he could say something about transnational cooperation. He replied that there was very good cooperation with overseas police forces. There was, for example, media training ongoing at that moment and he could happily furnish me with a list of all courses on which police officers had travelled overseas within the last couple of years. There was also a joint service coordinating council, involving the police and the chief of staff of the military that meets once a month. Beyond that, he couldn't say much because this was the remit of the Assistant Commissioner (Crime). As Assistant Commissioner (Administration and Training), his role was personnel, training, welfare, the police choir, the force band and public relations. I asked whether it would be possible for him to refer me to the Assistant Commissioner (Crime). Unfortunately not, he replied, that person was on long-term leave and would not be returning to the post. I asked whether it would be possible to be referred to his replacement. That, he said, wouldn't be a problem because only this morning he had himself been promoted to Assistant Commissioner (Crime). With that, the interview was concluded.

It is difficult to say what could have helped in a situation such as this. Clearly the power is with the Assistant Commissioner, who by his behaviour illustrates the low priority he gives to researchers. This is a relatively common attitude of powerful people in organisations. They are busy and have many other demands on their time. Although Ben Bowling is an experienced and well-established academic, he had to repeatedly return and not be put off by seemingly uncooperative 'front' staff – what might be called the gatekeepers of the gatekeeper. Researchers sometimes travel thousands of miles, having won hard-fought-over research grants to pay for the trip. They may be full of enthusiasm for the project, but are sometimes viewed as an irritation, something to be got out of the way as soon as possible.

This is not always the case, of course, but the interview below with Laura Piacentini illustrates the patience that is often necessary when conducting a research project far from home. Piacentini's work is concerned with Russian prisons, especially the experiences of women in the system. In the following conversation she is mostly referring to her book about surviving the system in Russian prisons (2004) and also to an article (with Pallot and Moran) about gender and the penal system in Russia (2009).

Interview with Laura Piacentini: getting into Russian prisons

At first access was no problem, because I did a pilot study that was enabled by Roy King, my PhD supervisor who had extensive contacts due to his work in Russian prisons. I spent a long time waiting around at the beginning, however – once I got over there – six weeks holed up in a library in a barracks. I spent my time reading and doing a spot of English language teaching as well as gazing out of the window!

A year later, when I arrived to do the main study it was a different story. I eventually got a 'letter' giving me permission to do the research, and that was my ticket (which had overall taken two years: I began preparing for fieldwork in 1997, and got access for the main study in 1999), but basically they wanted me out of the way, to send me to the prisons hundreds of miles away from Moscow. It was never part of the plan to go to Siberia, but actually it worked out much better.

It was always going to be a qualitative study, to explore the running of punishment in contemporary Russia. I wanted to go further than a survey, to look at the cultural mores, essential traditions and Russian-celebrating culture as a prelude to data collection. In this way I was developing an ethnography of closeness, reflecting on my personal values to understand the context of the study. I knew that the penal system was a 'material product' of socialism because it was designed into the ideology of utopian Leninist theory building. I therefore felt it was necessary to explore what it meant to punish now that the heaven-on-earth that was Marxism/Leninism had gone.

Overall the research design was done on the hoof, modified as I went along. There was a clear methodology and design to follow but it took the form of a checklist of areas to cover and a series of sub-questions beneath each area. It was a moveable framework that I reconfigured as I went along.

For example, in one prison a governor I was interviewing refused to allow me to write his responses or my notes in English (all the interviews were conducted in Russian). I had to show him my questions, and I felt very controlled and uncomfortable in terms of ethics. He refused to be anonymised in the writing up of the interview, and I didn't feel confident – I was controlled and regulated. There were sanctions on the work. In the end I didn't use his interview; I made the professional decision. I sometimes say to students, this is the point where you own your thesis, the stage where you feel confident enough to say that you won't use a particular interview.

Despite such difficulties, one of the successes of the study is that it has brought deeper understandings of Russian prison regimes – the second highest prison population in the world – to the discipline of criminology, and tried to say something different, so although people have explored the political and legal aspects, my study has also examined culture and identity and agency. No one had entered Russian penal territory before. Yet, the penal system is cited continually as both a model for how reform *can* work, while abuses still operate. When you deeply embed yourself in the culture that surrounds a penal society you learn about how cultural attachments are formed (or not formed).

It has been about internally navigating within a difficult world in a different language – in terms of both Russian and the prison language. It has asked, what is really different? And in some ways it seems that gender was ignored in the sense that for men and women nothing was very different, but in terms of differences between Russia and, for example, Britain, at least in British prisons the Human Rights Act would probably be being adhered to, or recognised as existing. But in Russia, well, it's a different story altogether.

One example was in the Siberian prison. When I arrived I was told that for various reasons the prisoners hadn't been let out into the fresh air for two weeks. They warned me that they were worried that there might be a disturbance of some sort. I felt very uncomfortable with this – and I felt I had to go to the governor and say to him that it might impact on my research (that I'd have to disclose what had happened) if there was a disturbance. He was, 'Yes, OK, I understand, things are being sorted out,' and I felt better in that I'd actually done something – I had to raise it with him. I felt the need to establish a position on this – I felt it was unethical of me to continue carrying out research in an environment that was on the brink of exploding.

I was concerned that there was some truth to the rumours of prisoners being denied the right to outdoor activity. I explained to him that this potentially made my position untenable and that I would have to reassess whether I could continue my work. Although I knew deep down that this would not have a lasting impact in terms of turning events around, I felt that by laying my cards on the table, I established my position, and hopefully my credibility, as a scholar who held opinions on rights and rights abuses and that this could be taken further by myself.

There is a problem in knowing too much about human rights abuses. People make disclosures in interviews, and this is a harmed and hurting population. Sometimes the first half of an interview will be just talking about the problems they have – their family can't visit, they haven't seen their son who lives 2,000 miles away and so on. What you have to be absolutely crystal clear about, and emphasise from the start, for instance in your letters to potential interviewees and in written material about the study, is that you are not there to monitor the prison (or other institution) but you will bring their concerns to the notice of the authorities. This is especially problematic in criminological research because the kinds of populations we encounter – often the powerless – are those who have been marginalised through the criminal justice system.

Also, it's about your own emotions. The topics we encounter in criminology can be depressing and emotional, and I think it's fine to talk about emotions in research, rather than writing emotionally. Prisons are troubling, dangerous places and they depress everyone! They represent lost faith in a section of society; poverty, isolation, pain, harm, violence and abuse are all present in the prison so it seems bizarre to me that we operate research as if this does not have an effect on one's emotions. The tricky task is to write reflexively about this and not to write, as you say, emotionally.

Research that involves coming into contact with some of the places, people and situations in criminology is especially difficult – the study of Russian prisons involved a hard-to-reach population and it was an extremely bumpy, emotional, teary and dangerous process. We might want to ask if the emotional sacrifice is worth it. Has it changed anything? My view is that one way of overcoming some of the emotional obstacles is to immerse yourself in a wide range of work and engage in a healthy and robust activity of discipline-hopping. Building intellectual dialogues demands that one balance how they engage with different ways of reading the prison world and it keeps emotions in check. In my current project on women's prisons, we employ a wide range of researchers who are Russian and it's been a fantastic process of self-critique because the Russian world-view is a different one, sometimes.

The way I think about it is that things might not change directly as a result of my study, but at least there are other ways that change might be less obvious. So, for instance, as a result of publishing my book and other studies, I'm sometimes asked to be an expert witness by organisations who might want information about human rights in certain countries – Amnesty, or in appeals against deportation – and I can give them that picture. So the information gets channelled in different ways, other fora – not necessarily directly changing 'the world' but having an effect in other ways. If that work hadn't been done or published, we probably couldn't say that would be the case. I think that what I am getting at here is the issue of wide dissemination. Away from the academe, there are all sorts of interesting and policy-focused fora that can be tapped into. I think that PhD students would do well to remind themselves that their work might not change the world, but if their work can take them into different dissemination environments, then they may produce some modest achievements.

Both these interviews illustrate the pitfalls of trying to get into difficult places to do research in crime and justice settings. They show that power relations are important to acknowledge in researching sensitive or 'closed' scenes such as prisons or the inner workings of police and security organisations. Although these conversations with Ben Bowling and Laura Piacentini might seem to present daunting situations to the uninitiated, in real life they represent the difficulties that all researchers will face at some point. Conducting interviews can be a frustrating and time-consuming method of obtaining data. The people you might want to interview, those you view as key to your project, may not share the level of importance with which you see the event. It is an artificial social encounter, with a conversational style that is not necessarily natural.

Perhaps these two examples illustrate clearly that the power dynamics of interviews are worth considering. Personal appearance and demeanour, including accent, personal history and even where the researcher lives can be things that may allow the interviewee to feel confident and able to open up to the researcher. Sometimes, despite appearances, people can feel intimidated by an interviewer 'from the university' coming to ask them potentially awkward questions. On the other hand, where the power is clearly in the hands of the interviewee, such as the Commissioner of Police above, or the person with the power to grant access to the national prison service, the interviewer needs to be tactful, friendly, responsive and appear relatively capable. Have your questions ready, and appear prepared but friendly and adaptable.

One of the tactics crime and justice organisations use may be to attempt to divert the researcher. The organisation may themselves have an issue they want researching, and see the interview as a way of moving the agenda. This might go along the lines of, 'Yes, we know you're interested in how women officers become detectives and join the murder squad, but we wondered if you could just, as part of your project, find out why they're not applying for traffic?'

To summarise, interviews are often the mainstay of qualitative projects and can generate a great deal of useful data. They can take various forms, from a set of questions asked from list requiring 'yes or no' answers, to a free-flowing conversation covering diverse areas. In crime and justice research, as in many other fields, there are power dynamics to be aware of and skills that will develop as the researcher progresses. Learning just the right amount of empathy or agreement, knowing when to prompt the interviewee and when certain topics should be abandoned, can only be learnt in 'real life' experiences.

The researchers quoted throughout this book, all very experienced senior academics, may seem to be talking about their experiences of research and interviews in a matter-of-fact way. One message they are trying to get across is that even they find things going wrong. Power dynamics and 'life' often intervene, spoiling the best-laid plans, but it is better to persevere because sometimes the unintended consequences turn out to be the most useful way into the problem. As Laura Piacentini remarks above: 'it was never part of the plan to go to Siberia, but actually it worked out much better.'

Focus groups

Focus groups, which could be described as rather like large-scale, multiple interviews, are much more complex and difficult to control than one-to-one interviews. The group might begin to argue, a mix of opinions and positions might emerge, and the researcher has to be in control: decide who can speak, try to encourage taking of turns and persuade people to speak one at a time. Focus groups can be a useful way to obtain lots of data quickly. They have been used to great effect by political parties and market researchers trying to obtain lots of opinions quickly and cheaply but also to generate debate on controversial topics. One problem with them, however, is that sometimes people get very loud and argumentative and unless the process is controlled the tapes are difficult to transcribe. Another problem can be that it is difficult to get people to talk, or disagree, or discuss issues with one another. These can turn into individual interviews within the group, where each tells of their opinions or experiences. In the worst case scenario no one has much of an opinion or everyone agrees.

The following describes a focus group where two groups of women police officers, who didn't know each other, came together for a discussion about 'barriers to promotion' for female officers (see Westmarland 1994). Some of the women were 'anti equal opportunities' (want to do it on my own terms, as good as any man) and others were from the 'policing is a man's world organised for men' position. Women from the first group expressed their satisfaction with their careers so far – one woman said that she had achieved her ambition to join the traffic department, as she'd wanted to 'drive fast cars fast'. Another said that she'd been in the CID for many years and had not been discriminated against. This sparked a reaction from other women who had sat silently up until this point. One woman, who had previously been working in the child and family protection unit (seen as a 'soft' option by some), countered this with her experiences:

> Once they found out I was pregnant it was like signing my own death warrant. The day I came back (from maternity leave) their opening line was 'Right, you're back to work (on the beat). We're having you out of that department and on shifts. Are you going to stop in the job?'

Another woman joined in at this point:

> When I first found out I was pregnant I was made to do Instant Response duties which meant that we worked from 10 p.m. to 1 a.m. in addition to our normal shift. I was told that if anything happened it was my fault because I chose to get pregnant and the job came first. I was made to work full shifts, with quick changeovers. When I came back to work I was told because I'd taken full maternity leave my disinterest in the job had been noted, and I was going nowhere. I could forget about applying for anything because I wouldn't get it because I had been off.

Another woman announced that when she had objected to being moved after returning from maternity leave her senior officer informed her that she should be on a discipline charge for insubordination. She said that when the case came to a tribunal the same senior officer claimed that she had been 'knitting baby clothes' while on duty!

As a result of these experiences being recounted, the other group of women in the focus group were visibly shocked and the mood of the room changed. The women in the formerly happy group said:

> Well, they go on about equal opportunities and how they understand that women get pregnant and they have babies, and it's all in the forefront, and this is going on and we don't even know about it.

> It's enough to make you stand for the Federation (the police officers' union).

> No wonder the HMI's going on about women and equal opportunities.

> I can't believe that they've actually sent a document around saying about job-sharing when their attitude's like that.

What had started as a seemingly pointless focus group, where everyone was completely happy with their situation, became a heated discussion about the way some colleagues had been treated. Although the point of the group discussion was to gather data on what women thought about applying for promotion in this particular police force, it turned into a supportive arena and was a useful example of how the organisation kept some people isolated from each other. It should be noted that this was data collected some years ago for a report to a particular force (Westmarland 1994); police practices have since changed with regard to maternity leave, and job-sharing has become more common.

Focus group discussions can become heated and the researcher has to moderate racist and sexist language and opinions. The advantages of the method are that lively debates can draw out opinions and are useful for discovering what 'the public' think, as opposed to just one person. In the case of public attitudes towards policing in a local area, for example (see Clarke *et al.* 2007), a wide range of opinions can be sought from similar groups of people (such as local residents) or those brought together by way of individual invitation (such as the women police officers in the focus group above).

Mixed methods

In the following interview Sandra Walklate points out the benefits of mixed methods. She explains the background and experiences from her project, which was funded as part of an ESRC programme conducted between 1994 and 1996. She has published, with co-authors, several papers and articles drawn from the project (see Evans *et al.* 1996, for example).

Interview with Sandra Walklate: the fear of crime debate

I should say something about what we were really concerned with. It was particularly the fear of crime debate, as it was then, and what we were trying to do was to unpick how it was in two small areas, two wards in fact – Oldtown and Bankhill, similar, working class, primarily white – and compare them.

When we started the project we always proposed a kind of mixed methodology – that was always in the game plan, because as a team that was what we were committed to and we felt at the time to get the funding we had to put a survey bit in there, a quantitative bit. So we did plan on doing our own version of a crime survey and we did borrow a lot from the British Crime Survey questions, but it was always planned as a longitudinal study. It was a two-and-a-half-year project so it was quite interesting from that respect, and it was always going to be a mixed method because what we wanted was to get a feel for, across the board, about how people were living with, managing and responding to crime. So it always included talking to community groups, residents, police officers, the professionals, the whole kit and caboodle.

That was the plan, and as the project unfolded – the first six months was about familiarisation in the areas – the two full-time researchers on the project spent time just hanging about places, going to the pubs, going to community forum meetings, just being seen around the areas. One of the first things we did as a team was to be taken on a walkabout by one of the community police officers, who was plain clothes, worked under cover, particularly in Oldtown. He took us on a walk around the area really early in the morning so nobody would see us out with the police, so that in his terms, the local 'scallies' wouldn't see us as associated with him. That was a really informative way of getting a feel for how the police thought, on the ground, about this particular location, and we did the same in the other area as well, with their equivalent officer, because they were actually policed quite differently, as we learned during the first six months.

So the first six months was about embedding, getting faces known in the location; it was also about refining the research tools and so on, training up people who were going to interview. It's kind of one of those happenstance things where it was luck we did that, because during that six months the Home Office had a survey team out there doing door-to-door interviews on intimidation. Through our contact with the local superintendent we learnt that they were 'asked' to leave.

We said, what do you mean, they were asked to leave, and we were told that they had to get off the estate – by day four they were told to get off the estate – and we went, oh-oh, we want to send people out interviewing there; and you know, we thought, how are we going to do this?

We discovered that part of the problem was that the Home Office interviewers were all your typical professional interviewers, you know, briefcases, smart suits and so on. We'd only ever planned to recruit postgrad students to do this and people who knew the locality, and had got local accents and that sort of thing. So when it came to training them it was about not carrying clipboards and briefcases but going out dressed as a student, and fortunately we didn't get any problems at all in getting people to talk to us in either of the locations. So from that bedding down process we learnt a lot – not only about the kind of quantitative data that was available for the area, so all your demographics and your ward data, and the stuff you can get from the census data to build up that kind of picture, but also we were getting more qualitative information about what the issues looked like, getting the local newspapers, going to community forum meetings, getting a bit involved in community groups. One of our researchers worked for a while as a volunteer in one of the locations just to get a feel for some of the issues and the other researcher at the time actually lived in the other location so we did get seriously embedded.

I suppose it depends what you're really interested in, but if you're really interested in community responses to crime or the fear of crime you've got to get a feel for what being there looks like from the grass-roots point of view if you can. The idea was to do the kind of more conventional sort of door-to-door survey in each of the locations – this was going to be our prime quantitative data base, apart from all the other sort of census data sort of stuff. This involved another different kind of learning curve, training the interviewers. First of all, we were very careful about managing the interviewers: there was always a member of the research team out with a group of interviewers at any one time, so we knew where people were going, if somebody disappeared into a house for too long. We could kind of keep a check on people and at the end of the day we'd debrief: OK, how did it go?

What we'd actually asked our students to do was to 'write anything down that people say to you', and we'd done one week in Oldtown and they said, 'It's not working, Sandra'. 'What do you mean, it's not working?' 'It's just people can't answer the questions we're asking.' 'They can't answer the questions?' 'Well, they're saying things like we kept getting all these qualitative quotes, such as, well, it's not like that round here if you're local, if we get a problem what's his face up the road'll sort it out. These questions about being afraid are not resonating with what people are actually saying to us, so we're not able to tick the answers, which is the conventional crime survey stuff, but what we've got is a lot of qualitative writing, on the interview schedules.'

And yet what was happening in the other area was that the questions were working fine, so we've got the same instrument, the same questions, that's working in one location but not working in the other location, and that was like, back to the drawing board – are we asking the right questions, or are we not?

Simultaneously to this – because you know research kind of evolves, in phases, so you do one thing with one strand of the research and you're doing another thing with another – we'd already started doing some focus group research with police officers, focus groups with professionals, which was coming out of our involvement, our kind of grounded work. So we'd already started doing that, and it was in one of those focus groups with the police officers in one of the areas, that one very, very experienced police officer said, 'Well, people just don't trust people round here, do they? They wouldn't even trust their own sons to do things for you.' And we thought, that's it! That's the clue, that's the missing link that we've been looking for. So we began to rethink – not that the data we'd been getting back was wrong, but it made us rethink how we were making sense of the data.

So from that we realised that the fear of crime was the wrong conceptual framework to be making sense of the data we were getting back, which led us into the whole trust and communities and dynamics of trust. Then, having made that link, that went on to inform how we further managed the focus group work with people who lived in the locality. It was a kind of cumulative thing. We started to ask them questions around, not so much about, fear, but we found different ways of getting them to talk about their experiences of crime, and living in that location; we didn't use fear as the word, because we were trying to see if they would talk about issues to do with trust as well. That happened, and it became clear that Bankhill was an area where the crime survey stuff worked, but in the focus groups they would talk very much about not trusting the professionals. They 'asked people to come and do things and they never do', whether that's the local authority to empty the bins, or the police to come. So you've got one area where people are clearly distrusting of their own neighbours but reaching out to the professionals to come and help them do things; you've got another area where there is much more trusting of neighbours and the people they know in the locality, and they wouldn't have anything to do with the authorities.

So I suppose it's that constant interaction, the unfolding research process, with the conceptual ideas, and seeing that as a dynamic rather than a kind of snapshot picture, which is what survey data would have given you. If we had just left it at that we'd have got, 'It didn't work', but if you're actually doing other stuff as well, that contextualises that, and you think, ah, but it might be working this way. We ended up in a completely different place from where we started, conceptually.

We couldn't do the survey again because it was a budgeting issue, so you have live with that and what it is that you've got, but there's different things you can do as a research team. You can either throw your hands up in the air in horror and say what a complete mess this is, or you can actually use it as a challenge. I think that's what we did as a team, we used it as a challenge. We thought, ah no, we can't say what people are saying to us is wrong, and we can't say what the interviewers are saying to us is wrong; what we've got to do is find a way of making sense of this disjunction, and that was the way we did it.

One of the downsides to that approach was actually convincing a wider audience that what we were saying made sense in relation to the data. I remember giving a seminar paper based on the research as we were starting to do the serious write-up and people couldn't believe that I wasn't talking about gender in relation to the fear of crime – they found it very difficult to take that it didn't come up. But people in our focus groups didn't talk about being afraid in the way in which the feminist literature would have expected them to talk about being afraid of crime. Now that is not to say that gender wasn't part of the overall picture, because it was, but it was in a different way.

If I could do it again, knowing what I know now, we might be more attuned to what was the role of the criminal gangs, the different roles of the criminal gangs in each area. Now you see, we started as a project on the fear of crime, never anticipating that the presence, or absence, of organised criminal gangs in either of these locations would be an ingredient in understanding the fear of crime, because we started with a very conventional set of hypotheses relating to the fear of crime debate. But then, as the project unfolded – and again, this was partly to do with the kind of police informants we got, partly to do with something that happened in one location in the course of the project, and then a serendipitous meeting on a demonstration about something else completely different – one of the researchers was introduced to someone who was presented to her as the press officer for the criminal gang in one of the estates where we were working. She interviewed him and he invited her to go to his house. He pulled out drawers of press cuttings on how the gang's activities had been reported in the local press, and we suddenly began to think, so when people say what's his face up the road will sort it out, they mean something quite specific. So that gave us another kind of insight that was about who you trust and who you don't trust. That was in Oldtown, where the presence of the criminal gangs was very, very organised, and they were called the 'Salford firm'. One of their key leaders was locked up for a very long time during the course of the project.

So what I'm saying, if we were starting again, is that you'd take that into account. You'd have to do health and safety stuff – you really are getting into dodgy areas. Before you needed clearance we used to get into schools and we did focus groups with secondary school kids, and they talked about the 'little Salford firm', in other words the lads who were aspiring to be in the criminal gangs. Then we were much more sensitive to the local residents who had a very sophisticated knowledge as to who was doing what in their area. So lads on pushbikes meeting up in the supermarket car park, they knew that was about swapping drugs, ferrying stuff, in a way in which if you didn't listen to folks you'd think they were just lads out on their pushbikes. So I think, anybody looking at those sorts of questions in those kinds of locations, I would advise them to start with a very different kind of agenda from what we started with.

The methods stayed the same, but our sense-making process of what they were producing changed completely, so we actually stepped right outside of the fear of crime debate at the end – I don't know how you actually avoid that kind of problem. I suppose the only thing you might do differently would be to do a bit more of that kind of intelligence-gathering before you started.

> At the end we had a three or four month dissemination period when we did presentations to the local authority. What that allowed us to do, we could talk meaningfully about the problems they had about attracting businesses and we could say yes, but that's because people perhaps see the process as open and interpretative and we were seen as too flaky.
>
> Talking about this reminds me of something I recommend to PhD students – it's like Sherlock Holmes' 'dog in the night time' – it's about being open-minded, it's having a hypothesis but not being driven by it. If you have negative findings it doesn't mean that you didn't find anything out; by having negative findings doesn't mean that there are no findings. Also, in terms of general advice, the usual things: keep a research diary, a reflective diary, good recommendations, don't believe everything you read in research method handbooks, beware of interview as therapy (the first bit I did on victims, interviewing an elderly woman on her burglary and it was quite clear it was therapy – be careful not to get drawn in). Also, switching the tape recorder off – I learnt more than once that the tape recorder was switched off and I'd stopped writing, so I was finding nooks and crannies to write down the exact phrases.

Sandra Walklate argues that the advantages of mixed methods are more contextualisation, a better understanding of the bigger picture, and, in the study she describes, a vital way of checking they understood some subtle cultural nuances. The existence of the organised gang, for example, would not have been discovered using a straightforward tick box survey. She also points out that they used quantitative data, such as existing population data, to begin their study. Another early part of the study was to be guided round the estate by the local police officer. These examples illustrate that as well as it being possible to mix qualitative and quantitative studies, both can be placed on a continuum or scale, from 'very hard' methods at one end (such as the raw data on numbers of crimes committed per population), to questions that have multiple choice answers, with therefore some 'human' aspect to the way they are asked and responded to, to the softer methods described in this chapter, interviews and surveys where respondents can make up their own answers, to open-ended interviews (see below).

This continuum extends further than this, however, because it includes the unstructured or 'naturalistic' methods, which will be discussed in the next chapter.

Continuum of research methods

Very hard	Hard	Soft	Very soft
Statistics	Closed question interviews/surveys	Open-ended question interviews	Observations/ ethnographies

Some studies use methods that set out to intentionally exploit the benefits of quantitative and qualitative methods. One example is a study by Matthews, Hancock and Gilling (2004) that aimed to look at the jury system. In particular the research team was interested in the jury members' 'perceptions, understanding, confidence and satisfaction in the jury system'. They surveyed six courts and used questionnaires and interviews to collect the data, and explained their rationale thus:

> The survey collected data of both a quantitative and qualitative nature, which was necessary to reflect the 'extensive' and 'intensive' nature of opinion formation. Since it was wished to map socio-demographic and other variables against those concerned with confidence in the criminal justice system, for example, it was important to use more than one type of data analysis method. As such, the research team employed the protocols common to most quantitative research in social science. Relationships between variables were analysed using SPSS 10.0 and N-Vivo (NUDIST) employed to analyse the qualitative data and to facilitate interfaces with statistical data. Data was 'indexed', 'charted' and 'mapped' (Ritchie and Spencer 1994) by the research team to explore the key themes this research was concerned with, to identify associations and to facilitate the development of explanations for the patterns generated by the data; a peer-checking system operated throughout.
>
> It was anticipated that the research strategy outlined above provides a more nuanced account of jurors' attitudes and experiences involving a combination of both quantitative and qualitative data.
>
> (Matthews *et al.* 2004: 24)

This study had government funding and approval from the Home Office. It therefore had 'official' status, which helped to facilitate access to jury members, the courts and the 'back areas' of the premises, which would have been difficult without such prior backing. The researchers surveyed six courts and interviewed and surveyed 100 jurors. Although they used a combination of quantitative and qualitative methods in order to be rigorous, to validate and 'triangulate' their data, this is expensive. Methods used that come under the 'qualitative' umbrella include interviews, focus groups, observational methods, and surveys, and 'semi-soft' methods such as discourse analysis, secondary analysis, documentary/policy analysis, historical research. Having said this, some of these methods can also be used in more quantitative ways.

So, for example, surveys may be simply a number of 'yes or no' answers, and may not have any room for 'qualitative' or interpretive answers. Similarly, interviews can be a series of questions taken from an interview schedule that is basically a tick box survey; a human being asks the questions, but this will still deliver the same data and results, namely the number of people who think 'x' or 'y'. It will go no further towards discovering why people think this, or allowing them to consider their answers or qualify their responses. In sum, no ambiguities or nuances are allowed to surface. As Lynn Hancock suggests in the following interview, these can be the key to understanding the research questions.

Interview with Lynn Hancock: citizenship and satisfaction – the effects of jury service

Have you looked at the questionnaire? It illustrates the sort of open-ended questions we had as well as the more closed-ended ones. It was really about what was most appropriate to our research questions. We put a proposal in and initially it was a broader enquiry – it looked at different kinds of people who come into contact with the criminal justice system, and the impact of that contact. For defendants, witnesses, jurors, etc., we were interested in how real contact with the criminal justice system shaped confidence, perceptions, understandings; because a lot of the existing research studies such as those generated through the British Crime Survey don't really recognise the nuanced, sometimes ambiguous, sometimes contradictory responses people have.

That [British Crime Survey] method doesn't really allow that to happen, so we were looking at the grounded experience of how that shaped it – it was part of the process of talking with the Home Office, we decided to narrow it down to jurors, and that was interesting for us in a major way because jurors, technically at least, come into contact with the system without particular axes to grind, so they are more disinterested than your victims or witnesses. So we were interested in that concrete experience and how it might shape perceptions and understandings of the courts.

They [the Home Office] were excited about that because at the time there was an interest in confidence in police, courts, judges, so there were these debates. Much of the existing data seemed to tap into perceptions at a 'surface' level, the 'how satisfied are you?' kind of thing.

So the methods were about looking at how people came into contact with the system, and their experience of it. We needed some demographics to do the analysis, such as responses to summonses and their perceptions before they came in. And we also wanted to dig deeper – to explore the kind of things that generated, that had an impact on, or inhibited factors that drove satisfaction. It wasn't just a satisfaction survey at a tick box level, we wanted to look at the conditions – the factors that generated these responses, that's why we needed the mixed methods. Also because of the nature of the study – because of the legal restrictions on what you can ask of jurors, and at that time there had been very little research on real jurors; there was quite a lot of psychology stuff on 'mock' jurors, but nothing qualitative on real jurors, especially in the criminal justice system in England and Wales, except for one very small study we'd come into contact with. We knew of other studies that had been done in the USA, and in New Zealand, and we looked at those studies – but people were quite anxious about that, the Home Office, court services. It is against the law to either ask or for the juror to answer certain questions; section 8 of the Contempt of Court Act 1981 prohibits asking about people's decision-making process and that's really important, so we had to be really very careful about the way in which we asked the questions.

So we went through quite a few drafts, and we had to have quite a big prompt at the beginning of the questionnaire, to advise our respondents about the questions we are asking. It had to be very carefully worded, and also it meant that some questions had to be closed-ended. We asked about the positive and negative aspects of doing jury service but we had to think through all the possible responses because we couldn't allow any aberration.

This is why it was necessary for the study to have a mix of methods – in order to address our research questions – but there were other sorts of considerations as well.

We wanted to make some sort of assessment in terms of demographics – we needed to know what the characteristics of our sample were, in terms of age, gender, ethnicity, occupation. We thought that things like education were important – because the media often raise questions about the capacity of jurors to undertake their role – and quite a few social background characteristics. It was about understanding our sample, and we did do some comparisons in the London-based courts and the census data, and in some ways it was broadly representative – ethnicity, for example.

We also wanted the depth that comes from a more qualitative enquiry, because concepts like perceptions were all central to our research question, and can be multi-dimensional and shaped by different factors. But recognising that sort of ambiguity and that things are more complex, we needed to allow people to explore and think things through, because quite a lot of public opinion research is quite surface level – it doesn't allow people to think through complex, nuanced ways in which people make sense of things. People are given a scenario and then told to respond to it, but the depth of people's perceptions, how they are generated or shaped, to what extent – those sort of things you need to explore.

It really did generate some quite interesting and novel material and answers because there are a lot of myths about jury service. Until then there hadn't been the real systematic look at who the jurors are, and what sense they make of it. Of course there are limitations; we would have liked a bigger sample. Nowadays, the Criminal Justice Act [2003], which closed off grounds for exemption, might have had some impact; we might have got an even more representative sample. At the time Lord Auld had just reported and it was quite disparaging about people serving on juries and how people wanted to get out of it and not taking it seriously, whereas our research showed very strongly that only a very minor proportion were reluctant.

We also found that those groups we actually think of as the least likely to have confidence in the criminal justice system – such as the victims, black people and minority ethnic groups – we found that they left jury service with a higher level of confidence. We found all kinds of things – and this is the value of the qualitative work – things came out of that talk: notions of citizenship, how the experience had reinforced their sense of citizenship, either in terms of national identity or social solidarity, but we didn't expect that at all. It's one of those delightful things that happens in qualitative research, given that at that time as well there was a lot of talk about citizenship, about how to promote it. There was also at the same time efforts to limit jury trials in some cases – in favour of judge-only trials – and attempts to limit the rights of defendants in mode of trial decisions, so there were interesting things which it added to. Perhaps more importantly, that sort of public opinion research, which works at a surface level, and those surveys that are very tick box that don't offer the opportunity to think through the depth of people's attitudes in criminal justice – I think it adds something to that.

One of the main difficulties was in the way juries are recruited – we weren't able to use those lists, so we didn't have a sampling frame. The only way we could recruit our respondents was through the courts – going into court on Monday morning and asking if we could talk to the group of jurors who had been assembled on that day, to ask if they would participate. Because there wasn't a sampling frame, we couldn't ensure a representative sample; we were concerned to know the characteristics of the sample, but we couldn't select a representative sample, that was impossible.

Regarding ethics – the big one was the legal issue – we didn't do all the interviewing ourselves, but we did training in a major way, especially about the importance of the prompt which we went through with jurors. We had both face-to-face and telephone interviews. But there was this big prompt – you must not stray – it was one of the most important things. We did have to close things off, but this was where the things that were important to the research might be discussed. We were thinking through all the possible things that people might want to say, but not allowing them to say too much about it. So you might tell your respondent, you must say 'yes' or 'no' to the following, and you could include things like the 'behaviour of other jurors' as part of a list of negative aspects of jury service; then they could indicate that whether or not was relevant, but they couldn't say what it was. That was a relatively minor point; other things were way more important but, interestingly, the press picked up on that.

I think juries are seen as an enigma – sometimes they are celebrated and other times castigated – so when the report was published there was a lot of comment about citizenship, quite a bit was made of that. At the same time there's been a systematic attempt to reduce the number of jury trials, seeing them as inefficient, expensive, and so on. It's at the heart of that due process/crime control conflict, so I think the impact it's had is subject to those wider issues of policy-making. The press picked up on some of the very minor points, so instead of talking about the overwhelming majority who said that juries are either essential, very important, or necessary to our system of justice, the focus was on the 33 jurors who were unhappy with the behaviour of other jurors, which was a very, very small proportion.

This study of juries clearly discovered some new and previously unexplored data. Other jury studies have either used 'mock' juries, which are often criticised for their lack of realism, or have not been able to ask about the sort of issues explored here. As the questionnaire prompt that Hancock mentions in her interview shows (see below) the interviewers had to be very specific about what they could and could not discuss.

Questionnaire

Jurors' perceptions, understanding and evaluation of the operation of the criminal justice system

Interviewer prompt

The aim of this research is to gather information about your experiences and perceptions of the criminal justice system both before and after your call to jury service.

It is important to make one thing clear. It is against the law for me to ask you to tell me some things about the case or cases on which you acted as a jury member. S8 of the Contempt of Court Act 1981 makes it an offence to obtain, disclose, or solicit any particulars of statements made, opinions expressed, arguments advanced or votes cast by members of a jury in the course of their deliberations in any legal proceedings.

We do **not** want to hear details about the actual case(s) in which you were involved. I must not ask you for details of what you and other jurors discussed or how you voted. I shall not ask you these things, and you must not tell me.

You must **not** tell me about anything you said or did (or which your fellow jurors said or did) in the course of your discussions about the case in the jury room. The questions I am going to ask are specifically designed to avoid this.

The things I am interested in are different. It is fine for you to tell me about aspects of your experiences as a juror other than what we've just mentioned: these may include how you were summoned as a juror, what the facilities at the court were like, what information you were given about your duties as a juror, and so on. Nevertheless, I want you to bear the warning in mind before you answer so that your replies do not inadvertently stray into that discussion stage. If you become worried that an answer you want to give might cover jury discussions, please tell me and I will explain further before you give your answer.

> Do you understand?
>
> This research is funded by the Home Office and has been approved by the Lord Chancellor's Department who have given permission for us to discuss these questions in order to consider how to improve the experience of jurors.
>
> No names will be used in our final report. Your *anonymity* will be ensured throughout. Anything you say will be treated in the strictest confidence.
>
> We will ask you a number of specifics but feel free to elaborate where you feel it is appropriate. I will let you know when it is not appropriate to do so.
>
> The questionnaire normally takes 30–40 minutes. We would like to thank you in advance for your cooperation.
>
> **Juror's questionnaire**
> Respondent number _____ contacted through _____ Court
>
> http://rds.homeoffice.gov.uk/rds/pdfs2/rdsolr0504.pdf

This extensive prompt was necessary because, as Hancock explains in her interview, there are strict rules about what can and cannot be discussed once the jurors have made their decisions. This has made research into the role and processes of juries very difficult. As Findlay (2001) explains, in complex trials it is assumed that jurors may have difficulty understanding the issues, especially in complex financial frauds. In a study of Hong Kong, Russian and Australian courts Findlay attempted to test the hypothesis that there is a 'largely untested correlation between complexity, confusion, and potential injustice' (2001: 58). His methods are described as follows:

> The Hong Kong study ran from 1988 through till 1990. Initially surveys were to be administered to jurors immediately after the delivery of their verdict. However, as a result of the withdrawal of essential access conditions the research reverted to a 'grab sampling' method, resulting in 58 completed questionnaires from recently serving jurors ... The sample in NSW covered 637 jurors in 57 trials, held in four courts over a four week period ... The NSW questionnaire was used as a model for the Russian instrument, being adapted to recognise the different status and functions of jurors, judges, victims and accused persons, as well as the specific format of the Russian verdict. This survey covered 142 juror respondents who had decided trials run in

three of the experimental court districts ... The research projects in Hong Kong and Russia also involved questionnaire surveys of lawyers and judges in the trials surveyed, or for Hong Kong of the bar and bench generally.

As these examples of mixed methods show, the complicated nature of some aspects of crime and justice require complex, ingenious and resource intensive projects. One major advantage, however, is that coverage of the issues can be much more sophisticated, with 'deeper understandings', as Hancock suggests in her interview.

Of course, many quantitative and qualitative studies also include some element that could be described as 'mixed' in that they have some element of counting or 'appreciative' methods.

Conclusion

Qualitative research has many variants and uses. As this chapter illustrates, it can be used in combination with other methods, in a mixed method study for instance. As the examples in this chapter have shown, qualitative data can be used to inform and add depth to quantitative data. The methods discussed in this chapter have all had some 'qualitative' aspect; that is, they include detailed research into the 'how' and 'why' questions, rather than simply 'how many'. Some of the examples have included the 'harder' end of qualitative research; this means that although the questions have been aimed at finding data that lend depth to the analysis, there are still elements of 'counting' to support the 'proof' or validity of the study. The following chapter will illustrate that this is a boundary line that is sometimes difficult to draw. The examples of interviewing individuals and groups have illustrated the power aspects of this process. Some of the ways in which 'softer' and more naturalistic qualitative data is gathered, analysed and used will be examined in more depth in the next chapters.

5 Soft and semi-structured research

Introduction

In the previous chapter it was explained that in some circumstances there are benefits to using mixed methods. In the descriptions of their projects, Lynn Hancock and Sandra Walklate both pointed out the depth of understanding that can be gained through using qualitative and quantitative methods to complement each other. Depth of understanding is what qualitative research is about, and in this chapter the 'softer' or less structured methods are explored. The term 'soft' in relation to research methods tends to be used in contrast against 'hard' science or purely numerical or statistical studies. The term 'semi-structured' means the sort of research where the whole game plan has not been cast in stone. In other words, it allows the researcher to be flexible, perhaps following up leads or areas of interest that were not initially anticipated.

The terms 'soft' and 'semi-structured' can apply to a wide range of different types of research. The list of these different methods is much more extensive than can be covered by this chapter. One of the main concepts underlying the idea of semi-structured research is the use of interviews where the schedule or list of questions to be posed includes areas of interest, rather than specific questions to elicit 'yes or no' answers. This might be a list of topic areas to be discussed, rather than a set of questions. The sorts of conversations that flow from semi-structured interviews allow a deeper understanding of the views and insights of the respondent. They are also less 'directive' and tend to lead to co-produced knowledge, in that the interviewee has a certain amount of freedom or power to decide the course and pace of the discussion. Some feminist researchers, for example, argue that the interview process is loaded with power differentials, and the way that questions are posed will lead to certain answers or slant the way the responses are phrased (see Stanley and Wise 1993; Roseneil 1996). One way to avoid this is to have semi-structured interviews which allow the respondent to have more control over the direction of the conversation, facilitating a free-flowing discussion rather than a question-and-answer session.

There are, of course, problems associated with this approach, including researcher bias (discussed in Chapter 6). This is also an issue for the sort of research discussed in this chapter, which has a long history in criminology and the studies of the sociology of deviance. It is a more 'naturalistic' method, in that it could be said to differ little from 'real' life. In some ways it does resemble the sort of activities people carry out in their normal day-to-day life. The term most commonly used to describe this type of research is ethnography. Essentially this approach involves the researcher spending time with the group of people they are researching. The aim is to see from the inside how the group or organisation operates. By becoming as invisible as possible over a period of time, the idea is for the researcher to understand the motivations, beliefs and feelings of a particular situation or group. In fact, sometimes this type of approach is classed under the broad category of 'field studies'. The idea of going out into the field echoes their origins in anthropology, where researchers would go to some under-developed site far from home and live the same sort of life as people from a very different socio-economic background, in order to understand their culture, way of life and belief systems.

Examples are included in this chapter that help to reveal the very softest end of criminological research, from semi-participant observational studies to full-blown ethnographies, showing their advantages, disadvantages and difficulties. Case studies from current and classic ethnographies and comparisons with feminist research methods are discussed looking at the researcher as 'insider' and 'outsider', at whom research is aimed at, and how should it be conducted. The issues raised also apply to anyone who planning to do qualitative work, such as interviews within an organisation, not just what might be classed as a fully fledged, in-depth 'insider' account. So far this volume has emphasised that researching issues connected to crime and justice relies on trust, unusual access arrangements and discretion. The studies discussed here have required these attributes in particularly important ways, illustrating these points for all researchers aiming to conduct projects using soft or semi-structured methods.

Ethnography

The word 'ethnography' means a description or account of ('-graphy') a culture or people ('ethno-'), and draws upon methods that are used in anthropological studies. The classic, or some might argue over-romanticised, view of this sort of approach is the young single graduate student, going to live in an exotic, unheard-of, off-the-beaten-track place. They learn the language, become immersed in the lives of the people, become a trusted friend. The aim of this approach is to live or walk in someone else's shoes, to see their point of view or, as some have described it, understand 'their world-view'. As Wolcott explains in the following extract, the need to explore 'culture' has often been seen as a central part of ethnographies.

> For the anthropologically orientated researcher, ethnography has always been associated with and intended for studying culture. Early assumptions that any research along these lines must necessarily be directed towards the study of 'primitives' and their 'tribal cultures' have given way to broadly defined concern for cultural scenes, microcultures, and to the interactions between and among groups with differing cultural orientations. The underlying idea is that culture is revealed through discerning patterns of socially shared behaviour. That idea rests a bit uneasily in the absence of satisfactory resolutions to provocative questions such as how much 'sharing' is necessary or how much agreement there must be as to just what we mean by culture to keep the concept viable.
>
> As viewed from *outside* its discipline of origin, however, ethnography has slowly become dislodged from the conceptual framework once so closely associated with it. As a consequence, for some researchers, an ethnographic question may simply be a question that is amenable to study through *techniques* (or *methods*, if you prefer) comparable to those employed by the early ethnographers. The orienting question need not call for interpretation at all, only description with finely *detailed* description substituted for, and perhaps even misconstrued for, carefully *contextualised* description.
>
> (Wolcott 1999: 67, emphasis in original)

The sorts of methods or techniques that Wolcott describes may seem fairly irrelevant to the study of crime and justice. For example, where are the 'undiscovered tribes' in criminology? What sort of 'cultures' can be explored and who can afford to spend many hours, months or even years living with a group of people to discover their ways of thinking or being?

In the past, however, studies have also been conducted by those already living within the cultures, who for some reason find themselves able to 'step outside' of it in order to observe the life and attitudes of the group of which they are a part. One example is the study of police officer 'occupational' culture in the late 1980s and early 1990s. Simon Holdaway, a serving police officer in the 1980s, made notes on his daily working life and the attitudes and beliefs of his colleagues (Holdaway 1983). Later, Malcolm Young conducted ethnographies of the cultural scene and the actors around him as a serving police officer (Young 1991, 1993). The problem of the 'insider/outsider' researcher is discussed later in this chapter, and refers to the way in which writers such as Holdaway and Young have provided us with access to a previously 'closed' group, although not without difficulties and problems.

This approach is sometimes dubbed 'cultural anthropology' and is used by people such as Malcolm Young studying aspects of crime and justice, because the methods are drawn from that discipline, and sometimes involve 'participant observation'. This means that the explanations of what they did will show that they were part of the 'action'. In some cases (see Westmarland 2001a, for example) researchers may not completely immerse themselves in the life of the group being studied, but they get close enough to understand and appreciate the lives and beliefs of the group. This is called non-participant or semi-participant observation. Another example in this volume is Laura Piacentini, who lived in a Russian prison to see for herself the conditions, and interviewed the prisoners, but did not become a 'participant' in the sense that she was one step removed form the actual 'lived experience'. On the other hand, later in this chapter Rob Hornsby explains that his study (with Dick Hobbs) was not an ethnography because they did not take part in the activities or witness them. They used semi-structured interview methods and social networking to obtain their data. The final example in this chapter, of Simon Winlow's covert ethnographic study of bouncers and organised crime, is an example of the most naturalistic and fully participant study.

These methods – observations, semi-structured interviews, 'ethnographic conversations' – are at the very furthest extent of contrast from the quantitative, statistical studies described in earlier chapters. Ethnographies rarely call upon representativeness to support their claim to validity or truth. They do not attempt to prove that the overwhelming number of people in a given sample believe a certain statement to be true or not. They are not aiming to supply percentages or chart the effects of certain variables. This is not to say that ethnographers never use statistics as a basis upon which to begin their studies, or do not include numerical data in their findings or publications. But it is fair to say that ethnographers will be more interested in the 'why' questions than the 'how many'. They are interested in becoming part of the scenery of the group to be researched or to 'blend in' and so make themselves invisible, minimising the intrusive effect they have upon the people they are studying.

In the following example, statistics are used in an ethnography to begin a discussion about what women are doing in the police. It compares female officers' arrest rates with those of their male colleagues. It shows that they are making as many arrests as male officers in some traditionally 'high status' types of arrest. The aim is to provide some background to an ethnography of gendered policing.

The idea that researchers become part of the culture, scene or environment that they are researching has a long and distinguished career in the social sciences. It began with the Chicago School of sociology in the late 1930s when researchers were encouraged to hang around with groups of young, disaffected 'street' gangs and to watch their activities. The cultural aspects of crime were studied – the ways in which friends, family and peer groups behave and interact with each other and their surroundings – relying on a belief that crime is culturally constructed. In other words, as explained earlier in Chapter 1, crime cannot be simply classified as 'breaking the law'; it covers a multitude of behaviours that might not be classed as 'illegal' or even harmful. In the 1960s the focus of this type of approach was illicit drug taking, as illustrated by the example from Adler's work later in this chapter. The idea was that 'naturalistic' studies could reveal social meanings, unpick stereotypes, and lead to a more critical approach to crime and justice research. It was argued that because the drug taking or other 'illegal' activities could be understood within a cultural milieu or context, the reasons behind the activities could be understood beyond the previously narrow explanations of 'good' and 'evil', or the legal/illegal binary.

As with other types of qualitative study, there are problems regarding 'researcher effect'; becoming part of a group can create ethical and procedural problems for researchers, which will be discussed later in this chapter and in more depth in the next chapter. There can be quandaries for researchers about 'blending' in with the group because friendships will be developed and confidences exchanged. As the hope is that people will behave in a more natural way once the initial effect of the presence of the researcher has been forgotten, it could be argued that the researcher is taking advantage of the people they are studying. This sort of research is called non-participant observation, in that it is known that the researcher is carrying out observations; the researcher does not attempt to get into the 'role' of the group being researched.

Participant observation, on the other hand, is where the researcher takes on the role of the researched. Examples might include police officers who carry out research within their workplace, sometimes covertly, or a researcher who joins and becomes part of a particular group, either openly or in secret, in order to investigate them. Obviously, ethical and personal problems can be raised about this type of research, but some would argue that the only way to find out 'the truth' is to be completely immersed in, and sometimes unknown to, the group being observed. As discussed in the next chapter, researchers are more aware than they used to be of the effects of their research and the harm it may cause. Ethics committees in universities have fairly stringent rules about disclosure and intent of studies that are conducted. That is not to say that covert research is not or cannot be carried out, but it has to be justified to a committee.

The problem that concerns the methodologist is how these cultures can be observed without the researcher changing them in some way. Can observations of cultures be valid, or have a claim to 'truth', if to record or detail them the researcher has to enter that world and possibly change the behaviour of the group?

One reason why this effect is important for ethnographers, cultural anthropologists and anyone attempting to enter an organisation or group to conduct research, is a problem of validity. Critics point to what is known as the 'Hawthorne effect' or 'researcher effect', arguing that the social scene, group or individuals will have acted in particular ways because the researcher was present, and this has implications for the plausibility of the findings of the study. In order to overcome these accusations that the research group might be 'playing up' to the researcher or otherwise acting in ways the researcher might want (or, in a contrary way, perhaps acting to annoy or upset the researcher), there need to be a number of ways of providing validity.

The study from which the term 'Hawthorne effect' is drawn was conducted in America in the 1920s. The project was set up to find out whether women working in a factory could be encouraged to work faster on a production line by changing certain variables, such as introducing free lunches, rest periods or financial rewards. As Schwartzman notes, this led to some puzzling results.

> The most interesting and controversial finding reported from this early phase of the study ... has come to be known as the Hawthorne Effect: the 'unexpected impact of nonexperimental outcomes' (Finlay, 1991, p. 1820). In the later experiments the researchers were once again puzzled by the fact that a general improvement in output for the operators was noted, but it rose independently of the specific changes in working conditions that were introduced, and it also rose when the rewards were withdrawn.
>
> (Schwartzman 1993: 6–7)

Of course, the researchers tried to find out why this was happening and asked the workers they were observing, who also expressed puzzlement. Although the study had been set up as a way of watching what workers did rather than what they thought or said they did, and 20,000 workers were interviewed, conclusions were, and still are, disputed. The investigators were aware of the potential effect of their presence, and tried to mitigate the effect by having different types of observers – the 'disinterested spectator' who watched and recorded group interactions in the work room, and an 'outsider' who conducted the interviews, but did not otherwise have any contact with the workers.

Today we assume from this study that any attention by observers will have an effect. In other words, if we know we are being watched or recorded, our behaviour will change, and we may not be aware that this is happening. The implications for researchers who base their findings on data gathered by observations are quite important. For cultural anthropologists and ethnographers the effect of always being there, affecting the scene, changing what people might do and say, are considerations and opportunities for reflexivity. This means that the researcher can discuss the effects of their presence as part of the study's findings. As the discussion below suggests, this approach may vary according to the status and identity of the researcher, particularly in 'closed' groups which may be encountered in research concerning crime and justice.

There are various positions for researchers who might encounter the difficulties of the effects of their presence. This is true for ethnographers who are trying to 'blend in' as well as for semi-structured interview methods. In each case they involve conversations based on trust and human interaction. They often involve the developing of friendships, mutual respect and the belief that someone understands their point of view. This type of approach sometimes involves the researcher and researched becoming friends, or at least close colleagues, and this can lead to emotional or practical difficulties.

Insider/outsider research

In her discussion of the various types of police research, Jennifer Brown (1996) identifies a number of 'positions' that can be occupied by people conducting research. She draws upon Reiner's (1992: 220) assertions about the nature of police research to include the following types (adapted from Brown 1996: 180–5):

Inside insiders: These are typically researchers who work for the agency for which they conduct the research. It could be an 'enthusiastic amateur' with little research training and the topics will be overwhelmingly 'operational'.

Outside insiders: A number of famous police studies have been conducted very successfully by this group of researchers who tend to consist of serving or recently retired officers, making observations on their colleagues. Having had some academic training, by studying for degrees, and in some cases entering academic careers, they could combine two vital skills. Their 'insider' knowledge together with their ability to observe, analyse and recount the activities, beliefs and in some cases misdemeanours of their co-workers led to a much enhanced understanding of the police officers' world.

Inside outsiders: These are researchers given 'official' access or rights to ask questions, obtain information and be treated as being on the same side as the institution they are researching. This includes market researchers, consultancy companies and in some cases in-house research officers. This latter group could be regarded in some cases as 'inside insiders' in the sense that their separation from the organisation is difficult to see very clearly. This sort of category includes the research officer, conducting research on police officers, for example. There are also numerous examples of police forces buying in academic expertise, where forces realise they need to have some 'independent' work carried out to verify or shape particular policies they are considering, or to try to solve a particular 'crisis'.

Outside outsiders: In her analysis Brown uses this category to include all 'external commentators' such as academics, independent organisations such as charities that fund research, and the Audit Commission, which at the time Brown was writing was becoming increasingly influential. Their analysis of police deployment, for example, called *Streetwise: Effective*

Police Patrol, was a 'bean counting' economics-based study, but nonetheless revealed some politically explosive data about how officers were spending their time. It made uncomfortable reading for police chiefs regarding the number of police officers available for front-line duties. It showed, for instance, that for every 2,500 police officers in a typical force, only 125 could be working the streets (Audit Commission 1996: 11).

A critic of these 'insider or outsider' categories might argue that researchers can move from one position to the other almost without making any reference to their changing places. For example, sometimes academics employ paid consultancies to provide a report to the police force or other organisation, and then use the data to publish more critical, theoretical pieces of work in academic arenas such as books or journals. As the discussions about crime and justice research ethics and emotions in Chapter 6 illustrate, this is an area that is debated and concerns criminologists due to the sensitivity, both personally and politically, of the data.

Taking these caveats into consideration, however, these four main categories are useful as a starting point: from complete 'outsider' to total 'insider' and various gradations of outside/insider and inside/outsider positions in between. Although Brown was specifically talking about police research, any study of criminal justice, its agencies or people will have similar issues. Just as researchers may feel to be 'other' or different from the people or situations they research, at first, as the study progresses they may become more sympathetic to the causes and ideas of the group they are investigating. At any point, and this may not be linear or continuous, the researcher may move from one position to another. So, for example, spending an evening at a social event with people from the researched group may make one feel like an 'insider'; the next morning viewing some act of brutality by the same group of people might make the researcher feel distanced from his or her new 'friends'.

This emotional aspect to research is something that is often overlooked and difficult to anticipate. For ethnographers, in particular, becoming part of the group, as everyone wants to feel they 'belong' and are liked, is difficult to separate from the 'professional' or 'real' reason they are there. The following excerpt, taken from an early ethnography of policing, conducted as part of my doctoral thesis, illustrates this:

> It might be asked whether there is any point in spending long hours conducting a police ethnography for any reason other than to blow the whistle on their indiscretions. As this type of research may involve encounters with violence, however, it raises certain ethical, practical and theoretical problems.

Just as the earlier discussion taken from Brown (1996) illustrates, although this work was technically conducted from an 'outside outsider' perspective, as a publicly funded (ESRC) PhD student, in reality, to obtain access and to help with living expenses I had taken a small research grant from the force, which included an arrangement to provide a report into 'barriers preventing women officers from being promoted' (Westmarland 1994). In effect, therefore, complete independence, or 'clean hands', where continuing access is vital to the ongoing study and its completion, is difficult to maintain.

One way to overcome this is through long-term personal or social contact, building up trust based on knowing who and why people are there. One of the ground-breaking studies was in the 1970s, in the USA, as Bryman reports:

Adler's study of upper-level drug dealers
Adler (1985) and her husband took up residence in California in order to attend graduate school in sociology. They soon made friends with a close neighbour (Dave, a pseudonym), who, it transpired, was a drug dealer. He was not a small 'pusher' of drugs who was trying to provide funds for his own habit, but someone who dealt in vast quantities and who received huge sums of money in exchange, that is an 'upper-level' drug dealer. They were encouraged by their supervisor, Jack Douglas, a prominent contributor to qualitative research on deviance (Douglas 1972, 1976), to infiltrate Dave's group of associates in order to carry out a study of such dealers, who are normally highly inaccessible. The nature of Adler's approach to data collection can be gleaned from the following passage:

> With my husband as research partner, I spent six years in the field (from 1974 to 1980) engaged in daily participant observation with members of this dealing and smuggling community. Although I did not deal, myself, I participated in many of their activities, partying with them, attending social gatherings, travelling with them, and watching them plan and execute their business activities ... In addition to observing and conversing casually with these dealers and smugglers, I conducted in-depth, taped interviews, and cross-checked my observations and their accounts against further sources of data whenever possible. After leaving the field, I continued to conduct follow-up interviews during periodic visits to the community until 1983.
> (Adler 1985: 1–2, in Bryman 1988: 7–8)

This illustrates some of the difficulties of researching an area of illicit or illegal behaviour. Adler used her close geographical proximity to gain access to the dealers, which afforded her their trust. Over a six-year period, a luxury of time that many researchers cannot hope for, they developed this trust and it led to being able to collect rich data that would have been very difficult to obtain in any other circumstances. This is one of the crucial questions for researching crime and justice using observational or other in-depth methods – not only how to access any given law-bending or lawbreaking community, but how to get them to trust you enough to conduct taped interviews or to observe their activities.

Aside from the ethical issues involved, there are other problems (addressed in the next chapter), such as, how do covert researchers such as Adler explain what they are doing? Did Adler tell the dealers she was going to use the information and observations from their social and professional activities? Usually the practical considerations of how to meet and introduce yourself to people actively involved in criminal activities is problematic. Perhaps this is the reason very few published academic articles attempt to use data from people currently or recently involved in criminal activities. One exception is an article by Hornsby and Hobbs (2007), about cigarette bootlegging, from which the following extract is taken. Rob Hornsby describes the project that was the basis for the article in his interview below. 'Jason', their respondent, got into the business in the mid-1990s, by taking coach trips across the Channel to France with groups of friends and family to buy cigarettes and hand-rolling tobacco in order to evade UK duty. In the case study Jason is asked how the system worked, and he describes the way he developed it from early beginnings.

> *Jason*: These runs were known as the pensioner day outs. Most of the people on the coaches were old-folks and doleys [benefit recipients] wanting to make some extra money filling up their bags with cigarettes and tobacco on the French side, and then handing the goods to me once we got back to Southshore. They were all told, 'If you get stopped by a Landwaiter [customs officer] and your bags get pulled, admit it's yours, you've bought the cigarettes and they're for your own personal use and let Customs keep them. You'll still get paid and no one's going to get into trouble.' I got the fags and baccy, they all had a nice run out, a laugh, a drink and got paid for it. The ferries were full of coaches where the same racket was going on.
>
> During those initial ventures with the 'pensioner days out' into France, Jason's mules consisted of friends, family members and acquaintances who drank in a club that he frequented. Those early and successful bootlegging incursions saw his pool of runners increase via local community and kinship networks that provided a flow of cigarette bootleggers willing to take seats on the coach to smuggle the contraband back into the UK. Within such networks, familiarity generates sponsorship, followed by acceptance. This is based upon the knowledge of network participants who are familiar by sight, referral or association, and convene via a network of acquaintances (Hunt 1990).

Jason was rather vague in his explanation to us regarding how he made the jump to operating on a much more ambitious scale, and he spoke of his expansion in a most matter-of-fact manner:

Jason: See, I knew this was a real earner as soon as we went into Europe [UK's entry into the Single Market] and I wasn't going to fuck about with some half-arsed scheme that might pay for a fortnight in Benidorm once a year. I went into Luxembourg . . . which created a lot more work in having to sort out the runs and then having to arrange the contacts to supply the goods to, the drivers, the digs, storage and the money. While I was running the pensioner day outs from Southshore, it was just a laugh really. No real effort required, hardly any risks associated with it at that time, just me driving the coach with a load of pensioners having sing songs and playing housey [bingo] . . . When I made my move into Luxembourg I had a lot of planning to sort out as it had became a serious business.

From a distribution base-camp in France, he employed six UK nationals for smuggling runs into Luxembourg, who returned with car boots and the back seats of the vehicles filled with contraband cigarettes and hand-rolling tobacco. The smuggling operation quickly became so profitable that Jason was able to rent one floor of a small French hotel to provide accommodation for his drivers, with another room set aside in order to store the contraband for distribution. A stream of increasingly professional UK bootleggers aiming to evade UK tobacco levies soon realised that Jason's cigarettes were significantly cheaper than the French and Belgian alternatives.

(Hornsby and Hobbs 2007: 555–6)

As Hornsby points out in his interview below, the level of trust required to tell a researcher about these activities must be a significant aspect of the methods employed. As Jason's activities are presumably ongoing, although not with the same commodities or methods, being exposed could lead to a significant period in prison. Any careless disclosures by the researchers could also lead to Jason's exposure and potential arrest. There are clearly ethical and practical issues here that need to be addressed. At the start of his interview Hornsby explained that the methods they used could not be classed as ethnography; rather, they used a technique of a series of semi-structured interviews, sometimes called 'ethnographic conversations', over a long period of time based on personal social networking. Below Hornsby reveals that this is a debatable issue because of the protracted nature of the negotiations prior to the interviews. He discusses the problems they encountered and how they overcame some of the difficulties posed by the project that led to this article. He explains how the original project (with Dick Hobbs) hit difficulties, but then ended up with some important and original data.

Interview with Rob Hornsby: accessing the bootleggers

Originally this project was a big EU project – international. We were involved in something which, if we'd known it was going to pan out that way, we wouldn't have been involved in. We were supposed to be reviewing 50 customs files, upper level cigarette cases that had been successfully prosecuted, and by upper level we mean a million plus cigarettes, per seizure.

So we started early, before the project was due to begin, in terms of getting access, getting hold of the gatekeepers, with different agencies, NCIS, Home Office, police forces, Customs and Excise and so on. We made approaches and they said, yes, this is great, this is just what we need, in terms of new ways of thinking within the agencies, and tackling this problem – a massive problem at that point in time – in terms of acquiring revenue for the Treasury. So it was a political issue as well in many aspects.

We got clearance from all the main players who expected to be involved and went to the Home Office who said, OK, you need security clearance, to counter-terrorism check level. That took for me ten months, and we were told in the meantime we couldn't approach people, well, by that time we'd already approached people, and we sort of went round the back doors with contacts we'd established in order to keep access to these law enforcement personnel open. But we couldn't get hold of the main substantive area of the research, such as the case files, and interview a sample of those who had been the main investigating officers on those cases.

In the end we didn't get the case files. Customs and Excise put the block on it despite earlier written and verbal agreements from that agency that they would fully cooperate with the research. The reason for it, we believe, was they were being dragged over the coals; their officers had been accused of perjury, convicted of corruption cases, there'd been suicides within the agency – an officer hanging himself because he was under a corruption investigation – and what they didn't want was a pair of nosey academics fishing about their case files and potentially doing further damage to the agency.

We didn't get over that, but in the end we carried on and through social networks we were introduced to 'Jason' the bootlegger. Now this had been under the surface for about 18 months: prior to the research I'd met him at a few parties, christenings, weddings, and slowly I was introduced by my gatekeeper to his uncle. The slow testing out, you know: these people don't just give you information, it's about building up trust and friendships. I still get this now – rogues, lesser players, not the rubbish at the bottom, but they're not the quality criminals – one of the guys I'm working with at the moment, covert systems have been placed against him. He doesn't park his cars by his own house, he parks in other streets, and other people are registered as owners of them because of the Proceeds of Crime Act: they say, we'll have that off you because you can't justify it, and his reply is, I'm only down on the insurance, it's his car really, all of those things ...

So anyway, Jason eventually got to trust me, and I said, well, how about giving us some interviews? At first he said, no, sounds a bit iffy to me. I said, you'll be safe – and it took a lot of reassurance from my gatekeeper to win him over and work on my part, and a considerable amount of money because 'we'll get a drink, we'll get a drink'. It's completely understandable that those involved within various forms of criminal activity are reluctant to talk to outsiders about their work. Why should they? What's in it for them? There's no money in it for them. From the villains' perspective there's always a danger that the researcher might possibly feed information to the police or be working covertly for law enforcement agencies.

He was testing me out all the time, and what I've noticed is that if you tell a story, you mention something, six months later they ask you to say it again, and I've been told this, to see if that story deviates in any significant way. Just about things that happened to you, things that happened at parties, things that you were engaged with, things that you know other people were engaged with, to see if you're telling the truth – because if it is the truth, usually you keep the content and context of the story the same.

I know he would have been asking around, and it took a considerable amount of time, and luckily the relationship I have with the gatekeeper is a very, very strong one, and now we've got family, babies, we've got that relationship, having a drink at social occasions, having a laugh, so it's about personality, trust, security.

From there to the interviews, that was a good 18 months, meeting him at functions, celebrations, even though we never put this down as an ethnography, because I think a lot of the stuff that's pushed out as ethnography really isn't – it's a qualitative piece. I'm not in and around them while they're doing their business, in their natural world, in their normal social settings, and it doesn't qualify as ethnography simply because I had a few drinks with the guy. You know that some of the data that we obtained would have come from some of those meetings, but not all of it was interview-based.

On the original project there was going to be a quantitative side of it, pulling out a lot of the quantitative data in terms of the composition, the *modus operandi*, the uses of transport – but basically it was all meaningless tosh. On the back of that we were going to do some interesting stuff by interviewing the officers, but we also planned in that research, and this is where it was poorly thought out – interview convicted imprisoned smugglers, trying to access to them via the Home Office. But that would be a project in itself, and that never happened; but we were the only ones of the original project to get the criminals involved. We were the only ones who brought any significant qualitative insights from those who'd been 'at it', in terms of smuggling cigarettes, as such, but these wouldn't have hit the benchmarks for the upper level. Although Jason would have probably been involved in the importation of contraband of tens of millions of cigarettes, because he was at it for so long. We did also manage to interview a number of customs and police officers who'd been involved in the investigation of cigarette smuggling, but the main substance of the original methodological approach in acquiring and analysing the case files never occurred due to the resistance of some senior officers within that organisation.

But you're looking at a long stretch of time, catching one person at it with ten million cigarettes, or three or four people at it with cigarettes, they're not going to talk about, yeah, well, we did this or that before: asset recovery was just coming in at that time. Jason was involved in commodity swapping, he was involved in mid-level marijuana distribution, counterfeit clothing, watches, any opportunity, an entrepreneur.

We took field notes and some interviews with customs officers but no tape recorders, getting access to people involved in the trade and getting over the no case files problem.

The outcomes of the study are that people are reading and citing our article: we've made an impact, but also in sociology and medical arenas – going across disciplines – there's the health, social harm perspective. Also, it's provided a good building block for more research. We've had policy-makers' recognition, and other research

> out of it that I'm developing is along the public health and social harm perspectives connected to organised crime and the ways in which such activities within the concept of organised crime impact upon public health.

In order to conduct this research and gain access to lawbreaking cross-border activities, Hornsby and Hobbs used a combination of some original and persistent methods. These are rarely used in criminology because of the difficulties Rob Hornsby describes, such as the time and money involved and the ability to develop appropriate social networks. A search of the internet or a journal such as the *British Journal of Criminology*, where the above article was published, reveals an absence of the voices or experiences of 'real criminals'. In other words, although authors and contributors talk about the existence of lawbreakers, their numbers, what they do and how and what to do about them, very few authentic voices such as Jason's are heard. This illustrates the difficulties of accessing or persuading people to talk about their activities. Of course, there are books and articles about 'unsuccessful' criminals (in other words, prisoners) who give accounts of their previous crimes and how they were caught. Martin Gill has written an account of armed bank robbers who, once caught and imprisoned, explained their motivations and ways in which they were caught (2000). Similarly, accounts of prisoners and 'reformed' or retired lawbreakers are available (see McVicar 1974, for example).

As explained above, this is an example of Brown's insider/outsider conundrum. Clearly Hornsby and Hobbs are 'outsiders' in the sense that they took no part in Jason's bootlegging activities. On the other hand, Hornsby had to spend significant periods of time (and money) developing a trust relationship with him. To what extent researchers can remain 'outside' the scene, physically or emotionally, in these situations is debatable. As Hobbs said in an earlier work describing an ethnography of police detectives of London's East End, he sometimes had to make compromises concerning his personal ethics to enable him to continue the study (Hobbs 1988).

As a result of the difficulties of obtaining access to current and active lawbreakers, there has been a tradition in the social sciences of covert research, as Adler's account above illustrates. Rather than declare your interest, you simply take part in or hang around the margins of the activities, record what happens and gain a 'clean' and unadulterated version of the social scene of a particular criminal world. Aside from the ethical difficulties, tackled in the next chapter, there are obvious dangers and drawbacks of this 'covert' approach, as the interview with Simon Winlow below illustrates.

So although Rob Hornsby is saying that his study was not an ethnography, it relies on personal contact, on the ability to gain someone's trust and to have the interpersonal skills to be able to persuade an unwilling and perhaps fearful respondent that it will be 'OK'. Just as Hornsby had to be very 'known' to his respondent Jason, Winlow had to be just the opposite. He had, as part of his covert research, to act out a role as a nightclub bouncer. His true identity was not known to his respondents. He pretended to be a pub and club doorman and carried out that role while conducting research on violence, the drugs trade and organised crime. There are obvious dangers bound up with this sort of approach, both physical and emotional, in addition to the ethical issues associated with this sort of study.

As a researcher aiming to infiltrate organised crime in a quite different way from Hornsby and Hobbs, Winlow's interview illustrates that being secretive and using covert methods was justified by the need to infiltrate the particular world of the professional doorman. The team behind the project explain their aims as follows:

> Our task was to research bouncers, or doormen, those individuals who are employed as private security guards in pubs, bars and clubs. We wanted to explore a culture that from our previous work (Hobbs 1995) we felt was grounded in violence, and we wanted to be so conversant with that culture that we could understand it from the viewpoint. We chose to employ ethnography as one of our research tools because we wished to explore the culture of a group that was becoming increasingly demonised . . . We felt that merely to accompany bouncers while they worked in an attempt to formulate data that are essentially observational would be inappropriate, potentially obtrusive, and unlikely to proffer data of sufficient depth and vibrancy.
>
> (Winlow *et al.* 2001: 537)

They go on to explain that despite considerations about difficulties gaining access and discussions about the ethical concerns, they decided to 'go in deep', drawing on Adler's methods of 'utilising personal observation, interaction and experience' (Adler 1985: 11). Later in the article they explain their methods in more depth, especially the need to be 'covert', not revealing to the other bouncers that any research was in progress.

> From the outset of our research it was apparent that if we were truly to understand the occupational culture of bouncers, it would be necessary to fashion some sort of covert access. Whilst it was appealing simply to hang around in bars and clubs and observe these men at work (and in our ethnography, but not all the interviews, all the bouncers were male), we were left in no doubt that the most fruitful avenue for analysis was to place a researcher within the occupation.
>
> (Winlow *et al.* 2001: 538)

Interview with Simon Winlow: reflections on organised crime

The background is that I was interested primarily in how criminal markets had evolved, especially post 1980s. Just as I started to get into that work, which was my first ethnographic work, I became increasingly aware that there was a considerable presence of door security firms involved in elements of the professional organised crime market that I was investigating; and it was at this time that Dick Hobbs suggested he could apply for some cash to do some research, and one piece of research seemed to bleed into another.

With regard to professional organised crime, there was a huge amount of literature, but one of the primary motivations was that we didn't think it was applicable to the world I wanted to investigate. In the organised crime literature there was lots of stuff on mafias and hierarchical organised crime groups but it just didn't seem to fit with the reality I knew existed, and so it was an idea to get an empirical look for myself, at a world that was changing very quickly.

It was really quite different but it's important to acknowledge that my primary introduction to the world of bouncers was facilitated by the connections I'd made in professional organised criminal markets; everything from counterfeit goods and importing tobacco – alcohol was big at the time, people were starting to do credit card and cheque frauds, and of course, drug markets were expanding very quickly. One of the key markets I looked at was the growth of Ecstasy in the night time economy.

The key aspect of the ethnographic work was that I needed a job. Getting a job as a bouncer is never something you're going to see in a shop window, you know, 'Bouncer required'. It required introductions that were really quite complicated, it was a really tricky process to negotiate. They needed to know me and we needed to build up a rapport before I even got a chance to work on the door, so it was crucial that I had these contacts to introduce me, to head doormen in most cases, but also to security company bosses.

There's an obscene amount of handshaking about the whole process; it's an important process because they are hugely reliant upon a particular type of man working for them. But right from the outset, they would see no point employing a sociologist or anyone who couldn't physically do the job.

I was advantaged because, in most cases, I talk like them, I didn't look too dissimilar; and although a lot of them were really very big,

I could act. There was a connectedness, we would feel comfortable slipping into established parameters of talk – you know, I wasn't going to start talking about Nietzsche – I could talk about the things they were interested in. Basically, what we're talking about is a kind of cultural similarity, which is absolutely crucial in terms of accessing these really quite hidden cultures.

I'm a kind of working-class guy anyway, and I was interested in violence generally speaking, interested in the same kinds of things as them. All of those traditional things that working-class parents teach their kids about what a man is, you know, was very much a part of how I negotiated everyday life. So I sort of slotted quite neatly into it.

A lot of it was natural. It's just a matter of talking to people, laughing at the same jokes, giving them a chance to get to know you and like you and doing the same with them, but it was by no means easy in every aspect of the research. For instance, I'd changed: I wasn't entirely like them any more, I'd been exposed to the liberal world of education. If they were sexist or racist, which they were sometimes, I would occasionally not be at ease in their presence or I'd find myself laughing at jokes which I really didn't want to laugh at, you know. And of course, the violence, which is why I was there in the first place.

I had to get some kind of detailed sense as to why these people did what they did, and interviews simply wouldn't reveal that. In many cases they don't know why – but they'll give you a kind of account that needn't be anywhere close to reality. In order to get that reality you have to be around them and see how they operate and see how the occupational culture of bouncers is structured, and what it means for a specific work group. How people put their hands on other people, what are the tipping points, where they'll put up with certain amounts of misbehaviour and when they'll act. How do they make sense of that? In many cases they seemingly observe rules: like, people weren't allowed into the bar or nightclub wearing trainers, but only on Sundays – I wondered why that was the case, but it actually reflected a quite detailed interpretation of drinking cultures in that city. People tended to go out all day drinking on Sundays, before the licensing laws changed, and often the people who were turning up at the bar or nightclub at 7 o'clock had been out since 11 o'clock and so were drunk. So it wasn't just a ridiculous rule, we don't allow people who wear trainers in on a Sunday, it's because the type of people who wear trainers on a Sunday are likely to have been out all day, drinking. You know, who knows that? You have to be around these people and see how they operate to try and kind of tease out the details, but generally ethnography also gives you the chance to see how everyday life is organised for this particular group of people.

I think that the big success of the study is that we create quite a visceral sort of picture for people. It gives them some insight into what, in many cases, is an aspect of everyday life that is completely alien to them. You know, these people are getting involved in violence, some are involved in illegal activities, and the immediate question is, well, who are these people and why do they do what they do? And I think ethnography is the only opportunity to get to the details, to get down to the real facts of the matter.

We're participants rather than just observers; I'm certainly a participant. Every violent incident that happened in the bar where I worked, most of the time I had to be involved in, even if it was just peripherally. You couldn't just stand on the outskirts and watch, or you'd have been found out very quickly and they would have got rid of you. You had to actually get involved and put your hands on people, and throw them out, and I think being involved at that level gives a more detailed appreciation of what these people do and why.

When I was working as a bouncer nobody knew what I was doing. It would have been impossible to work in these places and have people know I was in fact a sociologist. I didn't lie about it, but they don't ask those sorts of things.

I didn't have any qualms about not revealing why I was there . . . I did the job, but there were huge difficulties, as in many cases it was incredibly boring. Then I would have to do a four-and-a-half-hour shift, I didn't want to be there, at getting on for midnight, I'd much rather be at home in bed, but here you are in this place, doing this job, in some cases with absolutely nothing happening.

On the other hand, I think the lulls were sometimes just as revealing as the action points. It gave me the opportunity to talk to colleagues and that kind of thing, but of course, when you have a night such as that over and over again, the conversation dries up. You've exhausted all the avenues you have previously identified as potentially illuminating for the research, so it's not always the kind of exciting world that you read about in a book; it's a lot of hours, a lot of frustration, especially when you're doing the interviews that go alongside it – you're dealing with organised criminals or people with no concept of time.

Plus many other things as well: crime, for instance – in the covert role where do you draw the line about what you are willing to do or not willing to do? I was also involved in the professional organised crime research at the time. A suitcase full of fake designer shirts or something like that, you know – I can let you have them for this price, and everything above that's yours – to what degree do you actually take that on? If you turn every opportunity down they are going to get a little bit suspicious.

To anyone thinking of doing an ethnography, my advice would be to do a questionnaire instead! Ethnography is very time-consuming and I think if you do it right – that is, street ethnography – it should be quite emotionally charged, quite demanding, because you should have an empathy with the people you are working with, and it's a very tricky process. It's about you and your academic development, it is very demanding; especially with the bouncers, you see so much violence and that can be tricky, although I didn't really mind being around men fighting. I'd seen it many times before, but when it was directed at people who couldn't fight back, or women, I really struggled with that; you were then working with a guy who you knew had punched a woman – how do you negotiate that?

You have to go into it with your eyes open, to try to predict all the likely problems that are going to arise; there will always be problems, and there'll always be problems you can't predict, of course, but try and think through how you might deal with them. Realistically, I don't think you should be in any way guided by institutional practice about what is right and what is wrong. You should make your own informed decision about who you're researching, about their forms of behaviour, about political, economic and cultural issues, and then your place within that. You can't afford to be judgemental; you have to try and get on with people.

I think I was a good ethnographer because I was researching a social group that I could slip almost seamlessly into – if I was doing ethnography on some aspect of middle-class culture I'd be absolutely useless. But I get PhD students, and I think, there goes a natural ethnographer, somebody who's talkative, upbeat, in many cases the kind of person you want to talk to, knows how to tell a joke, with an easy manner, and people like their presence. Because you're going to be around a lot, and in many cases for a slightly unusual amount of time you're going to be sitting in their presence, not doing very much, so they've got to want you to be there, otherwise they're going to say, well, what on earth are you doing here? People, you know, if they're a little reserved, that can be quite tricky; one of the missing pieces of advice in a lot of methods books is that you should talk as much as the person you're talking to. A good ethnographic interview is a conversation, it's not just listening carefully to what the person says and asking them to expand, it's not just one question after another; because eventually the person who is on the receiving end of those questions is going to boil it down to one-word answers, and then they're going to tell you to shut up. It has to be an interesting conversation, for them as well, not just for you, for your instrumental purposes – you have to enjoy being a part of it.

In the early days, when you're getting to know each other, you should allow the act of ethnography to reveal the answer without you actually having to pose the question in formal terms. If I'm just recently arrived as a colleague, working with you on your door, if I suddenly start asking questions, you going to think, who is this guy, what's he asking these questions for, and you put up barriers. If I sort of sit there and try to copy what you're doing, say very little, look at the street and sigh, check my watch every five minutes and act as if I really don't want to be there, then we've developed a form of connectedness. I can see something similar in you, we're alike, and especially with bouncers, because you're spending so much time together, you don't have to be talking all the time – you can allow a lull – a lull can be quite useful for your purposes.

For instance, if I ask you about who you'll allow in and who you won't allow in, in many cases you haven't really thought an answer through; it might seem an unusual question, because I should automatically know who gets in and who doesn't get in, and so I might annoy you by asking that kind of question. Just by watching you work I can find out quite easily: you sit there for a four-hour shift, three nights a week, and I find very quickly that you don't like people who have facial tattoos, you don't like people who come in groups of more than three, or you don't like people who are obviously drunk, obviously on drugs. Or even that you are clearly biased against particular ethnic groups, on particular nights, because of the type of music they play or something like that. Without having to ask, and then have you vocalise a response, I can find out, and often in far more detail, just by watching you work.

It's about being conversant with culture as well, knowing when to speak and when to shut up, and if you know the culture, then these things will be automatic, and that's when ethnography works.

Conclusion

As Simon Winlow's account illustrates, ethnographies offer a method to access a group that is naturalistic, and can provide a wealth of information while avoiding problems associated with the Hawthorne effect. The interview also demonstrates the fallacy that ethnographic methods are simply a matter of doing what we all do in normal everyday life as casual observers. In Rob Hornsby's interview it was also clear that researching crime and justice issues that require accessing active criminal activities, and the people who carry out ongoing illegal activities, is problematic. Time and money are serious concerns for any researcher; all studies cost money and have to be 'costed' in terms of the hours spent against potential results. To predict these costs for ethnographic studies is very difficult because, as Winlow explains, no one can predict when nothing will happen, and the time spent 'hanging about' can be viewed by some as a waste of money.

Of course, all these issues are relevant to one of the central themes of this book, the realities of 'real life' research. Problems get in the way from the start, when research is proposed, costed, sent to an ethics committee for approval, and most of all, after these hurdles have been sorted out and the study actually has to be conducted, the data collected and written up. The two interviewees here and their associated team members have overcome barriers that illustrate the way real life does often intervene. Rather than simply thinking, when faced with the various obstacles, that it is simply too difficult or problematic, in each case they persisted, used methods that might not seem to be the easiest, and sometimes had to divert their path to the proposed end point.

This illustrates the second main theme of this book, which is that the most important aspect of choosing research methods is assessing their ability to deliver what the researcher aims to find out. As Simon Winlow says, he wanted to know about the lives and beliefs involved in violence, and to do so he felt it was necessary to have 'hands on' experience. Rob Hornsby explains that they suffered a setback when they were unable to access vital files for their study. This meant they had to use personal resources, to find people involved in the trade they wanted to investigate. They wanted to explain to the world about the realities of cigarette bootlegging. To do so meant that personal safety had to be risked: 'Jason' had to be protected from identification and ethical issues had to be confronted.

All of these issues occur in the field of researching crime and justice and none can really be predicted in advance. It is obvious that in a research team they will be debated and attempts made to negate any possible harm or danger. In real life, however, it is often impossible to predict just how everyone will act and behave. It is not the intention of this volume to suggest that researchers should place themselves in danger – quite the opposite – but to illustrate that all sorts of complicated and potentially illegal activities may come by the way. In the following chapter some of these issues are discussed in terms of ethics and danger, and the ways in which such perils may be, if not completely avoided, at least predicted so that the researcher can be prepared.

6 Ethics, emotions, politics and danger

Introduction

Combining the concepts of ethics, emotions, politics and danger in the research process may seem to be a diverse range of topics to cover in a chapter of a book about the 'realities' of researching crime and justice. One reason for discussing these issues together is that during the processes involved where 'real' research happens it seems that there are inextricably linked. As Liebling and Stanko observed in a special issue of the *British Journal of Criminology* in 2001, which focused on dilemmas in researching disorder and violence:

> ... we criminologists are professionals whose task is to observe and analyse account after account of the kinds of havoc individuals, groups or the state mete out ... We face moral turmoil, as we witness or become part of scenes of violence, struggle or maltreatment. Why is there so little dialogue on these matters?
> (Liebling and Stanko 2001: 421)

The intervening years have seen an increase in the number of book articles and journals concerned with research ethics (see, for example, Israel and Hay 2006; Rowe 2007; Mertens and Ginsberg 2009) and a rising bureaucracy of ethics micro management. Universities, government-backed funding bodies such as the Economic and Social Research Council (ESRC), and charitable funders, upon whom academic researchers often rely to carry out their projects, have become much more alert to and insistent about the way these matters are considered. As a result systems have been put in place to monitor and survey the way researchers consider ethics in the process of their studies and the risks associated with potentially dangerous situations. This means that aside from any feelings individual researchers may have, ethics, emotions, politics and danger are linked in the sense that principal and co-investigators will have to consider these issues. In the early 2000s applications for funds would include questions such as, 'Are there any ethical considerations?' These have now been replaced by much more stringent requests to outline whether 'anyone could be harmed by the research'; and if there are any possible risks, it is necessary to formulate extensive detailed plans to minimise that occurrence.

The possibility of anyone being harmed by a potential research project takes ethics, emotions, politics and danger as a set of possible concerns to be considered.

- **Research ethics** – a general category of how the moral rights and responsibilities will be managed throughout the project.
- **Emotions** – will anyone be harmed psychologically, what sort of issues might the researcher and researched confront?
- **Politics** – who says how the research is conducted and what happens to the findings once published? Will the study be used in ways that might lead to hurt, distress or some unintended outcome?
- **Danger** – will the researchers or participants be placed in any physical or psychological danger as a result of the project?

The links between these four issues will become clearer in the course of this chapter.

Research ethics

It is only in recent years, since the early 2000s, that the issue of ethics has become seriously considered in criminological research. In the early to mid 1990s it was regarded as a side issue which might be considered politically expedient to mention, perhaps if applying for funds to a major governmental or third sector charitable organisation, and particularly if the topic might be regarded as 'sensitive' for any reason. These supposedly sensitive topics included anything involving children, the abused, or groups considered vulnerable for some reason. Projects that might ask questions about sexualities, violence or illegal activities might also have been on the list.

Although no particularly scandalous or exploitative situations came to light, it gradually became clear to the social sciences research community that the issues of 'ethics', and sometimes danger to both researcher and researched, might be something to take into account when proposing to conduct a study. Feminist researchers had been growing increasingly vocal about the issue of ethics in research, asking, for instance, whose knowledge, whose issues? (see Stanley and Wise 1993). Perhaps as a result of the increasingly risk-averse attitudes of organisations including universities, the issues of protecting employees and the reputation of the institution became more important. Consequently, regulation of activities viewed as potentially 'risky' increased, and the recognition of the potential for problems arose in the minds of funders, supervisors and principal investigators (called PIs in research council funding speak). The bureaucracy's complicated downloadable and electronically submittable application forms now included a section on 'possible ethical difficulties'. Whereas in the past it was possible to insert 'N/A', now some input was required, and this involved in some cases creative thinking as to the possible dangers that researchers might encounter.

As a personal experience, an example of this arose in 2002 in the submission of a proposal for funding to the Economic and Social Research Council (ESRC). In collaboration with a colleague (Dick Hobbs) the proposal was to explore the issue of women bouncers or door staff. We wanted to combine our experiences – my work on women police officers and his on male bouncers. The application for funding was initially refused, and one of the reasons for this was that we had not considered the ethical and 'safety' aspects of the study. When the refused forms were returned to us we saw that the referees had mentioned that they thought it would be 'rather dangerous' for women researchers to be out late at night in busy city centres locating and approaching door security staff. We subsequently rewrote the proposal, indicating that we would ensure that researchers would have mobile phones, have someone to call in case of difficulties, and would take account of any instructions they were given regarding safety from police or security staff. As a result of the changes, our application was successful (see Hobbs *et al.* 2007 for detailed results of the study). The increasing acknowledgement by the ESRC of the importance of ethics in research has now led them to produce a *Research Ethics Framework* document outlining their requirements for consideration of any application for funded research. Their six core principles are reproduced below.

ESRC statement of the principles of ethical research

There are six core principles that inform the ESRC *Research Ethics Framework* (REF). They are as follows.

1   *Research should be designed, reviewed and undertaken in a way that ensures its integrity and quality.*

This principle is at the heart of the REF and needs little further elaboration. It means that researchers and research ethics committees (RECs) should ensure that from the start, the development and consideration of proposals is informed by a commitment to research that is accountable and of the highest quality. Accountability underlies each of the following principles, while quality is expressed through good scientific design, the anticipation of likely difficulties and how these might be addressed, and the ways in which objectives will actually be delivered during the work.

2   *Research staff and subjects must be informed fully about the purpose, methods and intended possible uses of the research, what their participation in the research entails and what risks, if any, are involved. Some variation is allowed in very specific and exceptional research contexts.*

This principle underpins the meaning of informed consent. Informed consent entails giving as much information as possible about the research so that prospective participants can make an informed decision on their possible involvement. Typically, this information should be provided in written form and signed off by the research subjects. Where consent is not to be secured a full statement justifying this should be provided. Paragraph 3.2.5.2 describes the circumstances where informed consent may need to be managed differently. The primary objective is to conduct research openly and without deception. Deception (i.e. research without consent) should only be used as a last resort when no other approach is possible. This principle also requires that research staff need to be made fully aware of the proposed research and its potential risks to them.

In cases of multi- or interdisciplinary research the definition of informed consent should be given very careful consideration. The relationship between researchers and researched may vary between disciplines or in projects using diverse methodologies. In the case of participatory social science research, consent to participate is seen as an ongoing and open-ended process. Consent here is not simply resolved through the formal signing of a consent document at the start of research. Instead it is continually open to revision and questioning. Highly formalised or bureaucratic ways of securing consent should be avoided in favour of fostering relationships in which ongoing ethical regard for participants is to be sustained, even after the study itself has been completed. Review mechanisms will need to enable this where appropriate.

In cases of international research or work that relates to non-majority culture, the conventional meaning of informed consent may be problematic because the conventional model of consent rests on the 'primacy of the individual'. The individual is seen as both the owner of rights and the bearer of reciprocal duties to the rights of others. This emphasis on the individual can seem inappropriate or meaningless in some cultural contexts, where the individual may take less precedence than broader notions of kin or community. This may be especially so when social scientists work in developing countries.

In cases where research involves vulnerable groups such as children, older persons or adults with learning difficulties, every effort should be made to secure their informed consent. However, in cases where this is seen as impossible or where the research subjects are considered not competent to give their assent to the research, the issue of honesty and consent may need to be managed via proxies, who should be either those with a duty of care or who can provide disinterested independent approval depending on the individual circumstances. In the case of research on children, one cannot expect parents alone to provide disinterested approval on their children's behalf. In such cases, every effort should be made to deal with consent through dialogue with both children and their parents (or legal equivalent). Again, there may be circumstances where this could jeopardise the research (again in some areas of deviance, such as research into teenage sexuality or teenage pregnancy). In such circumstances, researchers will need to regard the potential risk to the principal subjects of the research as a priority.

3 *The confidentiality of information supplied by research subjects and the anonymity of respondents must be respected.*

This third principle requires that researchers take steps to ensure that research data and its sources remain confidential unless participants have consented to their disclosure, and in this latter case ensure that plans have been made for their storage and access to them.

4 *Research participants must participate in a voluntary way, free from any coercion.*

In all cases of research, researchers should inform subjects of their right to refuse to participate or withdraw from the investigation whenever and for whatever reason they wish. There should be no coercion of research subjects to participate in the research. Consent has to be freely given in order to be valid. This is linked to the issue of covert research and deliberate deception. Deception by definition precludes consent and should only be used in a research setting where open and transparent research is impossible, whether because of the risks it might create for the researcher or participant, or in work where consent can be secured without providing the participant with full information about the project to avoid jeopardising its performance.

5 *Harm to research participants must be avoided.*

This principle requires that social science research should be conducted in such a way that it minimises harm or risk to social groups or individuals. Participants' interests or well-being should not be damaged as a result of their participation in the research, even though in the short term there may be experimental procedures that generate some limited risk.* At the same time, no group should be unreasonably excluded from the research. In regard to this last point, research should be commissioned, designed and undertaken in such a way as to respect the interests of all social groups whatever their age, disability, race, ethnicity, religion, culture, gender or other characteristics. Some research will focus on a specific group and it would be inappropriate to seek wider levels of inclusivity across social groups in such research.

In addition, researchers should attempt to avoid harm not only to an immediate population of subjects, but to their wider family, kin and community. Research designs should consider potential harm to respondents' organisations or businesses as a result of the work. There is no simple rule for getting the balance right between these potential risks and effects. In order to assist RECs to come to a decision, researchers should endeavour to explain the likely effects of the research beyond the immediate respondents, where this is relevant. A related matter is the way in which research is communicated, especially where material is sensitive, or where results could be misconstrued and subsequently used by third parties against the interests of the research participants or researchers themselves.

*There may be exceptional circumstances in some fields of research when, with the consent of the participant, some short-term and minimal degree of harm which causes no lasting effects nor prolonged personal discomfort might be acceptable, for example, in laboratory-based social science research, where exposure to minimal personal risk could produce results that will have longer-term benefit to the respondent and others.

6   *The independence and impartiality of researchers must be clear, and any conflicts of interest or partiality must be explicit.*

The research should be conducted so as to ensure the professional integrity of its design, the generation and analysis of data, and the publication of results, while the direct and indirect contributions of colleagues, collaborators and others should also be acknowledged. In addition, this principle requires that investigators ensure that there is no undeclared conflict of interest (which may be personal, academic or commercial) in their proposed work and that the relation between the sources of funding and researchers' control over results is made clear, specifically in relation to the ownership, publication and subsequent use of research data.

Researchers need also to consider more generally the form and context of the publication of research results, especially where they are approached by the media prior to full publication of their work. They should try to ensure that media coverage does not compromise research participants, co-researchers or funding bodies or breach confidentiality. It is essential that relations with the media be agreed by the research team and managed by the lead investigator. The ESRC's Communications Toolkit at www.esrcsocietytoday.ac.uk and the ESRC's communications team provide advice about the procedures that should be followed.

To summarise:

- Researchers and research organisations should ensure that appropriate governance procedures and mechanisms are in place to oversee social science research.
- The ethical principles of integrity, honesty, confidentiality, voluntary participation, impartiality and the avoidance of personal risk to individuals or social groups characterise social science research that is conducted in a professional and ethical manner.
- The key concept of informed consent needs to be understood by both researchers and RECs in light of the context, aims and objectives of the research and may require ongoing review and advice from fellow professionals or an REC itself.

In order to illustrate these points, the ESRC *Research Ethics Framework* provides a number of case studies, and the following example (adapted from ESRC 2010: 24–30) has some elements that might be common to other crime and justice researchers.

ESRC case study: homelessness, begging and drug use

Professor Andrews, a social anthropologist, leads a team of researchers, including a social worker, a pharmacologist and a statistician in the medical school, who are proposing to carry out a study of patterns of migration, homelessness, street begging and drug use in the city. The study is funded by the ESRC with additional support from the city council. The local drugs charities, and drug and alcohol action teams (DAATs), have agreed to cooperate with the research team. The research team intends to carry out ethnographic work in two areas where begging is most common and to recruit 100 individuals through hostels for the homeless for more formal interviews and urine testing.

Initiating research ethics review

This proposal would need to go to full review by an REC, given the sensitivity of the issues it raises and the potential risks to both researchers and participants.

Making an application

The applicant should consider a number of issues when addressing the ethical dimensions of this proposal, including its potential benefits, the risk of harm, the processes of recruitment, mechanisms of gaining consent, privacy, confidentiality of information and any additional information that would be requested by the REC (e.g. information sheets). How might informed consent be properly defined in this proposal, especially where subjects are vulnerable and may be reluctant to give consent? It might make sense for consent to be given at different stages of the project rather than via a one-off agreement.

Reviewing the application

There are a number of questions that would need to be addressed by the REC in handling this application, including:

- How would the review be organised within the committee? Who on the committee would look at this proposal (everyone, discipline specialist, methodological specialist)? Would the ethnographic component be considered by different people or using different criteria from the interviews and the urine testing?

- What criteria (or guidelines) would be used in assessing it? Would these be generic or specific to the disciplines and approaches taken? In particular:
- How would the Committee go about assessing the level and diversity of risk?
- What procedures and documentation would it require in relation to informed consent?
- What other concerns might be identified – the university's reputation, legal position, etc?
- Would the involvement of the City Council be considered relevant to ethics review? Would the collaboration of DAATs be considered relevant?

There are no 'obvious' answers to these questions: they require debate within the Committee itself. An REC might also invite the applicants to explain or defend their proposal in person.

Reporting back to applicants

Good practice would suggest that RECs should be able to report back within two to three months of receipt of an application, or sooner, depending on the frequency of meetings. This would also fall within the ESRC REF's three-month period between notification of funding and start of the project.

Feedback might include commentary on issues for consideration or elaboration, or set out what the committee requires to be done to gain approval.

The university REC might also need to consider how it might respond if contacted by a charity for the homeless which expressed concern about the study.

Ethical restrictions on criminological research

Given this list of requirements and regulations, some researchers might ask whether it is now feasible to carry out any worthwhile research in the field of crime and justice. The principles the ESRC prescribe, of which the above are but a summary of a much longer document, may place particular restrictions on criminological research because as Winlow *et al.* note, 'Deviant cultures have little to gain by allowing researchers access to their daily lives and various illegal activities' (2001: 538). In stressing the need for informed consent, avoiding deception, risk and harm, the designers of these codes of ethics are perhaps thinking of a more ordered world where people are happy and willing to be open about their activities if assured of anonymity. Essentially, the ESRC is attempting to set a gold standard for research in the social sciences and is expecting individual universities' research ethics committees (RECs) both to act as the initial point of contact and to carry out a policing function in requiring staged ethics approval and final reports.

As mentioned in previous chapters, this book does not aim to be a collection of prescriptive hints as to how to do research and certainly is not intended to be an ethics handbook. The interviews with well-established researchers have aimed to present evidence of 'real life' experiences and a broadly practical approach to the sort of problems people encounter. In this vein a number of questions are tackled in this chapter:

- What are the 'ethical' concerns around researching crime and justice?
- How do politics affect what is research and how it is done?
- What has emotion got to do with research?
- How to manage danger and the research process?

In researching crime and justice, very often the people who are the participants can be disadvantaged, relatively powerless or described as the 'harmed and hurting', as Piacentini notes in her interview in Chapter 4. As researchers are human, and the people they research have feelings, the problems faced are often connected to ethics, emotions and the politics of any particular project. To address this, the ethics and emotions of research are discussed in the following sections of this chapter by analysing some excerpts that were not used in the main interviews earlier in the book. Where interviewees mentioned the subjects of ethics or emotions, these data have been extracted for analysis in this chapter, and are discussed in terms of the ethical codes and bureaucracies of ethics that are part of current research practice. A discussion of the politics of research follows later in the chapter, linked to a summing up of some of the theoretical approaches that criminological research is based upon. This takes the form of an explanation of the way a piece of research can be come politicised in various senses, related to the following questions:

- Who uses the research?
- Who might appropriate it?
- Upon what sort of premise is it based?
- In whose interests are the researchers working?

Crime and justice specific ethics?

In describing the way criminologists may have to hide dark and guilty secrets, Liebling and Stanko further their useful debate about the potentially 'special' aspects of researching crime and particularly violence (2001). They argue that the topics criminologists choose to investigate present particular ethical concerns, especially around whose 'side' the researcher may find themselves defending. The worry about the objectivity of data as a result of these ethical concerns is acute, because, they argue:

There are, for example, inherent uncertainties in the way we choose our allegiances in the field. Take for instance the need for social scientists to protect the confidentiality of research subjects. Who or what is our allegiance to when, for instance, a police officer hits an arrestee or a bouncer roughly ejects an abusive drunk from a night-club? Whose confidentiality should be protected? Researching violence of police, bouncers or prison life assumes that we can agree on the nature of the distinctions between legal and illegal use of violence in particular contexts.
(Liebling and Stanko 2001: 424–5)

In effect this is a discussion that is core to this volume – the way real life intervenes to make researching crime and justice so interesting and important. Although other researchers have asked which side 'we' are on, as Liebling and Stanko point out criminologists have to deal with the frequent dichotomy and debate of the line between legal and illegal. The stakes are higher for people who might see police officers breaking the law, because of the sanctions that may follow for those officers, because of the powerlessness of the victim, but also because of the inaccessibility of the research site due to lack of trust. The organisation of criminal justice bodies will often mean that there are many excuses for not allowing access, and unless this is achieved and maintained it is impossible to proceed. The simple rule to maintain confidentiality and to be overt in all our dealings is perhaps not as straightforward as for other academic disciplines.

Some key practical questions for criminologists could include:

- In researching 'crime and justice', what sort of challenges might there be to ethical codes and principles?
- What are the fundamental ethical difficulties associated with criminological research, such as the unequal relationships between the powerful and powerless? Physical and emotional risk or danger?
- Does gender/ethnicity/race/class or some types of vulnerability add another dimension?
- Are some research methods more 'ethical' than others in criminology? For example, are ethnographies more ethical than surveys?
- What about 'insider/outsider' loyalties? When promises are made by researchers, there may be expectations of change as a result of the research.

From my own experience in the field of police ethnography, a number of ethical dilemmas have arisen, from many small 'molehills', as Rowe (2007) has described fairly unimportant incidents, to larger, more troubling ones. The sort of issue encountered during my study of gender and policing included police officers telling witnesses what to say in statements, by 'coaching' them as to the best way to put things, in order to make the case stronger. In incidents where they felt some challenge could be made to their account of events, officers would often discuss what they were about to write in their pocket book accounts of the incident, and in the process enhance or elaborate the evidence. They frequently used 'ways and means to justice' that involved threatening suspects with unpleasant outcomes if they did not cooperate. There was a significant amount of 'cuffing' jobs, time-wasting, filling in boring periods with 'non-police' activities. There was frequent witnessing/hearing sexist/racist language or behaviour during the fieldwork, and a constant flow of accepting free or reduced price food, takeaway meals and drinks.

Some of these issues might be viewed as more 'serious' than others but it could be argued that any small breach of trust, such as accepting a free cup of coffee, can be the start of the 'slippery slope'. On the other hand, the most serious and certainly the most disturbing type of police misbehaviour I witnessed was brutality and excessive force.

The following are four examples of brutality that attempt to illustrate the sort of dilemmas I faced during the fieldwork for *Gender and Policing* (2001a).

1 The first case involves where violence is explained as an unintentional outcome, and highlights problems associated with defining what is 'excessive' force. A number of examples of this type of violence by the police were witnessed during the fieldwork. Many were related to assaults in the home, which seemed to be inflamed rather than soothed by the presence of police uniforms. In this particular case, however, the 'domestic' had started in a public place, the centre of a city's night life area on a busy Saturday evening. While driving around the city centre a crew, including a female officer, drove past a woman whose male companion seemed to be assaulting her. The van came to a sudden halt and the woman officer jumped out to check whether she needed any help. At this point it became obvious that the woman was very drunk and she started shouting and abusing the police officer. After a warning she was arrested and physically bundled into the back of the 'cage' in the police van. Upon reaching the custody suite she sobered up somewhat, but then decided to become very uncooperative, refusing to give her name and address. At this, the woman officer who had arrested her grabbed her in a headlock, twisted her over the bench and made her scream that she would provide the required information.

2 In the second example, violence is used as a 'punishment' by the police. On patrol early one morning at the end of a long night shift, some officers were dragging a 'druggie' out of the back of a police van, along the ground. His bare skin was being grazed along the concrete leading up to the custody suite door. He was then picked up by four of the officers, one at each 'corner', and his head was used as a battering ram to attract the attention of those inside operating the automatic doors.

From most people's perspective, this would be excessive, as the emaciated heroin addict did not pose a physical threat to the much larger, stronger officers who in any case outnumbered him. His 'crime' had been to be 'lippy' to the officers who were arresting him for suspected possession of illegal substances and to refuse to submit to a body search.

3   In this case, violence is used to lighten the situation and as revenge due to annoyance, and involves an attempted suicide. A seemingly deranged young man had taken a large number of tranquillisers, then climbed down an icy cliff to lie in wait for the incoming tide. In the dark and bitter cold the police officers, who were not amused at being called out of a cosy canteen, dragged the man, on his back, down the steep path to the ambulance rather than carrying him. On the way over the cliffs they were also trying to revive him so that he could stand up and they would be relieved of their burden. One of the officers slapped the man's face and violently crushed his ear lobe, shouting at him to wake up. When he didn't respond they bounced and slid his body down the snowy sand dunes, with some hilarity, making jokes about downhill slaloms and about it not hurting him a bit. As he was being lifted into the ambulance, he regained consciousness a little and started protesting about the rough treatment he had received. In response the police officer received a great appreciative laugh as he turned to the assembled group of officers and onlookers in mock amazement and announced: 'Well! You try to save someone's life and that's the thanks you get!'

4   In the following case officers were acting in order to save face. It involves a failed escapee who tried to make a dash for freedom while in police custody. He was standing in front of the charge desk and was informed that because of his numerous previous visits to the cells recently, police bail was being refused. Realising that this meant a long weekend in custody he suddenly broke free from the circle of officers around him and ran for the door. Inadvertently I was standing in his path and acted as a barrier so that the officers could catch him as we collided. He was dragged back into the cells as his personal property – shoes, belt and so on – was being forcibly and roughly removed. Officers were shouting at him, as he cried out in pain and protest, that it was his own fault as he had attacked 'a woman' and someone who was 'not even one of us'. Later one of the officers, clearly embarrassed, apologised for her suspect having attempted to 'attack' someone who was an innocent bystander.

The following excerpt is taken from an article in a special issue of the *British Journal of Criminology* in 2001, and takes these issues of politics and ethics (and later emotions and danger) as things to be concerned about. The article was about 'blowing the whistle' on police violence.

In this article the dilemmas faced by fieldworkers when they witness deviance in the form of violent acts are discussed. Indeed, although being present when something 'illegal' occurs is a fairly universal problem for participant observation studies, at the beginning of a project ethnographers rarely have an instruction manual which goes further than the general methodological issues ... [where] the ethical ambiguities of fieldwork are raised, but few practical resolutions are suggested.

(Westmarland 2001b: 523)

One of the problems was that as the research progressed it became clear that ethical issues were going to arise continually. Police violence and brutality, one aspect of the study that might be considered worthy of a whistle-blower's attention, were regular occurrences, and in one sense the fact that the police were comfortable committing these acts while I was present was a good sign, as evidence that trust and a certain level of researcher invisibility had been achieved. On the other hand, some of the incidents made uncomfortable viewing, and led to dilemmas about what to say, and do, and whether to publish the material. As the four case examples above from the fieldwork illustrate, the everyday physicality of police work is often at a level not previously experienced by individual academic researchers.

In an attempt to help rationalise these dilemmas, various professional bodies and associations, such as the British Society of Criminology, have developed a set of guidelines to which researchers can refer. As explained above, the ESRC, as one of the main funding bodies of academic research in the UK, also have a guide, the *Research Ethics Framework*, to what they expect of researchers applying to them for funding. Whoever they are funded by, however, most projects involving 'human subjects' will need to be submitted to the relevant university's research ethics committee (REC) if they are to be conducted by students, staff or in the 'name' of that organisation.

This application usually means completing a form, and then awaiting comments from the committee, perhaps followed by making changes to the proposed methods. In the proposal the researchers will make assurances about the sort of ethical guidelines they will follow. Depending on the type of methods and the sensitivities of the issues proposed, a more detailed form or explanation may be necessary. The following extract is part of a code of ethics taken from the British Criminology Society's website. This is part of a much longer document, but provides a flavour of the sort of framework the university's ethics committee will expect in an application. These codes are available for other subject disciplines, such as psychology (www.bps.org.uk) and sociology, in addition to this one from the British Society of Criminology (BSC). The British Society of Criminology's guidelines are available at www.britsoccrim.org/ethical.htm.

Researchers' responsibilities towards research participants

Researchers should:

(i) Recognise that they have a responsibility to ensure that the physical, social and psychological well-being of an individual participating in research is not adversely affected by participation in the research. Researchers should strive to protect the rights of those they study, their interests, sensitivities and privacy. Researchers should consider carefully the possibility that the research experience may be a disturbing one, particularly for those who are vulnerable by virtue of factors such as age, social status, or powerlessness and should seek to minimise such disturbances. Researchers should also consider whether or not it is appropriate to offer information about support services (e.g. leaflets about relevant self-help groups).

(ii) Be sympathetic to the constraints on organisations participating in research and not inhibit their functioning by imposing any unnecessary burdens on them.

(iii) Base research on the freely given informed consent of those studied in all but exceptional circumstances. (Exceptional in this context relates to exceptional importance of the topic rather than difficulty of gaining access.) Informed consent implies a responsibility on the part of the researchers to explain as fully as possible, and in terms meaningful to participants, what the research is about, who is undertaking and financing it, why it is being undertaken, and how any research findings are to be disseminated. Researchers should also make clear that participants have the right to refuse permission or withdraw from involvement in research whenever and for whatever reason they wish. Participants' consent should be informed, voluntary and continuing, and researchers need to check that this is the case. Research participants have the right to withdraw from the research at any time and for any reason without adverse consequences. Research participants should be informed about how far they will be afforded anonymity and confidentiality. Researchers should pay special attention to these matters when participation is sought from children, young, or vulnerable people, including consideration of the need for additional consent from an adult responsible for the child at the time participation is sought. It is not considered appropriate to assume that penal and care institutions can give informed consent on research on young people's behalf. The young people themselves must be consulted.

Furthermore, researchers should give regard for issues of child protection and make provision for the disclosure of abuse. Researchers should consider the possibility of discussing research findings with participants and those who are the subject of the research.

(iv) Where there is likelihood that identifiable data may be shared with other researchers, the potential uses to which the data might be put should be discussed with research participants. Research participants should be informed if data are likely to be placed in archives, including computer archives. Researchers should not breach the 'duty of confidentiality' and not pass on identifiable data to third parties without participants' consent. Researchers should also note that they should work within the confines of current legislation over such matters as intellectual property (including copyright, trademark, patents), privacy and confidentiality, data protection and human rights. Offers of confidentiality may sometimes be overridden by law: researchers should therefore consider the circumstances in which they might be required to divulge information to legal or other authorities, and make such circumstances clear to participants when seeking their informed consent.

(v) Researchers should be aware, when conducting research via the internet, of the particular problems that may arise when engaging in this medium. Researchers should not only be aware of the relevant areas of law in the jurisdictions that they cover but they should also be aware of the rules of conduct of their internet service provider (including JANET – Joint Academic Network). When conducting internet research, the researcher should be aware of the boundaries between the public and the private domains, and also any legal and cultural differences across jurisdictions. Where research might prejudice the legitimate rights of respondents, researchers should obtain informed consent from them, honour assurances of confidentiality, and ensure the security of data transmission. They should exercise particular care and consideration when engaging with children and vulnerable people in internet research.

(vi) Researchers should be aware of the additional difficulties that can occur when undertaking comparative or cross-national research, involving different jurisdictions where codes of practice are likely to differ.

This code is useful when thinking about formal approval for a project that will have contact with 'human subjects' (that is, research participants or, put more simply, people). As explained earlier, any project carried out in the name of a university, whether as a member of staff or PhD student (usually), and occasionally in undergraduate work, will probably have been referred to an ethics committee, which reviews proposals and provides suggestions and hopefully approval. The types of issues that concern ethics committees include:

- **Consent** – will the people taking part in the study be told what it is about and have the opportunity to agree to take part? This is called 'informed' consent.
- Will the people involved be able to **withdraw** from the study, and have their information removed from the database?
- Will the people involved be assured of **anonymity**?
- Will the data be shared with anyone (recordings of interviews, for example) and will they be kept **securely** under lock and key?
- If any children or young people are involved in the study, have the researchers undergone suitable **security checks**?
- Will the people taking part in the study be able to **contact** someone if they wish to withdraw from the study or make a complaint?
- Will the **findings** be shared with, or fed back to, the participants of the study?

Researchers are often required to complete a pro forma, a guide to the sort of information the committee will require. The following, adapted from the Open University Human Participants and Materials Ethics Committee (HPMEC) guidelines (June 2010), gives suggestions as to the questions that may be asked by committees.

Title of project
A short, descriptive title.

Schedule
Time-frame for the research and its data collection phase(s).

Abstract
A summary of the main points of the research, written in terms easily understandable by a non-specialist and containing no technical terms.

Source(s) of funding
Details of the external or internal funding body (e.g. ESRC, MRC).

Justification for research
What contribution to knowledge, policy, practice, and people's lives the research will make?

Investigators
Give **names** and **units** of all persons involved in the collection and handling of individual data. Please name one person as **Principal Investigator** (PI).

Published ethical guidelines to be followed
For example: BERA, BPS, BSA, BSC.

Location(s) of data collection
Give details of where and when data will be collected. If on private, corporate or institutional premises, indicate what approvals are gained/required.

Participants
Give details of the population from which you will be sampling and how this sampling will be done.

Recruitment procedures
How will you identify and approach potential participants?

Consent
Give details of how informed consent will be gained and attach copies of information sheet(s) and consent form(s). Give details of how participants can withdraw consent and what will happen to their data in such a case.

Methodology
Outline the method(s) that will be employed to collect and analyse data.

Data protection
Give details of registration of the project under the DP Act and the procedures to be followed re: storage and disposal of data to comply with the Act.

Recompense to participants
Normally, recompense is only given for expenses and inconvenience, otherwise it might be seen as coercion/inducement to participate. Give details of any recompense to participants.

Deception
Give details of the withholding of any information from participants, or misrepresentation or other deception that is an integral part of the research. Any such deception should be fully justified.

> **Risks**
> Detail any foreseen risks to participants or researchers and, based on a risk assessment, the steps that will be taken to minimise/counter these. If the proposed study involves contact with children or other vulnerable groups, please confirm that an enhanced Criminal Records Bureau (CRB) Disclosure has been obtained for each person involved in these contacts.
>
> **Debriefing**
> Give details of how information will be given to participants after data collection to inform them of the purpose of their participation and the research more broadly.
>
> **Declaration**
> Declare here that the research will conform to the above protocol and that any significant changes or new issues will be raised with the HPMEC before they are implemented.

There are no hard and fast rules to a successful application to a research ethics committee. The key issue is to read and digest the guidelines that are relevant to your study and to think yourself into the place of the research participants – your potential data providers. Work out what might go wrong, how you would feel as a researcher or if you were one of the participants, and aim to provide safeguards and reassurances that when real life happens you will have at least thought about the possibilities of difficulties and solutions. One common question committees ask criminologists is around the issue of 'disclosure'. What will you do if someone tells you something that you feel you may have to share with the 'authorities'? This could be knowledge of ongoing child abuse, or even where the bodies are hidden. As Liebling and Stanko conclude, 'we cannot avoid squalid politics and ethical predicaments when researching crime and violence' (2001: 421). Can you demonstrate to the REC that you are prepared for this in an interview or during fieldwork observations?

Most universities currently have an electronic application process, which includes a set of guidelines and an appeals process. If possible, look at an example of a successful proposal, such as an application a colleague has submitted in the past. In the case of students, the advisor or supervisor of the project should be available to help with this process.

The politics of researching crime and justice

In criminological texts, when the politics of research is discussed it is not usually in the sense of party or even governmental politics. Despite the supposed link between criminology and criminal justice policy development, very often the topic of the politics of research refers to the micro politics of the process, outcome or findings of the research. Who funded the research, how 'independent' were the researchers, was there a hidden or underlying agenda? Were the findings 'appropriated', ignored, misrepresented or denied? Whose 'side' did the researchers appear to favour?

In the description of the violence research above, where the ethnography depended on ongoing access to police activities and the trust of individual officers, dilemmas arise as to whether to report certain behaviours. It is clear that to do so would seriously inhibit the procedure of the study. Dealing with the micro politics and daily occurrences in 'real life' research is not easy. In a study of police culture and behaviour on patrol, for example, Smith and Gray (1983) 'decided to purposefully respond in a contradictory way to overtly homophobic behaviour' (Westmarland 2001a). They reported that officers became confused by their apparent condoning of their attitudes. Rowe also reports his difficulties with knowing whether or not to report behaviour that could affect the outcome of his study. He describes that there were several times when he was unsure as to the best course of action:

> On another occasion, I was left with a comparatively junior PC and a suspect in the station 'chute' where prisoners are held before being formally 'booked in' to the custody suite. As we chatted I noticed the prisoner surreptitiously put something in his mouth and swallow it. The PC did not seem to notice and I was unsure whether to mention it to him. I was concerned that if the prisoner had swallowed drugs this might have serious repercussions for both him and the officer. Methodologically, however, I did not want to interfere in the situation and influence the way in which events unfolded. Eventually I decided that the potential impact on both the prisoner and the officer was primary, and when the opportunity arose I discreetly mentioned to the officer what I had seen. He thanked me and discussed this with his more experienced colleague, and the two of them decided to 'keep this between ourselves'.
>
> (Rowe 2007: 42)

Whether or not to say anything in this sort of situation might be seen as ethical dilemmas, but it is also about the politics of the situation. If researchers make the wrong call the impact upon the study may be damaging or lead to the whole project being abandoned. Reiner, for example, when deciding whether to reveal some information that he believed could have been politically explosive, came to the conclusion that his job, future access and the career of his informant were not worth risking (2000: 223). Even if the incident was a comparatively minor matter, due to the nature of police culture and the way it encourages group solidarity, one of the 'hazards faced by whistleblowers' can be the 'cold shoulder treatment' (Chan 1996: 121). In other words, it can lead not only to the individual officers being no longer willing to give their free consent to the study, but also to them telling their colleagues of the 'danger' the researcher poses. Similarly, if the researcher is 'overenthusiastically' reporting all incidents of misdemeanour to senior officers, they might feel that it is politically expedient to halt the research, perhaps fearing an *exposé*, either to their superiors or to a more public audience.

Negotiating the political minefield – a research note

The following discussion attempts to address some of the key questions about the politics of research, from my own experience. This is not meant to provide the 'answer' to the problem of what to do in practical situations, just some reflections on my own practice.

As I explained above (and see Westmarland 2001a), one dilemma was about reporting violence, as other behaviours seemed 'par for the course'. In other words, I had expected the 'cuffing' of jobs they did not wish to attend, the acceptance of free meals, giving out summary justice, and so on, as I had read about this from the numerous books on police culture, including the extensive work done by my PhD supervisor, Dick Hobbs. The violence, however, was a much more 'political' issue, as in many cases it was clearly excessive and illegal. Although it did not happen every day or even very frequently, the shocking and often gratuitous nature of it seemed to invoke a 'something needs to be done' reaction. At the same time it was difficult to judge exactly what this should be, and as it was I was trying to become invisible, not to make judgemental comments, and was aware that 'trust needs to be continuously cultivated' (Reiner 2000: 224).

The issue of gender, as the focus of the study, was clearly a personal/political issue. As a woman researcher, a non-police 'outside outsider' (Brown 1996), my position was 'other'. This was my first encounter with 'real' research; I was very naive and nonplussed when police officers, being experts at what Goffman would call 'impression management' (1969), would state to all within earshot, 'So this report, then, it's about women and you're a woman so it's going to be biased. They should have got a man to do it, then it would have been fair' (Westmarland 1994). As mentioned earlier, at an initial access interview for this research (such as that described by Ben Bowling in Chapter 4 of this volume), a senior woman police officer had asked, 'What will you do if you see an officer assault a suspect and they call upon you as a witness?' Questions such as these, fired at speed and with the expertise of professionals who have experience of respondents who attempt to cover up the truth, are often unnerving.

In such ethical dilemmas you don't really know what you would do and so the only honest response is a seemingly unprofessional but perhaps best policy answer of, 'I don't know until it happens'. Another dilemma involved the trust and friendship built up with individual officers: having lived through what seemed like half a lifetime with them in various shifts, become their confidante, seen their weaknesses and foibles, then having to publicly denounce their intimate thoughts and confidences offered in moments of high drama/emotion.

The second political issue was that people often believe (as you do yourself at the time) that 'something will happen' as a result of the research. For example, there were few women in some departments, such as the firearms, and in these sexist behaviour and language were rife. One research project will not fix this sort of endemic problem. As a woman in a male-dominated research environment I might have been seen as the 'voice' of oppression and defence of supposedly 'weaker' female officers, supposed to be able to answer all questions around the 'problem of women'. Also, being in the minority as a woman in largely male groups of workers, and with the topic of the research being about gender – interpreted as 'equal opportunities' in their eyes, an often hated and denigrated term – caused tensions. As Stanko commented about her research in various parts of the criminal justice system, she was subjected to sexual harassment, partly due to the way officers are 'welded together' (1998: 38) in their occupational cultural ways of dealing with potential danger.

Some of these problems can be avoided by ethnographers by being covert: if not in their presence, but perhaps in terms of the topic of investigation. It might be argued (as the ESRC framework suggests above) that this is less ethical, but it can be politically expedient. As Simon Winlow explains in his interview for this volume, it meant that he was simply 'one of the boys' and he presumably experienced no dilemmas about not reporting any illegal behaviour, as this would have blown his cover.

Of course, there is a distinction between telling the whole truth and being slightly vague about the purposes of the research. In one study I conducted the aim was to observe homicide detectives making decisions about which murders to investigate fully and energetically and which they might make less effort with. This project drew upon ideas from Martin Innes' study of symbolism and victimhood in detectives' views of 'innocence' and guilt in homicide cases (2003). My aim was to conduct an ethnographic study shadowing the Washington DC Homicide team in their daily work attempting to solve murders across the city, mostly the sudden and unprovoked shooting of young black men (Westmarland 2009).

I had initially aimed to observe the way officers make decisions and to what extent they were using some sort of police-specific moral code to decide which cases to pursue, how to do so and their attitudes and feelings about their behaviour. Regarding the politics of these situations, as with all ethnographies, personal relationships are built up, intimate views expressed and all the 'backstage' moments are impossible to hide. Therefore, the officers' views about their actions, tactics and so on become open to the researcher's selectivity and interpretation. One aim of this study was to discover whether any moral bias exists, as Innes suggests (2003), in the detectives' decisions about who to pursue as a suspect. In an ethnographic situation this leads to an obvious focus upon any misdemeanours, or biased, 'unethical' decision-making, by the officers, when this might be the exception rather than the rule.

One problem I had was how much information to give out. If I was to announce to the officers that I would be studying their decisions and ethics and how this related to the effort they put into various homicide investigations, this would have had potentially damaging effects. First, it would have been difficult to gain their trust and for them to allow me to hear their 'true' reasons for certain professional decisions; second, it might have affected the way they conducted the investigations; and third, it would have been a difficult project to sell to senior officers – it sounds as if the researcher is checking on their officers' 'morals' in their beliefs and actions.

As a result of these political considerations, I made a decision to be fairly economical with the truth about the underlying reason for the research. In other words, rather than announcing upfront to each detective I encountered when they asked the inevitable, 'What's this all about?', I would explain in a rather vague way that I was comparing their methods of clearing up homicides with that of UK detectives. This made for an interesting opener for conversations, as they were keen to know about the so-called 'murder-solving computer system' they had heard British detectives were using (this has the acronym HOLMES, which stands for Home Office Large Major Enquiry System – see Innes 2003 for a fuller explanation). Once rapport was established with each officer, it was revealed to them that the study was about the way the different homicides might be viewed as a result of circumstance, victim and perpetrator.

Practical suggestions for research in the field

- It is obvious that the data and the individuals' identities need to be disguised, if only for the sake of the defendants and witnesses, or others encountered in the field, even where police ask, which page of the book will I be appearing on? Or in the case of one chief officer, a condition in agreeing to his force being involved in the project that they should be named.
- See no evil/speak no evil, but publish everything later – the 'ethnographer's escape clause'. Any intervention will 'spoil the scene' or affect what would have happened if the researcher were absent.
- Try to intervene subtly where unacceptable (to the researcher) behaviour or racist or sexist language happens. Wait until the heat has passed, then bring up the events; or be obvious not to collude and they might do it for you.
- Try not to make judgements on the spot – reflecting on the events rather than making quick remarks or interventions in the heat of the moment

are more valuable long term. Things look very different (sometimes better, sometimes worse) in hindsight.
- Work out why people act in certain ways without getting overly sucked into their world-view.

It could be argued, therefore, that our dilemmas are very similar to those experienced by other social scientists and so standard methods to avoid or mitigate the problems can be used. One of the differences, perhaps, is the gendered power differential that exists in the criminal justice world, particularly in policing. Power, secrecy and a certain aspect of police culture that allows officers to believe that they are acting for the public good or 'right', in the sense of mission and morals, combine in this research field to provide situations that create multiple ethical dilemmas for researchers. Like police officers' work, in the field no two situations are alike and cannot therefore be predicted. Codes of practice, similar to police rules and regulations, cannot cover all eventualities and the role of the ethical researcher requires the use of 'discretion', just like police work. In this way perhaps a commonality can be seen, and an understanding of how and why actions and beliefs are held, endure and seem to be part of police culture can be identified through the difficulties researchers experience when they enter the field. Rather than seeing 'ethics' as a problem for researchers, therefore, it can be used in the understanding and analysis of data gathered in an environment that is fraught with ethical dilemmas of its own. Research data can be viewed through an ethically aware lens, while reflecting on the moral dilemmas the researched group are attempting to struggle with and contain.

Emotions

With regard to the emotional aspect of researching crime and justice it is obvious that, as with the ethical and political concerns above, some studies will be more troubling than others. And as with those two previous concerns, it is also difficult to make hard and fast rules or give specific advice. Writing in 1999, Wolcott argues, in offering advice to ethnographers he did not want to be too 'preachy/teachy' (1999: 283), that even then he thought ethics advice had become too prescriptive. Ethnographers and other researchers often form friendships or emotional bonds with their research participants, and may then go through tortuous decision-making processes in deciding what to do in certain situations. Emotions are involved when deciding, for instance, whether writing up the research will be 'tale telling': participants will have been assured of anonymity, but perhaps they will be able to work out where the researcher's loyalty lies, making for uncomfortable reading. For example, in one study Tunnell explains that his sympathies lay with 'known felons' (1998: 217) rather than with the police.

As Carter and Delamont (1996) explain in the introduction to their collection of essays about the study of qualitative research and the emotions, researchers are often unwilling to reveal their feelings about the projects they have conducted. Furthermore, they argue, emotions and disturbing feelings about projects sometimes arrive unexpectedly, even if injustice, pain, power, violence, and even death, are to be expected in the researching of crime and justice.

The following is an example from my own experience. Although I had viewed several dead bodies during the research for my PhD, and got used to it, in a later study of detectives in the USA, investigating homicide and ethical decision-making (mentioned above), one particular call had an effect on me that was unexpected.

Field notes from DC 2004

It was just another call to a shooting. Two young black men, the fifteenth and sixteenth bodies I had viewed at the scene of an incident during the past two weeks of fieldwork. Not particularly bloody or physically disturbing. Two bodies in the front of a moderately sized family car, with their heads, with eyes closed as if sleeping, resting peacefully on their respective airbags. It seems from the neat and slightly oozing bullet holes each had received (one just behind the ear, the other towards the back of the head) that they had died before the car had crashed at a fairly low speed into a lamp standard at the side of the road.

All was proceeding as normal, no witnesses wanted to be interviewed, no one had heard or seen anything, despite the close proximity of well-kept houses within a few feet of the crash scene. We hung around in the hot dark DC night waiting for the 'meat wagon' to arrive to transport the bodies to the medical examiner's office. As each body was extricated from the car and laid on a stretcher to be slotted into one of the bunks in the back of the nondescript removal van that had arrived, and wrapped in a white cotton sheet, their pockets were checked for identification, drugs, weapons or other evidence of potential wrongdoing.

At this point someone noticed the feet and trainers of the passenger. They seemed unusually small – and feminine. At this the rather strange-looking but matter-of-fact driver of the removal van stopped proceedings, pulled up the top clothes of the passenger and revealed a crop-top bra – exclaiming 'hey – this is a girl'. Even the detective I was accompanying was surprised – the victim's cornrow hair, jeans and tee shirt had given her a masculine, or at least androgynous appearance. For some reason, perhaps as I was a long way from home, family and friends, a bit overtired, and the dead girl reminded me of my two daughters at that age, I felt, on getting into bed in my rented apartment in the early hours of the morning, more affected than I had expected to be.

(Westmarland 2009)

Even secondary material such as case files can be disturbing, especially if the individual nature of the items cannot be anticipated in advance. The following description of a study of suicide shows that there are sometimes unexpected triggers, such as photographs or notes of an extremely personal nature. In a study of case files collected by a coroner's court, Fincham *et al.* (2007) describe some of the more distressing aspects of their research.

> The most affecting material in the files is the original copies of suicide notes. While they do not necessarily carry the dramatic impact of photographs, they are often the most potent relics of the last moments of a person's life contained in the files. The condition of the notes, the material they are written on, the handwriting and the language used in them can make for exceptionally moving data.
> (Fincham *et al.* 2007: 10)

In analysing their reactions to the type of material they were reading, the researchers reflected on why and how certain issues can have a particular impact.

> Both detail and a lack of detail can have an impact on our emotional reactions to the suicides as well as our intellectual and analytical responses. An initial human reaction to the lack of detail in a case file could be to assume that this is a lonely or shunned person, whereas more detail could suggest a picture of somebody who is loved, or perhaps loathed. The emotional content of the statements of friends and family is high. These documents are suffused with expressions of love, bitterness, regret, anger, blame, loathing, confusion and sorrow.
> (Fincham *et al.* 2007: 12)

In this study Fincham *et al.* report that the three people in their research team each found their own way to deal with the emotions involved in reading and analysing the material. They also found the means to express to each other when something was affecting them and ways in which they could take 'time out' from reading the files. This is perhaps preferable to the experience recounted by Moran-Ellis (1997), who experienced difficulty in getting away from the pain invoked by reading case files:

> I felt appalled by what I was finding out, and I felt much pain by proxy for the children who had been subjected to what amounts to physical as well as emotional and sexual assault. I could barely contemplate the pain they had felt . . . And yet I found I couldn't not think about it.
> (Moran-Ellis 1997: 181)

Emotions in research situations demand what Hochschild (1983) coined as a syndrome the 'managed heart'. She describes the way that female aircrews, as a result of being continually bombarded with demands and sometimes abusive customers, find ways to manage their emotions. She argues that it is not a case of becoming hardened to the feelings that are invoked in these situations, but rather learning to keep a pleasant and smiling outward persona while carrying out the required processes to function in the job. Hochschild does not suggest that this is an ideal situation; in fact, she regards it as stressful and debilitating at first, and then as becoming potentially damaging, in that the surface acting they have to do becomes a deeper, ingrained response that is almost natural, and this, she argues, is even more injurious to health.

Talking about the dangers of the 'managed heart', Homan (1980) said that the stress and the later feelings of betrayal can be problematic for the researcher once they have left the field. This ties in with Hochschild's claims that continual 'acting' can, as a result of being habitual, become automatic, and cause stressful changes to notions of self and personality. The female aircrew member, in keeping a smile on her face, soon became an automaton, the smile becoming 'part' of the woman's identity; instead of simply 'acting' the good attentive customer servant, she became one.

Some have suggested that a potential solution to being troubled by distressing emotional issues in the research process is to have a colleague with whom the stressful and upsetting issues can be talked through. In their special issue of the *British Journal of Criminology* in 2001 on researching violence, Liebling and Stanko discuss the difficulties of obtaining reliable objective and valid data in potentially dangerous situations. They claim that few researchers share their problems with others: 'While there may be many reading this issue who have not faced the raw emotions emanating from these dilemmas, we think that there are many more who have. Few of us share how we resolve or understand them' (2001: 424).

Another suggestion where emotional or dangerous situations arise is to have a counselling service to which respondents can be referred, perhaps if the interview becomes an offloading session for the respondent. This can be difficult, however, if the research is covert, as the researcher is expecting the confidant to take part in what is essentially a deception. Israel and Hay (2006) note that the issue of covert research is an area of heated debate, surrounding whether 'deception by lying, withholding information, or misleading exaggeration', such as employed by Fountain in her study of drug dealing, which she conducted covertly (1996: 73). Fountain noted 'that she often felt that she was betraying subjects who had treated her as a friend, unaware that she was conducting research' (cited in Rowe 2007: 39). Regarding his decision to use overt methods for his study of the police, Rowe observes:

> ... an overt approach was preferable in this case, since the pressure of sustaining a covert project would have been considerable and the risk of losing the data too great in the event of being 'uncovered'. One sergeant reinforced my confidence that I had followed the best course when he noted – in no uncertain terms – that I would have been physically thrown out of the police station had officers suspected that I was an undercover researcher.
>
> (Rowe 2007: 39)

Israel and Hay (2006) note that there have been other researchers who have justified covert research.

> Several researchers have argued that covert strategies may be justified in limited circumstances (Bulmer 1982) ... Other researchers have been concerned about the effect of the known observer on participants or the desire of 'powerful or secretive interests' (British Sociological Association 2002, Socio-Legal Studies Association n.d.) to block access by social scientists ...
>
> Although he acknowledged powerful arguments against covert research and believed that the need for such research was frequently exaggerated, Bulmer concluded that some covert studies, voluntarily undertaken, *had* produced good social science ...
>
> (Israel and Hay 2006: 174)

In terms of the validity of the research one of the aims of covert methods is the desire to eliminate 'reactivity' or the Hawthorne effect, explored in Chapter 5. Essentially, the plausibility of the study is increased if the people concerned did not know they were being watched and recorded, or observed making mistakes or remarks, being violent. So while covert research can facilitate ease of access, for example by pretending to be a bouncer, it has its ethical difficulties, aside from being potentially dangerous.

Danger in the research process

Apart from the ethically dubious and emotionally draining aspects, danger can be involved in conducting covert research. For example, if someone is open that they are a researcher, but secretive about their real reasons for being there, if found out they may be subjected to physical threat or personal humiliation. As Rowe reports above, regarding his thoughts about doing covert research with police officers, if he had taken this approach and been found out, he would have been physically thrown out.

On the other hand, some topics are very difficult to research openly, and the presence of researchers may cause reactions that would make the study impossible. It could be argued that in some cases less harm could come to researchers and respondents if they did not know the true nature of the project. Knowing that a researcher is trying to find out about your illegal drug dealing is perhaps more stressful than simply treating him or her as a friend or customer. Potential fields for covert studies in crime and justice might include corruption, ethical behaviour, equal opportunities, illegal violence and brutality, and illicit drug use.

The danger and stress incurred concern being found out before the end of the study and the potential reactions of the deceived. Attempting to access the unregulated and often violent world of organised crime, as reported in the interviews with Winlow and Hornsby in this volume, clearly involve dangers. Similarly, although not a covert study, Sandra Walklate and her researchers were carrying out door-to-door interviews in an estate that turned out to be controlled by an organised criminal gang. One researcher had an encounter with the gang's press officer, while a previous, unrelated, team of researchers had been told to leave the estate a few months earlier.

Some of the respondents for this book raised the fact that the regulation of research by committees and funders could obstruct or prevent good research, and this has recently become if not intolerable, at least obstructive. Other researchers talked about the way things used to be done that could not be carried out now, and the way the law obstructs the collection of certain data. Talking about Winlow's project in 2001, which was eventually published in full (as Hobbs *et al.* 2003), the researchers say that:

> Complying with formal academic ethical codes when we seek to understand the complex interaction of social worlds that do not acknowledge such bourgeois conceits is an unrealistic tactic, in particular for ethnographers ... Indeed, our researcher was recruited precisely because of his familiarity with the night time milieu ... The willingness of our researcher to use [legal] force of varying degrees to escort drunks and recalcitrant customers from the premises, and to defend himself and his colleagues from attack was crucial in gaining the respect of other denizens of the night, and reflexively rendered the sociologist vulnerable to the ravages of the field.
>
> (Winlow *et al.* 2001: 547)

As one of my reflections in an early chapter drawn from my PhD illustrates, the issues of how committees viewed such behaviour were apparent. In this section I was talking about the benefits of feeling fearful, but using it as a way of experiencing solidarity with the police officers I was researching:

> In the cases which are discussed here it will be apparent that there is an absence of applicable 'rules' to deal with the numerous situations arising in the field which research training courses and departmental guidelines cannot anticipate. Indeed, as a newly funded PhD student,

finding myself hiding behind a tree, facing the threat of being shot, in the course of a police firearms containment, I did wonder whether the potential attractions of ethnographic tradition, of 'telling it like it is' were worth the risk.

(Westmarland 2000b: 27)

Conclusion

Despite the glamorous, slightly illicit aspects of their covert study, Winlow *et al*. point out that they were not 'thrill-seeking' and yet there were some particularly disturbing incidents where people were seriously hurt (see 2001: 545 for an example). As I have argued previously, ethnographers in the field of crime and justice may well take part, or be very close to potentially life-threatening situations; examples exist of armed stake-outs, gang warfare, violent close encounters with suspects. In 'real life' research that involves observing groups who use violence or toughness as part of their occupational toolkit, this can be difficult to avoid. As Uildriks and Mastrigt observe, violence is often *required* in dangerous situations (1991: 160).

Similarly, what constitutes violence and danger in a specific situation is difficult to define. In the heat of the moment, it might seem to be just another policing incident, but afterwards, reflecting on the 'what ifs', it may seem to have been more risky. With regard to the police research on gender referred to earlier in the chapter:

> Ethnographers who are taking part in potentially life-threatening situations may have their view of excessive force coloured by the danger they face. Once the incident has been resolved, and the violent parties quelled, researchers may feel relieved that the officers they were accompanying acted in the ways they did. In other words, violence by the police might be regarded as self-defence by the observer who is threatened by an 'outside' agent. It might seem extremely unethical to report the actions of someone you perceive to have saved your skin.
>
> (Westmarland 2001b: 529)

7 Analysing evidence of crime and justice

Introduction

One of the central ideas of this book has been the importance of 'real life' research in crime and justice, the focus being on the various methods that others have used, with their advantages and pitfalls. To this end a number of established researchers were interviewed to elicit their views on their own practice, and to allow them to reflect and hopefully suggest some ways around some of the common things that go wrong when 'real life' intervenes. The interviews have illustrated various methods that are commonly used in criminology, without suggesting, of course, that the full range of possibilities has been explored. They give explanations of the studies the interviewees have undertaken, with excerpts and references to the work they have done.

In addition, in Chapter 6 I tried to bring in the interviewees' experiences, and also to use some relating to my own research, to illustrate the difficulties of conducting research in a political and ethical quagmire. These include some of the field notes from the ethnographies I have conducted, in order to reflect on the potential difficulties researchers in crime and justice might encounter. Again, these are not comprehensive, or even particularly representative of the files of criminology. For that chapter I drew largely on a special issue of the *British Journal of Criminology* from 2001, which contained a number of broad-based subject areas – from nightclub bouncers to historical studies of prostitution – yet pertinent papers discussing the issues of ethics and violence in the research process.

The following section summarises the methods discussed by the interviewees in the book.

What the interviewees said

Below are summaries of what the interviewees said about the choice of particular methods for research.

John Muncie

Throughout the interview, John Muncie talked about the difficulties of doing good, robust research with existing statistics. He argued that the research stands or falls on the way these statistics are gathered and there are several things that make international or comparative analysis problematic. He pointed out that the way prison numbers are counted varies from country to country; and even the classification of what is a child cannot be standardised across the world. Muncie's suggestions included 'triangulation', in other words, trying to find other statistics that would support or contradict a particular position, or to narrow down the analysis to a smaller, more manageable project, such as looking at just one jurisdiction. His main point regarding the choice of methods was that the validity of conclusions of any study based on statistics relies upon how they were collected in the first place.

Ben Bowling

Ben Bowling's conversation described the difficulties and realities of interviews and gaining access to gatekeepers, especially in countries far from home. It also illustrated that an interview is not simply about finding a respondent, sitting them down and asking questions. Ben Bowling had to be persistent, overcoming gatekeepers to gatekeepers – the secretaries, assistants and 'front people' who often guard the gatekeepers in large organisations. As Bowling illustrated, once access is achieved, the interview is often about convincing someone in an organisation such as the police that you should be allowed largely unfettered access to people within that organisation. In other words, the interview is not solely about gleaning information, but is as much about relations of power: how the researcher passes the test and manages the performance.

Laura Piacentini

Laura Piacentini talked about the benefits for her research of being able to live near and among the group she was researching, in Russian prisons. She described the problems of persuading the prison authorities to allow her access to the prisons and the people she wanted to interview. Another difficulty was convincing the people she encountered that she was serious, and not just coming in to expose or hurt them. She did this by credentials such as being able to speak their language, being interested in their poetry and culture; but she describes how she still got into some difficult situations. Power relations in the interviews, the way the authorities 'sent her to Siberia', which was never in the original plan, and the human rights issues for the inmates. Piacentini was also clearly affected by the situation of the people who were in prison and their circumstances and talked about the emotional issues of the 'harmed and hurting' population she was trying to research. The strength, validity and plausibility of this study, and others like it, rely on the way Piacentini writes about these issues, using her in-depth knowledge of the situations she encountered.

Sandra Walklate

Sandra Walklate's study was in some ways a classic 'mixed methods' project in that it involved a combination of data analysis of the existing statistics about the locale to be studied, some observations and time spent living around the area, door-to-door interviews, and focus groups. The study was conducted over some years, so it was also longitudinal, and changes over time could be observed. She argued that these methods allowed a deeper and more contextualised picture to emerge than if the team had simply knocked on doors with tick box questionnaires. The aim of the study was to investigate aspects of the fear of crime debate in two areas; the team was surprised when respondents in one of the areas 'couldn't answer the questions', and the questionnaire was found to be 'just not working'; whereas in the other area the questionnaire was working fine. One of the successes of the study was the way the methods allowed the team to interrogate the local police in the two areas they chose. Throughout the project the findings from one method, such as observations on the estate, talking to local police officers, were used to ask questions using another method, such as during the focus groups. This allowed the team to understand the way the estate was organised, and to go beyond the standard fear of crime debates, such as the BCS.

Lynn Hancock

Lynn Hancock talked about the struggles of conducting a study in the public domain – jury service and its associated processes – which also has its secret back stories that have never been explored. As part of a team she won the money and permission to conduct a large-scale survey, but argued against conducting a 'tick box' survey. She wanted in-depth questions and to find out something of importance about the experience of serving on a jury. To achieve this the team devised a questionnaire that allowed for answers that encouraged in-depth reasoning about the experience of the respondents as jury members, which was used to conduct interviews. This questionnaire had to be prefaced by a very well thought through 'prompt', which explained to the interviewees that certain issues regarding the jury service were off limits as it would be illegal to talk about them, and made it clear how the matter would be controlled by the interviewer if the discussion strayed.

Rob Hornsby

Rob Hornsby, in a similar way to the other interviewees, chose a group of people to research that are difficult to access, and almost impossible to research as a general population. His access to the cigarette bootleggers was through one respondent – 'Jason' – who opened up the world, meanings and methods of the illegal trade with which he had been involved. Perhaps as a quintessentially 'criminological' topic, Hornsby's interview shows the difficulties facing researchers who want to pursue this field. First of all, the authorities claimed that the files they needed were too secret to reveal. Next, 'officials' were unwilling to talk. The problem of 'where to go next' was solved by Hornsby using his existing social networks, and persuading his resulting contact to be interviewed. Interpersonal skills, social background and persistence finally resulted in his being able to obtain the data to write a unique account of the world of the bootleggers. Hornsby claims that what they did was 'not an ethnography', as it did not involve any direct observations or participation in the actions or behaviours they were researching. On the other hand, it did require similar resources in terms of time, money and the potential for failure – coming away with no interviews or data being the risk they faced. In terms of success, however, it would be difficult to imagine how this study could have been conducted in any other way, the dearth of similar studies being evidence of the difficulties they overcame.

Simon Winlow

This final interview described what might be called a 'classic' ethnography. Simon Winlow conducted an ethnography as a 'full participant'. His study involved 'deep' and covert fieldwork in that he became a nightclub bouncer; played the role, almost 'became' the research subject. In other words, the line between identities – as researcher and as bouncer – became blurred. He argues that he could move in and out of this role easily; he had been around the edges of that world before commencing the study, and so to some extent knew how to act the part. The disadvantages of this sort of study, as Winlow explains, is that you spend long hours with the same people when nothing much happens; boredom can set in and you feel you would really rather be somewhere else. For ethnographers to collect even small amounts of data they have to spend inordinate periods of time just observing. Not that he claims this time was wasted, but it is an important consideration. In terms of the successes of the study it is clear that the sort of organised crime activities he witnessed would have been difficult to achieve if he had not been in a covert role. The violent culture of the bouncers might also have been curtailed if they had known Simon Winlow was a researcher.

Summary of the interviews

The methods or approaches this book has described have involved a journey from quantitative studies involving little or no contact with human participants, accessing international databases to explore, for instance, the comparative nature of youth justice, to studies involving fully immersed, participant observation. As various methods have been explained and explored it has been pointed out that although research is a political process, in that the emotions, attachments and passions are real, there is not one method that is agreed to be superior to another in criminology. In fact the whole book has been aimed at analysing the advantages and disadvantages of different methods with the aim of steering the reader to think over the most important point to choosing a research method – the appropriate fit of method with the research questions. In other words, can this method deliver, or hope to possibly deliver an answer to the question or questions the study is hoping to address?

The experienced researchers who generously agreed to be interviewed about their work, methods and experiences provide a real life view of the perils and pains of research, but also the successes. Their insights about the research process are used in the following section to explore how evidence is analysed and theorised. Research can be hard work, but it is the part of academic life that sustains many professionals. 'Doing' the research is the fun part; in the next sections ways of analysing the evidence are discussed, together with theorising and writing up, as the eventual aim is, of course, to let everyone know about the research you've been doing.

Analysing evidence

Researching crime and justice, like other social science research, is about collecting credible evidence, then about using that evidence to support arguments and debates that may or may not have wider implications such as for policy change. In some ways, then, it seems that researching crime and justice, within a criminological framework, is special and different from other branches of social science. As explained throughout this book, although it is often argued that criminology is simply another term for the sociology of crime or deviance, there are some aspects of the studies outlined here that seem to form a collective that can be named as a separate field. Others will disagree, but it is useful to have a classification that covers actions, individuals and processes connected with crime and justice. This collection of fields of interest, while being disputed, comes under the broad identification of criminology.

Despite this seemingly identifiable category of criminology research, it has been argued throughout the preceding chapters that there is no single, right or superior way to conduct research. It is vitally important to consider whether the particular methods chosen will deliver (or are potentially capable of doing so) what the aim of the study is to discover. Two main points of this debate are as follows.

First, in terms of the quantitative/qualitative debate, it is impossible to dictate when one or other is exclusively preferable; it must be asked what the research seeks to discover and then be ascertained whether the chosen methods will deliver. It is also important to consider who the audience of the research will be, so that the information supplied will be useful and valid in terms of the understandings and needs of that group.

Second, research does not happen in a vacuum. There are ethical, political and emotional aspects to consider when planning or carrying out any project – perhaps more so now due to regulatory frameworks which may affect the choice of methods. This has been illustrated by the constant references to researching crime and justice in the 'real world', together with reflections on whether researching crime and justice is special, and if so, in what ways does it differ from other social science research.

Theoretical concerns

In the analysis of material from the interviews for a discussion in this last chapter, it is necessary to say something about theorising criminological research. What follows is not intended to be an exploration of what might be described as the 'canon' or entire range of named criminological theories. Many excellent books exist that do this (see, for example, Walklate 2003; Newburn 2007). A methods handbook would have done this and certainly raised the issue of criminological theory much earlier in the text (for example, Coleman and Moynihan 1996). It is a matter of some debate in research circles as to whether is it better to 'locate' your research in a certain theoretical place or 'tradition', as broadly similar groups of related theories are sometimes described, or to wait until the evidence is collected, and in the process of analysing it allow theory to develop from the material.

As explained in Chapter 2, some researchers begin with a clear theory to 'test', and aim to gather information that supports or disproves that theory. Some of the theories people aim to prove (sometimes called hypotheses, as they are a collection of ideas that are being tested, and are not yet a fully formulated theory) are based on the 'big' theories of criminology that form the canon. In other words, they take a broad criminological theory, some of which are described below, and within that broad theory take an idea of their own, and attempt to test their ideas by collecting data. Their data or evidence is then analysed in the light of not only their own idea, but also the theoretical tradition upon which their ideas were based. This might sound confusing, and people often struggle with, and try to avoid, theorising their research. The following, however, is a simple example of this process.

In my own research on women in policing, the project was based on some 'big' theories of gender and beliefs about the role of men and women in society. This set of theories or traditions was around the social construction of gender, particularly the 'performance' of being male or female. These ideas were initially drawn from a book by Brittan (1989) in which he explored ideas about the way men and women are socialised into their respective roles. He argued that people act out these beliefs throughout their daily lives at work, in the family and with friends. Within the broad categories of 'male' and 'female' there can be multiple gendered identities, such as for men, 'father', 'breadwinner', 'mate', sportsman' and so on. Brittan's claim was that for men it is especially difficult to maintain these multiple roles and to do so involves a sort of competition or 'race' to succeed, as they are constantly comparing themselves with other men, and feeling inadequate.

With regard to this theory of gender and masculinities, the hypotheses for my study of women in the police were concerned with the way women may or may not be appropriating these difficult, competing, 'male' roles. From initial research I thought that perhaps women might be 'acting like men' in the police, or at least trying to compensate, in a largely male-dominated world, by copying so-called 'male' characteristics. Once the project began, however, I realised that the evidence I was gathering would not fit neatly into these original theoretical frameworks. In fact, what I observed were unexpectedly complicated issues around occupational competence being judged by a set of police cultural rules that had gender as one of the categories, but not necessarily of the most importance. Collegial respect and belief in ability and comradeship were acknowledged to be much more about 'body capital' or the ability or willingness to get involved in physically demanding or threatening situations. Although women would be dismissed as 'useless' if they were unwilling to fight or stand up to people in physical situations, the same would apply to men.

At the end of the study, in the writing up and analysis stages, it was necessary to change my main approach from being about the 'race' that men have to run to achieve 'masculinity' to the ways in which 'the body', and how it is presented, used and maintained, is an important determinant of policing competence. In effect, the study had developed in a way that needed a whole new framework of theories to explain the evidence. Some of the findings would not explain or support the original hypothesis, and so a new set of ideas had to be used to allow the study to make sense, say something about the situation and explain some of the ways policing and gender work within their occupational cultural framework (see Westmarland 2001a, Chapter 1 for a fuller discussion).

It is clear that theory is an important part of the way evidence is analysed and collected, which adds to the significance of the choice of methods. As important as the choosing of a method that is capable of delivering answers to the research questions is the underlying theory or assumptions about the methods the study is going to use. The next section provides a potted history of some of the traditions of criminology which have been used to research crime and justice from its inception. This is followed by some further examples linked to the interviews in this book that reveal insights into theorising in research.

A short guide to criminological theories

Criminology's historical traditions begin with what is often called the classical school of criminology. This was the established theory of the eighteenth century, which tried to explain why people commit crime and what to do to prevent this happening.

Classicists argue that:

- People commit crime because they are rational actors, and given the means and opportunity, people will knowingly and purposefully break the law.
- In order to prevent crime, people must know that if they are caught they will face severe, sure and swift punishment.
- Such punishment must be quickly administered, so that the wrongdoer (and importantly anyone else thinking about committing a crime) realises the link between the crime and the pain of punishment. It should be certain, sure and the same for everyone.

This was the general approach – what we might call the social policy of the time – which went largely unchallenged until the mid-nineteenth century, when the rise of 'science' and attempts to use it to understand human behaviour, led to a collection of theories grouped under the label of 'positivism'.

Positivists argue that:

- People commit crime due to faulty reasoning. They believe that it is better to commit crime than to work for a living, for example.
- To prevent crime people need to be re-educated – shown the error of their ways.
- People can be 'reformed' and changed into useful and productive members of society.
- Punishment should be adjusted to fit the criminal, in other words depending on what reformation requires.

These two competing approaches did not cancel each other out, nor did one replace the other. Classical (sometimes termed 'neo-classical' to differentiate a modern, supposedly less harsh version of the approach) and positivist ideas are still in evidence today. For instance, the modern 'welfarist' approach of the 1960s was firmly based in the positivist school of thought, whereas the 'prison works', 'tough on crime' approach of the 1990s and right of centre political parties shows firm anchors in classicist crime polices.

Positivism is split into two main sets of theories: individual or biological, and sociological. The differences between the two involve whether the individual, or society, is the site of concern.

- **Biological positivism** is based on the idea that an individual's physical or psychological make-up leads them to be predisposed to becoming 'criminal'.
- **Sociological positivism** argues that it is society's influences – the family, the media, schools and peer groups – that decide whether an individual will follow a life of crime or be an upstanding member of the community.

So the two broad schools of thought – classicism and positivism – each rest upon a crucial premise around the motivation and treatment of people who commit crime. For classicists the emphasis is on free will: people choose the 'pleasure' of crime and its rewards, but can be deterred by the threat of the 'pain' of punishment. For positivists there are certain aspects of crime that are not totally within the control of the individual; in the case of sociological positivists, although society does not cause people to commit crime, it serves a social function – namely that a society without crime would stagnate, be totalitarian and lack order.

In the 1950s and 1960s, a range of theorists came along who challenged both of these approaches. The 'new criminologists' became known as the critical or radical schools of criminology. Aside from their political approaches – largely class-based Marxist – these criminologists were given to approaching crime as 'realists', in that they believed that crime is a 'real' problem' that affects 'real' people's lives. Later, one group that emerged from the general approach, left realists, argued that it is the poor who are in prison partly because that is the group who are targeted by law enforcers. They also said that it is likely to be the poor who suffer from crimes such as burglary and violence in the home, as they are less able to protect their property and escape violent situations.

Another group, the right realists, while believing that crime is a 'real' problem, argue that it is the problems of young men, perhaps third or fourth generation of a family who have never worked, living on estates where few men are available as role models, that lead to a cycle of lawbreaking and an endemic disregard for the rule of law.

For the critical or radical criminologists not only do the poor suffer more crime as victims, they are also 'labelled' as criminal. Unlike the middle and upper classes, they are subject to a higher level of monitoring and surveillance, and some of their activities may be seen as 'criminal' when similar actions in other classes may be less visible and regarded as civil matters. One example the theorists use is to compare benefit fraud with tax evasion. Despite the former being a much lower national total loss to the exchequer, it is seen as cheating society, and campaigns are mounted to encourage anonymous reporting; but tax fraud, financially at least ten times the value in terms of loss of revenue, is viewed as 'OK if you can get away with it'.

These broad explanations of categories of criminological theories may help to clarify the earlier discussions about choosing research methods. It is possible to see, from reading the interviews, that methods are not decided on in a vacuum. Methodological approaches are chosen not only as to their suitability in practical terms – those 'how many' versus 'why' issues discussed at length in Chapters 2 and 3 – but also as to their theoretical underpinnings. It will have been clear that the researchers interviewed did not simply approach their topics dispassionately, without any pre-existing beliefs. The research that is explored throughout this book has underlying beliefs and theories about the way the world is organised, and criminology, just like any other academic discipline, has a set of basic theories or paradigms that guide and organise the thoughts and research that are carried out.

As with other issues in this volume, there are, of course, textbooks fully devoted to the discussion and exploration of the many nuances of the innumerable theories that are available in the criminologist's toolkit. This chapter aims to provide just a short guide to these theories, using examples from the interviews earlier in the book to illustrate where theories can support and facilitate research. These theories may become clearer in the following analysis of the main themes of the interviews, intended to be an example of the way interviews can be analysed and theorised.

The themes that have arisen from the interviews

In this section some of the responses to the problems and pitfalls of researching 'real' criminology are explored. These emerged in response to questions posed to the interviewees, although as these were all experienced researchers themselves, the prompts and suggestions of the interview schedule tended to result in conversations rather than question-and-answer sessions. In addition the respondents had seen the list of suggested areas of discussion in advance and so potentially had had a chance to prepare, coming up with responses and areas of interest. Following the interview process the data files were transcribed and analysis began, exploring the issues that had been discussed, and this led to the emergence of a number of themes. In the analysis process, what appeared to be the most pertinent aspects of the discussions, in terms of the book's aims, were listed and then arranged into themes. Following this, examples from each of the interviews were grouped together as evidence of these themes.

The three most useful groups of ideas or 'themes' from the interviews emerged as:

- Power relations in research situations, including access to data, people, and the power to define the 'problem' and what counts as data.

- Potential harm and violence, particularly around the research process – physical dangers, but also the issue of disclosures, and the way researchers might deal with information.
- Ethics and what happens to data, research and the politics of the research process.

Power relations and access

To take the first theme, power relations and access, each of the respondents mentioned some aspect of power in the research process.

In the first interview John Muncie explained his difficulties in ascertaining whether the UK is indeed the most punitive country in Europe, or the world, in terms of juvenile justice. The power to define, and to gain access to data on, the imprisonment of children, while appearing initially straightforward, is in fact closely bound to the political process of data collection in individual countries. This affects the ability to investigate or verify a country's definition of 'prison', for example, and individual countries, let alone researchers, lack the power to insist on each country overcoming reporting differences, where the notion of a 'child' varies between 8 years of age in some countries to 18 in others.

In terms of physical access, Ben Bowling talked about having to wait around for hours in overpowering heat, arriving for interviews that were cancelled, for several days in succession. When he finally achieved access to the officer he wanted to talk to, he was then denied access to information, in that the officer claimed not to be able to answer his questions. The micro dynamics of power in the interview itself were evident, where the Deputy Commissioner watched the television over Bowling's shoulder throughout the interview.

In another example of power relations in the research process, Laura Piacentini talks about being kept waiting in a prison library for six weeks while her access was secured. She recounts being physically controlled in that she was literally sent to Siberia. The power to keep researchers 'in their place' is an issue that is often raised by social scientists, but for criminologists there are some special aspects worth noting. Very often the places criminologists want to investigate are 'closed' in more senses than simply as a result of physical barriers. It can seem that the officials who control spaces such as prisons, police forces, courts and so on have myriad means of justifying their inability to allow access. Piacentini explains how she had to work in a second language, to 'prove' that she was really interested in their culture by discussing poetry, and endure attempts to control what she wrote and saw.

Access to groups was also discussed by Sandra Walklate in her description of how it was discovered that one of the estates they were researching was controlled by an organised local gang. They only realised the significance of this fact during the course of interviews and focus groups, and through a lucky encounter between one of the researchers and the gang's 'press officer'. The power relations of research are illustrated here because despite the gang's seemingly well-organised structure (as evidenced by their having roles such as 'press officer') their organisation is discreet if not secret, and yet, on the estate, everyone (including the children interviewed) 'knows'.

Similarly, the power to access people and populations was raised by Lynn Hancock in her exploration of jury service. It might be supposed that a project approved and funded by the government through the Home Office, hence demonstrating their interest in the findings, would have few difficulties of power to access the groups and data they needed. This is, however, a good illustration of the way power works in the 'real' world of researching crime and justice. A naive researcher might think that a government-funded study would allow access to the necessary information. The team needed the names and addresses of jury members to be interviewed, to be able to approach them directly, and that the sample would be representative in numbers by age, ethnic group, class, gender and so on, as well as the details of those called who asked to be excused, and why they were able to waive or delay their jury service duty.

In fact, Hancock and her team had to present themselves at court on Monday mornings as each new cohort of jurors arrived, and seek permission from court officials to talk to the new jurors, asking them to take part in the research. In a similar way, Rob Hornsby explains that in his study with Dick Hobbs, which was again government-funded (via the European Union), they struggled to achieve access to official files of customs cases, first of all due to 'security' issues, and later due to infighting and power struggles within the criminal justice agencies. At the other end of the spectrum Simon Winlow's experiences of undercover 'covert' ethnography illustrate that access to criminal underworlds relies on taking part. To protect his cover, he had to appear to at least condone the activities of his supposed colleagues. As he said, suspicions would have been aroused if, for example, he never took the chance to buy stolen goods when they were offered.

To summarise, the analysis of the interview data, in terms of the theme of power relations and access, shows that for some researchers it is about physical access – being granted permission to talk to certain officers, or denied it by being sent to prisons far from the centre of the 'action' – for others, it is overcoming government or 'official' barriers; and for others it is about personal decisions and relationships. The conversations with the researchers show that their strategies for overcoming the problems often involve working with and around the difficulties. A useful starting point can be to accept that power relations exist, and that access will not be straightforward, even where 'official' permission exists. Being flexible and having an awareness of what is happening, together with learning and adjusting as things unfold, were all commonly thought to be important in the reflections of these experienced researchers.

Potential harm and violence

The second theme, of potential harm and violence, particularly around the issue of disclosure, is by no means exclusive to researchers in the field of crime and justice. It is an issue especially pertinent to research involving sensitive topics such as sexualities, or financial matters, in that it is concerned with personal, private, potentially embarrassing or commercially sensitive information. For criminologists the main areas of potential disclosure concern the lawbreaking or violations of two groups: the 'criminals', and those supposedly controlling, trying or punishing them. In other words, this means disclosures about criminal activities on either side of the 'blue line' but not necessarily the law. The field of crime and justice is concerned with 'offences', 'harms', violations of codes and official directives (such as, for instance, the just and fair treatment of prisoners). As explained in Chapter 1, the definition of crime and justice can be messy and complicated.

In her analysis of Russian prison life Laura Piacentini talks about the revelation on arriving at one of her research sites that the inmates had not been out in the fresh air for two weeks and that a disturbance was anticipated. Reacting to this sort of information from a researcher's point of view is difficult on several levels. A researcher has to consider the ethics of disclosing this sort of situation to the world. As a 'trusted confidant' of the officer giving the information the relationship is one of trust and perhaps friendship. On a personal level the researcher will be aware of the violations of legal human rights but also of humanitarian feelings and collusion.

Similarly, Lynn Hancock talks of the difficulties of conducting a research project under the shadow of the criminal law preventing disclosure of the decisions made in the jury room. Their efforts to prevent their respondents placing themselves in a position of breaking the law were complex and time-consuming. The rules the researchers had to adhere to also potentially stifled some very useful and interesting data being collected.

Just as Rob Hornsby had to spend long periods drinking and socialising to obtain the trust of his gatekeeper and informant. Simon Winlow had to occasionally be seen to take part in criminal activities, which may have had harmful aspects, not least to the researcher if his real identity had been revealed. To avoid suspicion Winlow explains that he had to occasionally take stolen goods when they were offered for sale, otherwise he would not have fitted into the group where such behaviour was normal and expected.

Ethics and politics

The interviewees in this book would all be classed as experienced researchers in their field, having conducted ground-breaking studies. To break new ground often involves risks and experimenting with ideas and methods. The academics interviewed here have reflected on their methods in terms of ethics, because of what some have described as a new climate of ethics. In other words, academic departments in universities have become more aware of the ethical issues surrounding research and the potential harm research may cause; also, in a more bureaucratic sense, they have formed committees and developed procedures that must be followed before any project can be approved or in some cases funded.

This is a relatively new phenomenon, and some of the interviewees reflected on how it used to be. Sandra Walklate describes how they conducted focus groups with older school children for her project, gleaning useful information from the teenagers, and she remarks that it would be impossible to do similar research now. Similarly, Simon Winlow and Rob Hornsby both admit that the ethical control over researchers now prevents certain data being collected and some studies from being conducted due to perhaps over-zealous committee members who may have little or no understanding of the processes of real crime and justice research. One of the interviewees talked about a professor of English language being unqualified to judge the safety or otherwise of meetings with criminal underworld participants.

In her discussion of human rights Laura Piacentini is concerned by ethics and in particular the way she might report the situation of the hurting and vulnerable groups she researches. Whether or not to continue with certain lines of enquiry, how interviews are conducted and how to deal with the knowledge she gains from insider status are all obviously troubling to her. Researching crime and justice will often involve encountering powerful groups – those with the power, for example, to define what is a crime, to enforce the law (or not), to impose or bend certain rules, and to regulate – and also those with little or no power, the regulated, society's non-conformist so-called 'deviant' groups, who can be stigmatised, labelled and controlled. The power differential between these two groups may be blurred but it will always be present in crime and justice research. The ethics of how to deal with this differential – how to report abuses of power or deviance, whether from the powerful or so-called powerless – is one of the unique aspects of crime and justice research. In other words, criminological research has particular ethical and power-laden aspects that make it especially interesting and sometimes problematic, but definitely worth pursuing.

The writing up process

Writing up is naturally one of the last aspects of the research process. As emphasised throughout this volume, it is necessary to keep in mind what you aim to find out when choosing methods. It is also useful to know the format of what you intend to eventually write (a report, a book, a PhD), and your intended audience will perhaps play a part in deciding how the research is carried out, which methods to use. Researchers and academics often find it difficult, however, once the data has been collected, all the interviews are transcribed, and the field notes colour-coded, knowing where to start. Organising the data into sensible and coherent chapters of a book or sections for a report can be troubling and cause sleepless nights. Although there may have been a plan at the beginning of what the study aimed to discover, and which appropriate methods to use, sometimes (in fact, often) the research throws up unexpected findings, or as Sandra Walklate suggests in her discussion, no findings of a particular type that were expected.

Analysing data for the writing up process

There are many ways data can be analysed, from earlier discussions (see Chapter 3) it is clear that, for instance, statistical data have certain accepted methods. Even studies that rely on simple percentages have basic and obvious rules. In his international comparisons, John Muncie describes how he takes statistics from various sources to attempt to find 'ball park' numbers initially. He then goes on to compare different countries' methods of statistical collection in order to interrogate their validity. Both Sandra Walklate and Lynn Hancock describe their studies as having certain similarities to the British Crime Survey, which uses published statistical methods to arrive at results. In some cases this involves numbers or percentages of respondents who agree or disagree with certain statements or arguments. In Hancock's study of juries it resulted in significant numbers of people feeling more 'citizen-like' as a result of their participation.

It might seem fairly obvious that a statistical survey would be analysed in terms of the numbers of responses to various questions that are asked, but studies that rely on discussions or observations may appear to be more difficult to analyse. Typical quandaries that arise might include which quotes to use, and how to represent what your respondents have said faithfully. Constructing a narrative or 'story' around your findings can be a difficult and time-consuming aspect of research. Experienced researchers have a number of ways they overcome these difficulties.

1   Look back at the original question or aims of the study and select data that seem to have some bearing on these questions (there will often be quite a lot that will not).
2   Attempt to develop a series of themes that emerge from the data that answers the questions the study aimed to answer.
3   Make a list of all the obvious themes, but also those data that do not seem to fit into any of those that answer the question (because this type of data may be very important if the study turns up 'unexpected' findings).
4   Try to theorise the meaning of the data within the themes. For example, one of the themes of the data collected for the interviews for this book

was around the ethics of research. There was a question about ethics in the interview schedule. One of the unexpected themes to arise was the way the 'rise' of the regulation of ethics in modern university systems has changed. This could be theorised in various ways:

(a) University ethics committees have become part of a university managerialist project that is growing exponentially and needs to be controlled.
(b) Researchers see university ethics committees as unnecessary controls on their professional judgement and expertise.
(c) Ethics within academic research has, quite rightly, been raised up the agenda by conscientious researchers who see the field they are working within as being potentially harmful.

The process of theorising is simply about competing ideas of how the world might be viewed. Each of these three positions could be further theorised using paradigms or approaches such as Marxism, feminist theory, managerialist approaches to organisation and so on. Each could form the basis of a research project to investigate the way ethics and committees and regulation within universities works and is viewed by those within the system. As you will see, it is hoped, from this chapter, the process of analysis, deciding on themes, answering questions, fulfilling aims and so on, can be systematically developed into theorising and 'answering' questions. Also, as displayed, this process throws up a number of new questions.

Conclusion

In summary this book has been about the way 'real' research happens. The pitfalls and problems are fairly obvious – research in crime and justice is about 'real' people and issues, situated in a politically controversial and fast-moving field. Unlike some other types of social research there are certain sensitivities around the nature of the topic of enquiry. Some of these topics cannot be 'told' due to their negative association with lawbreaking, and this can place researchers in a difficult position. In common with most other research, however, researchers are required to be aware of these sensitivities and difficulties. Overall the book has tried to convey the message that in 'real life' research things may go wrong, but they do so for everyone. Researchers deal with this by working out a way around the problem or regarding it as a 'finding'.

Another key message of this book is that there are no right or wrong methods, just different ones that suit various types of criminological questions. Whether or not these methods are any different from those used by other social scientists is a moot point, but this does not change the issue that the most important consideration when choosing research methods is to consider if they are appropriate for the question in hand. Is it possible, if everything goes right (and it rarely does), that these methods can deliver the answer (or an answer) to the question posed? If the answer is definitely 'yes!', you may have to think again because, as the examples throughout the book have shown, certainty is in short supply in research. If the answer is 'maybe, depending upon all the pieces of the jigsaw falling into place', then you are probably going along the right lines. Good luck . . .

References

Adler, P. (1985) *Wheeling and Dealing: An Ethnography of an Upper Level Drug Dealing and Smuggling Community*. New York: Columbia University Press.
Audit Commission (1996) *Streetwise: Effective Police Patrol*. London: HMSO.
Becker, H. (1963) *Outsiders: Studies in the Sociology of Deviance*. New York: Free Press.
Bolling, K., Grant, C. and Donovan, J. L. (2009) *British Crime Survey (England and Wales) Technical Report Volume I*. London: Home Office.
Bowling, B. (2009) 'Transnational policing: the globalisation thesis, a typology and a research agenda', *Policing*, 3(2): 149–60.
Bowling, B. (2010) *Policing the Caribbean: Transnational Security Cooperation in Practice*. Oxford: Oxford University Press.
Brace, N., Kemp, R. and Snelgar, R. (2009) *SPSS for Psychologists*, 4th edn. Basingstoke: Palgrave Macmillan.
Brittan, A. (1989) *Masculinity and Power*. Oxford: Basil Blackwell.
Brookman, F. and Maguire, M. (2004) 'Reducing homicide: a review of the possibilities', *Crime, Law and Social Change*, 42: 325–403.
Brookman, F., Maguire, M., Pierpoint, H. and Bennett, T. (eds) (2010) *Handbook on Crime*. Cullompton: Willan Publishing.
Brown, J. (1996) 'Police research: some critical issues', in F. Leishman, B. Loveday, and S. P. Savage (eds) *Core Issues in Policing*. London: Longman.
Bryman, A. (1988) *Quantity and Quality in Social Research*. London: Unwin Hyman.
Bulmer, M. (1982) *Social Research Ethics: An Examination of the Merits of Covert Participant Observation*. New York: Holmes and Meier.
Carter, K. and Delamont, S. (1996) *Qualitative Research: The Emotional Dimension*. Aldershot: Avebury.
Chan, J. (1996) 'Changing police culture', *British Journal of Criminology*, 36(1): 109–34.
Clarke, J., Newman, J., Smith, J., Vidler, E. and Westmarland, L. (2007) *Creating Citizen-Consumers: Changing Publics and Changing Public Services*. London: Sage.
Cohen, S. and Taylor, L. (1972) *Psychological Survival*. Harmondsworth: Penguin.
Coleman, C. and Moynihan, J. (1996) *Understanding Crime Data: Haunted by the Dark Figure*. Buckingham: Open University Press.
Cresswell, J. W. (2010) *How Sage has Shaped Research Methods: A 40 Year History*. London: Sage.
Douglas, J. D. (1972) *Investigative Social Research*. Beverly Hills, CA: Sage.

Drake, D., Muncie, J. and Westmarland, L. (2010) 'Interrogating criminal justice', in D. Drake, J. Muncie and L. Westmarland (eds) *Criminal Justice: Local and Global*. Cullompton: Willan Publishing in association with the Open University.

Economic and Social Research Council (ESRC) *Research Ethics Framework (REF)*. Online at: www.esrcsocietytoday.ac.uk.

Evans, K., Fraser, P. and Walklate, S. (1996) 'Whom can you trust? The politics of "grassing" on an inner city housing estate', *Sociological Review*, 44(3): 361–80.

Ferrell, J. and Hamm, M. S. (eds) (1998) *Ethnography at the Edge: Crime, Deviance and Field Research*. Boston, MA: Northeastern University Press.

Finch, J. (1984) '"It's great to have someone to talk to": the ethics and politics of interviewing women', in C. Bell and H. Roberts (eds) *Social Researching: Politics, Problems, Practice*. London: Routledge and Kegan Paul.

Fincham, B., Scourfield, J. and Langer, S. (2007) *The Emotional and Analytic Impact of Working with Disturbing Secondary Data*, NCRM Working Paper Series 8/07. ESRC National Centre for Research Methods.

Findlay, M. (2001) 'Juror comprehension and complexity: strategies to enhance understanding', *British Journal of Criminology*, 41(1): 56–76.

Finlay, W. (1991) 'Review of *Manufacturing Knowledge*', *Science*, 254: 1820–1.

Flatley, J., Kershaw, C., Smith, K., Chaplin, R. and Moon, D. (2010) *Crime in England and Wales 2009/10: Findings from the British Crime Survey and Police Recorded Crime*, Home Office Statistical Bulletin. London: Home Office.

Fountain, J. (1996) 'Dealing with data', in D. Hobbs and T. May (eds) *Interpreting the Field: Accounts of Ethnography*. Oxford: Clarendon Press.

Garland, D. (1988) 'British criminology before 1935', *British Journal of Criminology, Delinquency and Deviant Social Behaviour*, 28(2): 1–17.

Geberth, V. J. (1996) *Practical Homicide Investigation: Tactics, Procedures and Forensic Techniques*, 3rd edn. New York: CRC Press.

Genn, H. (1988) 'Multiple victimisation', in M. Maguire and J. Pointing (eds) *Crime Victims: A New Deal?* Milton Keynes: Open University Press.

Gill, M. (2000) *Commercial Robbery: Offenders' Perspectives on Security and Crime Prevention*. London: Blackstone Press.

Goffman, E. (1969) *The Presentation of Self in Everyday Life*. Harmondsworth: Penguin.

Gomm, R., Hammersley, M. and Foster, P. (2000) 'Case study and generalisation', in R. Gomm, M. Hammersley and P. Foster (eds) *Case Study Method: Key Issues, Key Texts*. London: Sage.

Haig, B. D. (1997) 'Feminist research methodology', in J. P. Keeves (ed.) *Educational Research, Methodology and Measurement: An International Handbook*, 2nd edn. Oxford: Elsevier.

Hammersley, M. (ed.) (1993) *Social Research: Philosophy, Politics and Practice*. London: Sage.

Hobbs, D. (1988) *Doing the Business*. Oxford: Oxford University Press.

Hobbs, D. (1995) *Bad Business*. Oxford: Oxford University Press.

Hobbs, D. and Westmarland, L. (2006) *Women on the Door: Female Bouncers in the New Night-time Economy*, Full Research Report, ESRC Reference Number RES-000-23-0384. Online at: www.esrcsocietytoday.ac.uk.

Hobbs, D., Westmarland, L. and O'Brien, K. (2007) 'Connecting the gendered door: women, violence and doorwork', *British Journal of Sociology*, 58(1): 21–38.

Hobbs, D., Hadfield, P., Lister, S. and Winlow, S. (2003) *Bouncers: Violence and Governance in the Night-time Economy*. Oxford: Oxford University Press.

Hochschild, A. (1983) *The Managed Heart: Commercialization of Human Feeling*. Berkeley, CA: University of California Press.

Holdaway, S. (1983) *Inside the British Police*. Blackwell: Oxford.

Homan, R. (1980) 'The ethics of covert methods', *British Journal of Sociology*, 31(1): 46–59.

Home Office (1996) *Criminal Statistics: England and Wales 1995*. London: The Stationery Office.

Hornsby, R. and Hobbs, D. (2007) 'A zone of ambiguity: the political economy of cigarette bootlegging', *British Journal of Criminology*, 47(4): 551–71.

Hubbard, G., Backett-Milburn, K. and Kemmer, D. (2001) 'Working with emotion: issues for the researcher in fieldwork and teamwork', *International Journal of Social Research Methodology*, 4(2): 119–37.

Hughes, G. (2000) 'Understanding the politics of criminological research', in V. Jupp, P. Davies and P. Francis (eds) *Doing Criminological Research*. London: Sage.

Hunt, D. (1990), 'Drugs and consensual crimes: drug dealing and prostitution', *Crime and Justice*, 13 (special edition: Drugs and Crime): 159–202.

Innes, M. (2003) *Investigating Murder: Detective Work and the Police Response to Criminal Homicide*. Oxford: Oxford University Press.

Israel, M. and Hay, I. (2006) *Research Ethics for Social Scientists: Between Ethical Conduct and Regulatory Compliance*. London: Sage.

Jupp, V. (2006) 'Victim surveys', in E. McLaughlin and J. Muncie (eds) *The Sage Dictionary of Criminology*, 2nd edn. London: Sage.

Jupp, V., Davies, P. and Francis, P. (eds) *Doing Criminological Research*. London: Sage.

Kimmel, A. (1988) *Ethics and Values in Applied Social Research*. London: Sage.

King, R. D. (2000) 'Doing research in prisons', in R. D. King and E. Wincup (eds) *Doing Research on Crime and Justice*. Oxford: Oxford University Press.

Klockars, C. B., Kutnjak Ivkovic, S. and Haberfield, M. R. (eds) (2003) *The Contours of Police Integrity*. London: Sage.

Lewis, S., Maguire, M., Raynor, P., Vanstone, M. and Vennard, J. (2007) 'What works in resettlement? Findings from seven Pathfinders for short-term prisoners in England and Wales', *Criminology and Criminal Justice*, February, 7: 33–53.

Liebling, A. and Stanko, B. (2001) 'Allegiance and ambivalence: some dilemmas in researching disorder and violence', *British Journal of Criminology*, 41(2): 421–30.

Loftus, B. (2008) 'Dominant culture interrupted: recognition, resentment and the politics of change in an English police force', *British Journal of Criminology*, 48(6): 756–77.

Lois, J. (2003) *Heroic Efforts: The Emotional Culture of Search and Rescue Volunteers*. New York: New York University Press.

Maguire, M. (1994) 'Crime statistics, patterns and trends: changing perceptions and their implications', in M. Maguire, R. Morgan and R. Reiner (eds) *The Oxford Handbook of Criminology*. Oxford: Clarendon Press.

Maher, L. (1997) *Sexed Work: Gender Race and Resistance in a Brooklyn Drug Market*. Oxford: Clarendon Press.

Matthews, R., Hancock, L. and Briggs, D. (2004) *Jurors' Perceptions, Understanding, Confidence and Satisfaction in the Jury System: A Study in Six Courts*, Home Office Online Report 05/04. London: Home Office.

McVicar, J. (1974) *McVicar by Himself*. London: Arrow.
Mertens, D. M. and Ginsberg, P. E. (2009) *The Handbook of Social Research Ethics*. Los Angeles: Sage.
Ministry of Justice (2010) *Reoffending of Juveniles: Results from the 2008 Cohort*. Online at: www.justice.gov.uk/publications/docs/reoffending-juveniles-2008-cohort.pdf.
Moran-Ellis, J. (1997) 'Close to home: the experience of researching child sexual abuse', in M. Hester, L. Kelly and J. Radford (eds) *Women, Violence and Male Power: Feminist Activism, Research and Practice*. Buckingham: Open University Press.
Muncie, J. (1996) 'The construction and deconstruction of crime', in J. Muncie and E. McLaughlin (eds) *The Problem of Crime*. London: Sage/Open University.
Muncie, J. (1999) *Youth and Crime: A Critical Introduction*. London: Sage.
Muncie, J. (2004) *Youth and Crime*, 2nd edn. London: Sage.
Muncie, J. (2005) 'The globalisation of crime control – the case of youth and juvenile justice: neo-liberalism, policy convergence and international conventions', *Theoretical Criminology*, 9(1): 35–64.
Muncie, J. and Goldson, B. (2006) 'States of transition: convergence and diversity in international youth justice', in J. Muncie and B. Goldson (eds) *Comparative Youth Justice*. London: Sage.
Muncie, J., Talbot, D. and Walters, R. (2010) 'Interrogating crime', in J. Muncie, D. Talbot and R. Walters (eds) *Crime: Local and Global*. Cullompton: Willan Publishing in association with the Open University.
Myhill, A. and Allen, J. (2002) *Rape and Sexual Assault of Women: Findings from the British Crime Survey*. Home Office Research Findings, 159. London: Home Office.
Newburn, T. (2007) *Criminology*. Cullompton: Willan Publishing.
Newiss, G. (1999) *Missing Presumed . . .? The Police Response to Missing Persons*, Police Research Series Paper 114. London: Home Office.
O'Brien, K., Hobbs, D. and Westmarland, L. (2007) 'Negotiating violence and gender: security and the night time economy in the UK', in S. Body-Gendrot and P. Spierenburg (eds) *Cultures of Violence in Europe: Historical and Contemporary Perspectives*. New York: Springer.
Parker, H. J. (1974) *View from the Boys: A Sociology of Down-town Adolescents*. Newton Abbot: David and Charles.
Pawson, R. (2006) *Evidence-based Policy: A Realist Perspective*. London: Sage.
Pawson, R. and Tilley, N. (1997) *Realistic Evaluation*. London: Sage.
Piacentini, L. (2004) *Surviving Russian Prisons: Punishment, Economy and Politics in Transition*. Cullompton: Willan Publishing.
Piacentini, L., Pallot, J. and Moran, D. (2009) 'Welcome to *Malaya Rodina* ('Little Homeland'): gender and the penal order in a Russian penal colony', *Social and Legal Studies*, 18(4): 523–42.
Powell, C. (1996) 'Whose voice? Whose feelings? Emotions; the theory and practice of feminist methodology', in K. Carter and S. Delamont (eds) *Qualitative Research: The Emotional Dimension*. Aldershot: Avebury.
Punch, K. F. (2005) *Introduction to Social Research: Quantitative and Qualitative Approaches*. London: Sage.
Reiner, R. (1992) 'Police research in the United Kingdom: a critical review', in N. Morris and M. Tonry (eds) *Modern Policing, Crime and Justice*. Chicago: Chicago University Press.

Reiner, R. (2000) 'Police research', in R. D. King and E. Wincup (eds) *Doing Research on Crime and Justice*. Oxford: Oxford University Press.

Ritchie, J. and Spencer, L. (1994) 'Qualitative data analysis for applied policy research', in A. Bryman and R. G. Burgess (eds) *Analysing Qualitative Data*. London: Routledge.

Roseneil, S. (1996) 'Greenham revisited: researching myself and my sisters', in D. Hobbs and T. May (eds) *Interpreting the Field: Accounts of Ethnography*. Oxford: Clarendon Press.

Rowe, M. (2007) 'Tripping over molehills: ethics and the ethnography of police work', *International Journal of Social Research Methodology*, 10(1): 37–48.

Saward, J. (with W. Green) (1995) *Rape: My Story*. London: Pan.

Schwartzman, H. B. (1993) *Ethnography in Organisations, Qualitative Research Methods*, Vol. 27. London: Sage.

Sharpe, J. A. (1988) 'The history of crime in England 1300–1914', *British Journal of Criminology, Delinquency and Deviant Social Behaviour*, 28(2): 124–37.

Skolnick, J. H. (1975) *Justice Without Trial: Law Enforcement in Democratic Society*. New York: John Wiley.

Smith, D. J. and Gray, J. (1983) *The Police and the People in London: Vol. IV, The Police in Action*. London: Policy Studies Institute.

Stanko, E. A. (1998) 'Making the invisible visible in criminology: a personal journey', in S. Holdaway and P. Rock (eds) *Thinking about Criminology*. London: UCL.

Stanley, L. and Wise, S. (1993) *Breaking Out Again*. London: Routledge.

Temkin, J. (1997) '*Plus ca change*: reporting rape in the 1990s', *British Journal of Criminology*, 37: 507–28.

Temkin, J. (1999) 'Reporting rape in London: a qualitative study', *Howard Journal*, 37(4): 507–28.

Tunnell, K. D. (1998) 'Honesty, secrecy and deception in the sociology of crime: confessions and reflections from the backstage', in J. Ferrell and M. S. Hamm (eds) *Ethnography at the Edge: Crime, Deviance and Field Research*. Boston, MA: Northeastern University Press.

Tyler, T. R. (2005) 'Policing in black and white: ethnic group differences in trust and confidence in the police', *Police Quarterly*, 8: 322–42.

Uildriks, N. and van Mastrigt, H (1991) *Policing Police Violence*. Boston, MA: Kluwer Law.

Walklate, S. (1998) *Understanding Criminology: Current Theoretical Debates*. Buckingham: Open University Press.

Walklate, S. (2000) 'Researching victims', in R. D. King and E. Wincup (eds) *Doing Research on Crime and Justice*. Oxford: Oxford University Press.

Walklate, S. (2003) *Understanding Criminology: Current Theoretical Debates*, 2nd edn. Buckingham: Open University Press.

Walklate, S. and Mythen, G. (2008) 'How scared are we?', *British Journal of Criminology*, 48(2): 209–25.

Walters, R. (2007) 'Critical criminology and the intensification of the authoritarian state', in A. Barton, K. Corteen, D. Scott and D. Whyte (eds) *Expanding the Criminological Imagination*. Cullompton: Willan Publishing.

Westmarland, L. (1994) 'An investigation into possible barriers to equal opportunities for women in Durham Constabulary', unpublished report, University of Durham, Department of Sociology and Social Policy.

Westmarland, L. (1995) 'Domination and deprivation: policing the city', paper presented to the British Society of Criminology Annual Conference, Leicester.

Westmarland, L (2000a) 'Taking the flak: operational policing, fear and violence', in G. Lee-Treweek and S. Linkogle (eds) *Danger in the Field: Risk and Ethics in Social Research*. London: Routledge.

Westmarland, L. (2000b) 'Telling the truth the whole truth and nothing but the truth? Ethics and the enforcement of law', *Journal of Ethical Sciences and Services*, 2(3): 193–202.

Westmarland, L. (2001a) *Gender and Policing: Sex, Power and Police Culture*. Cullompton: Willan Publishing.

Westmarland, L. (2001b) 'Blowing the whistle on police violence: gender, ethnography and ethics', *British Journal of Criminology*, 41(2): 523–35.

Westmarland, L. (2002) 'Challenges of policing London: a conversation with the metropolitan police commissioner, Sir John Stevens', *Police Practice and Research*, 3(3): 247–60.

Westmarland, L. (2003) 'Policing integrity: Britain's thin blue line', in C. B. Klockars, S. Kutnjak Ivkovic and M. R. Haberfield (eds) *The Contours of Police Integrity*. London: Sage.

Westmarland, L. (2005) 'Police ethics and integrity: breaking the blue code of silence', *Policing and Society*, 15(2): 145–65.

Westmarland, L. (2009) '"Snitches get stitches": the problem of solving homicide cases in Washington DC', unpublished conference paper, the Open University.

Winlow, S., Hobbs, D., Lister, S. and Hadfield, P. (2001) 'Get ready to duck: bouncers and the realities of ethnographic research on violent groups', *British Journal of Criminology*, 41(2): 536–48.

Wolcott, H. F. (1999) *Ethnography: A Way of Seeing*. London: Sage.

Young, J. (1971) *The Drug Takers: The Social meaning of Drug Use*. London: Paladin.

Young, M. (1991) *An Inside Job: Policing and Police Culture in Britain*. Oxford: Oxford University Press.

Young, M. (1993) *In the Sticks. Cultural Identity in a Rural Police Force*. Oxford: Clarendon Press.

Index

Added to a page number 't' denotes a table.

academic research 9, 10
access
  negotiating 46, 170
  power relations 179–80
  to difficult/closed areas/groups 93–9, 119, 179
  to groups 'inside' and 'outside' the law 18–19, 125, 131, 167
  to institutions 19–20, 149
  to official sources 58
accountability 59, 142
acting, continual 165
Adler, P. 121, 125–6
administrative criminology 51
agreed parameters 10, 64
aide memoires 85, 88
allegiances 149
analytical computer packages 74
annual statistics 54
anonymity 144
anthropology 118, 119
appearance (personal) 100
audience(s) 174
autopsies 57

Becker, Howard 33
begging case study 146–7
'being reckless' 56
'best' method 10, 16
betrayal, feelings of 165
bias (researcher) 118
'big' theories 34, 174–6
biological positivism 177
blending 121
'blue skies' research 16t
BMRB Social Research 66
bodies (discovered), and statistics 56
booster samples 43
boredom 172

bouncers study 120, 132–7
  see also female bouncers study
Bowling, Ben 92, 93–6, 170, 179
British Crime Surveys 38, 65–72
  comparability with police recorded crime 69, 70–1
  developments in 2008–09 survey 66
  findings 69
  methodological information 43, 45
  origins 71–2
  questionnaire 67–8
  rationale for research 66
  trends discovered by 69
British Journal of Criminology 6–7, 131, 140, 151, 165
British Society of Criminology 152
brutality study 150–1
burglary 70, 71

case files 164
case studies 84, 85–9
cause of death 57
cause and effect 15
causes of crime 9, 33, 51
Centre for Prison Studies 62
Chicago School 25, 51, 120
child protection 154
children, research involving 143, 153
cigarette bootlegging study 126–31, 172
class 177
classic ethnography 172
classical criminology 176, 177
closed areas/groups 93–9, 119, 122, 179
closed questions 90
coercion, freedom from 144
colleagues, talking with 165
communication, of research 145
Communication Toolkit (ESRC) 145
comparative studies 59–64

computer packages, analytical 74
conclusions 15, 170
confidentiality 144, 149, 154
conflicts of interest 145
consent 91, 144, 155
    see also informed consent
constructionism see social constructionism
contextualisation 108, 119, 171
continuous interviewing 66
control
    over researchers 179, 182
    over results 145
costs, ethnographic studies 138
counselling 165
counting, of homicides 57
court verdicts 57
courts, access to 19
covert research 160
    danger in conducting 166–8
    ethical issues 131, 144
    example 133–7
    impact on emotions 165
    justification of 166
    potential fields for 167
    problems with 125–6
credibility 40, 41, 65
crime
    defining 1–2
    discretion in recording 64–5
    overall fall in 71
    police recorded 68, 69, 70–1
    researching see criminological research
    unreported 65
Crime in England and Wales 68–9
crime science 9
crime scientists 18
crime statistics 170
    'dark figure' of 17, 50, 65
    homicide 53–9, 63
    see also official statistics
Crimewatch 56
criminal justice organisations
    access to 19, 149
    diversion of researchers 100
Criminal Statistics England and Wales 54–6, 68, 81
criminals, access to 18, 131, 180
criminological research
    danger 138–9, 141, 166–8
    emotions 123, 124, 141, 162–6
    ethics see ethics
    explaining likely effects to RECs 145
    initial ideas 15–16
    key features 8

methods see research methods
obstruction 167
politics 9, 42, 141, 157–62
problematising 1–21
    criminology as an organising discipline 6–7
    defining 8–9, 13–14
    'how and why' questions 9–10
    real research 4–6
    see also real-life research
    'who or what' questions 10–13
process 15
public 49
purposes 13, 45
research areas 2
themes arising from 178–82
theoretical concerns 174–6
types of headings 24, 25
writing up 182–4
criminological theories 176–8
criminologists 25
    see also new criminologists; researchers
criminology see criminological research
critical criminology 177
critical statistics 50
critical theorists 44
cross-disciplinary research 15
cross-national research 59–64, 154
cultural anthropology 119, 121, 122
culture(s)
    ethnographies 118, 119, 121
    official statistics 59–64
    studies of police 12–13, 119, 158, 175
    working with non-majority 143
custody, use of 59

danger 138–9, 141, 166–8
'dark figure', crime statistics 17, 50, 65
data
    robustness 84
    sharing 154
    see also qualitative data; quantitative data
data analysis 183–4
data collection 34, 43, 64, 65
databases (homicide) 57
death, establishing cause of 57
deception 143, 144, 165
decision-making, statistics and 81
deep knowledge 29
defensive interviewees 91
definitions, agreed 64
demeanour (personal) 100
description 119
detail, emotional impact of 164

diaries 85
'Dirty Harry' syndrome 79
disclosure 91, 121, 157, 181
discovery of bodies, and statistics 56
discretion 64–5
diversity 60
drug dealers study 121, 125
drug use study 146–7

Economic and Social Research Council (ESRC) 10, 140, 142–7
electronic applications 157
elite groups, access to 19
embedded criminology 8
emotions/emotional aspects 123, 124, 141, 162–6
ethical behaviour, survey of police beliefs 75–80
ethical codes, conformity with 167
ethical dilemmas, police studies 149–52, 158, 159–60
ethics 10, 140–57
  criminological research
    disclosure 181
    restrictions 147–8
    special aspects 148–57
  ethnography 121
  interviews 91
  Research Ethics Framework
    case study 146–7
    principles 142–6
  research methods 182
  research questions 15
ethics committees 121, 142, 144, 148, 152, 155, 167
ethnographers
  emotional aspects of research 124
  life-threatening situations 168
  researcher effect 121, 122
ethnographic conversations 120, 123, 127
ethnography 118–23, 138
  classic 172
  costs 138
  examples 160–1
  full immersion 32
  observational 85
  police *see* police
evaluative research 18, 53, 73–4
evidence-led research 51
experiments 53
external commentators 123

facts 41, 44
fear of crime 69

fear of crime debate study 103–8, 171
female aircrew study 165
female bouncers study 30–2, 85–9
female researchers 159, 160
feminist researchers 44, 117, 141
feminist theory 184
field studies 118
Findlay, M. 115–16
focus groups 84, 100–2
fraud 177–8
friends (victims'), access to 47
friendships, in ethnography 121, 123, 162
funders 12, 167
funding 16t
'funnel' approach 34

gatekeepers 19, 46, 92, 96, 170
gender performance/identities 175
Gender and Policing 150–1
gendered policing *see* women, in police
generalisability 80
globalisation 60
'governing through crime' 54
government-funded studies 180
Greater Manchester Police 56
groups, access to 18–19, 167, 179–80

Hancock, Lynn 109, 110–15, 117, 171, 180, 181, 183
Handbook on Crime 24
hard data 32, 46, 51
hard science 42, 44
harm 144–5, 181
Hawthorne effect 121–2, 138
health of a country, statistics and 54
hidden crime 17, 19
Hobbs, Dick 120, 127, 131, 142, 180
Home Office 10, 13, 17, 18, 19, 51, 52, 53, 54, 57, 64, 180
Home Office statistical bulletin (2009–10) 71
Home Office Statistics Unit 66
homelessness, ESRC case study 146–7
homicide(s) 55, 56, 81
  detective study 160–1
  statistics 53–9, 63
Hong Kong study 115–16
Hornsby, Rob 120, 126, 127, 128–32, 138, 167, 172, 180, 181, 182
hostile interviewees 91
Hughes, G. 9
human element, data collection 64, 65
human rights, ethics of discussing 182
hypothesis testing 33, 115–16, 174

identities, gendered 175
ideographic research 33
ideological basis, homicide statistics 57–8
immersion in research 32, 120, 121
impartiality, of researchers 145
impression management 159
in-depth knowledge 88
in-depth reasoning 171
in-depth research 15, 84
inaccessible groups, access to 18–19
independence, of researchers 145
independent variables 15
individualisation 11
infant deaths 57
informed consent 143, 153, 154
insecurity 54, 92
inside insiders 123
inside outsiders 123
insider/outsider research 19, 119, 123–37
Institute of Justice 53
institutions, access to 19–20, 149
integrity
　police study 75–80
　professional 142, 145
intellectual property 154
intent, of studies 121
inter-disciplinary research 143
international research 143
internet research 154
interviewees
　finding out about 92
　hostile/defensive 91
　summaries on choice of research methods 169–74
interviews 84, 110
　dual purpose 92
　examples 93–9
　power dynamics 100, 117
　preparing for 91–2
　process 89–90
　semi-structured 117, 118, 120
　things that can go wrong 90–1
　time aspect 90

Jupp, V. 65
jury service studies 109–15, 116–17, 171, 180, 181, 183
justice 1, 2, 3–4
'Justice for Julie' campaign 3–4

'killing with intent' 56
knowledge 15, 16, 29, 42, 88

labelling theory 33

law
　concept of crime and justice 2
　obstruction of research 167
lawbreaking, crime as 1–2
lawbreaking community, accessing 126, 180
left realists 177
legal-illegal dichotomy 149
life history research 33, 85
life-threatening situations 168
lived experience 25, 120

mainstream criminology 51
'managed heart' 165
managerialist approach 184
manslaughter 56
market research companies 43
Marxism 177, 184
Matthews, R. 109
'means justifies the end' principles 79
media, relations with 145
medico-legal autopsies 57
micro dynamics, of power 179
Ministry of Justice 10, 51–2
mission statement, Ministry of Justice 51–2
mixed methods 26, 171
　advantages 47, 102–16
　example 29–30
modules, BCS questionnaires 67–8
multi-disciplinary research 143
Muncie, John 1–2, 59–63, 64, 72, 81, 170, 179, 183

narrative construction 183–4
National Missing Persons Helpline 56
natural sciences 44
naturalistic methods 25, 34, 108, 118, 120, 121
new criminologists 177
New Labour 51
nomothetic research 33
non-human contact 46
non-participant observation 120, 121
Northern Ireland Crime and Victimisation Survey 43
'not guilty' verdicts 57
'not proven' verdicts 57
notes, reflective 85

objectivity 148
observational studies 34, 85
　see also participant observation
occupational culture study 119
offenders
　access to 18

subjects of research 27
official sources, access to 58, 180
official statistics 17, 25, 49, 50, 81
  critiquing 64–72
  interrogating 59–64
  as partial and socially constructed 63
open-ended questions 90
organised crime
  accessing world of 167
  study 120, 133–7
original data 80
outside insiders 123
outside outsiders 123, 124, 159
overt research 149, 165–6

paradigms 33, 184
partiality, of official statistics 63
participant observation 119–20, 121, 125
  see also non-participant observation;
    semi-participant observation
participation, voluntary 144
performance (gender) 175
permission, right to refuse 153
personal appearance/demeanour 100
personal approach 46
personal safety 138
physical access 179
physical barriers, to access 47
physical control, of researchers 179
Piacentini, Laura 96–9, 120, 148, 170–1,
    179, 181, 182
plausibility 37, 40, 41, 65, 88, 89, 121
police
  recorded crime 68, 69, 70–1
  sources, access to 58
  as subject of research 27
    access to 19–20, 46–7, 92
    beliefs regarding ethical behaviour
      75–80
    beliefs and wider police family 12–13
    deployment analysis 123
    ethnographic studies 120, 124, 149–52,
      158, 159–60
    issue of rape 35–42
    occupational culture 119
    overt approach 165–6
    policing the Caribbean 92, 93–6
    public judgement 27–9
    women see women
Police National Computer 18
Police Strength England and Wales 68
Policing the Caribbean 92
policy intervention studies 74
political importance, homicide statistics 56

political influence, official statistics 63
politicisation 82
politics 9, 10, 42, 141, 157–62
the poor, in criminology 177
positivist criminology 9, 44, 45, 176–7
power differentials 117, 182
power relations 99, 100, 170, 179–80
powerful groups 182
practitioners, criminologists as 25
pre-designed questions 43
primary data 53, 74–81
principal investigators 141
prisoners, resettlement study 73, 83
prisons, as subject of research 27
  access to 19–20, 47
  reform 74
  Russian prison 96–9, 120, 170–1, 181
problem sharing 165
proformas 154–6
property crime 71
psychological barriers, to access 47
public criminological research 49
publication, research results 145
punitive cultures, comparison of 59–64

qualitative data 32
qualitative methods 8, 23, 26, 82–116
  criticisms 88
  main strength 47
  questions 84
  reliance on personal approach 46
  versions of 84–102
  versus quantitative methods 9, 17, 22–48
  see also ethnography; focus groups;
    interviews; life history research
quality 142
quantitative data 27, 32
  advantages 52
  main types 50
  use of 29
  see also primary data; secondary data
quantitative methods 8, 23, 26, 49–81
  critiquing official statistics 64–72
  defined 50–3
  increasing importance 51
  instruments 46
  interrogating official statistics 59–64
  justification 39
  main strength 47
  questions 83
  reliance on non-human contact 46
  using primary data 74–81
  using secondary data 53–74
  versus qualitative methods 9, 17, 22–48

see also crime science; questionnaires; surveys
quasi-experimental approach 74
questionnaires 43, 46
  examples
    BCS 67–8
    female bouncers study 86–8
    jury system study 114–15

radical criminology 177
rape, tackling issue of 35–42
rapport 47
raw data 53, 57
'real life' research 1, 5, 14–20, 22, 32, 46, 138, 158, 168, 169
real research 4–6, 184
'real world' constraints 12
realist criminology 74, 177
realistic evaluation 74
reassurance 54
reclassification, homicide cases 57
recording, homicide statistics 58
reflexive diaries 85
regulation, of research 141, 167
relationship, researcher and researched 143
reliability 37–9, 63, 64
replicability 37, 84
Reporting rape in London: a qualitative study 35–8
reporting rates 69
representativeness 37, 88, 120
research designs 144
Research Ethics Framework (ESRC)
  case study 146–7
  principles of ethical research 142–6
  see also ethics
research methods 7–8
  agreed 64
  'best' method 10, 16
  British Crime Surveys 42–4, 45
  choosing 22, 23, 32–5, 138, 178, 184–5
  continuum 108, 109
  ethics 182
  limitations 22
  potential to deliver answers 22, 173–4
  practical considerations 44
  scientific 10, 42–7
  self-interest 12
  summary of interviewees responses 169–74
  see also mixed methods; qualitative methods; quantitative methods; soft and semi-structured research
research participants
  distance between researchers and 46

researchers' responsibilities towards 153–4
  see also interviewees; subjects of research
research questions 34
  complicated nature of 15
  deciding on 23
  'how' and 'why' 9–10
  pre-designed 43
  'who' or 'what' 10–13
research results, ethical issues 145
research staff, ethical issues 142–4
researcher bias 118
researcher effect 121–3
researchers
  academic 10
  distance between subject and 46–7
  diversion of 100
  ethical control over 182
  feminist 44, 117, 141
  independence and impartiality of 145
  inside/outside positions 123–37
  physical control of 179
  relationship between subject and 143
  responsibilities towards participants 153–4
  semi-detached workers 19–20
  women as 159, 160
  see also crime scientists; criminologists; ethnographers
responsibilities (researcher) 153–4
right realists 177
right to refuse permission 153
rigour 84
risk aversion 141
'risky' activities, regulation of 141
Rowe, M. 158
Russian prison life study 96–9, 120, 170–1, 181

sample populations 37, 42, 88
scepticism, need for 63–4, 65
scientific research 9, 10, 42–7
Scottish Crime & Justice Survey 43
secondary analysis 50
secondary data 53–74, 164
security 180
self-interest 12
self-report studies 50
semi-detached workers 19–20
semi-participant observation 118, 120
semi-structured research 117
  see also soft and semi-structured research
sensitive topics 47, 141
social constructionism 17, 63, 81, 175
social networking 120, 131, 172

social statistics 52
socialisation 175, 181
sociological positivism 177
sociology of deviance 25, 51, 118
soft data 32
soft science 42
soft and semi-structured research 117–39
   ethnography 118–23
   insider/outsider research 124–37
'solved' homicides 58
SPACE 61
SPSS 74–5
standardising 43
statistical analysis 74–5, 183
statistics
   conclusions based on 170
   in ethnography 120–1
   see also crime statistics; social statistics
Streetwise: Effective Police Patrol 123
subjects of research 26–7
   ethical issues 142–4
   see also police; prisoners; prisons; research participants
Sudden Infant Death Syndrome (SIDS) 57
suicide notes, disturbing nature of 164
surveys 89, 110
suspects, subjects of research 27
suspicion, avoiding 181

tax evasion/fraud 178
technical reports (BCS) 43
technology 91
Temkin, Jennifer 35–7
theft 70, 71
themes (research) 178–82
theoretical concerns 174–6
theory development 33, 34
theory testing 27–9, 33
theory-driven research 33
theory/theorising 33–5, 184
tick-box surveys 89, 108, 110, 171
time aspects 90, 138
trans-disciplinary research 15
triangulation 72, 170
trust 125, 127, 149, 181
truth 41, 44, 72, 120, 121, 160, 161

United Nations 61
universities
   electronic applications 157
   ethics committees see ethics committees
unreported crime 65

unrepresentative samples 88
'unsuccessful' criminals 131
User Guide to Home Office Crime Statistics (2010) 69

validation 88
validity 15, 33, 37, 39–42, 44, 58, 72, 89, 120, 121, 174
value-free facts 44
value-free science 44
variables 15, 42, 53, 74, 75
vehicle crime 70, 71
verdicts (court) 57
victimisation studies 45–6
victimisation surveys 50, 65
   see also British Crime Surveys
victims
   access to 47
   as subjects of research 27
   typologies 45
violence 159, 168, 181
violent crime statistics 54
visual methods 85
voluntary participation 144
vulnerable groups 143, 153

Walklate, Sandra 8, 45–7, 102, 103–8, 117, 167, 171, 179, 182, 183
welfarist approach 176
'what works' 18, 51, 59, 73, 83
What Works: Questions and answers about prison reform 74
whistleblowers 159
whistleblowing 151–2
Winlow, Simon 120, 131, 132–7, 138, 167, 168, 172, 180, 181, 182
Wolcott, H.F. 118–19
women, as subjects of research
   factory work performance 122
   female aircrew emotions 165
   female bouncers 30–2, 85–9
   in police
      arrest rates 120, 121t
      barriers to promotion 101–2
      'big theories' of gender 174–5
      issue of promotion 29–30
      rape victim experiences 35–42
   see also female researchers
writing up 162, 182–4

'yes' people 91, 92
youth crime study 60–6